BETRAYAL OF GANDHI

O.P. Dhiman

KALPAZ

Betrayal of Gandhi

Rs. 750

ISBN: 978-81-7835-746-1

Published in 2010 in India by
Kalpaz Publications
C-30, Satyawati Nagar,
Delhi-110052
E-mail: kalpaz@hotmail.com
Phone : 9212729499

Lasser Type Setting by: Quick Media, Delhi
Printed at : Gian Ridhi Offset Printers, Delhi

BETRAYAL OF GANDHI

Dedicated

to

those who died

and

those who live

to uphold

Gandhian Principles

Contents

Preface

MY first encounter with Gandhiji was when I read a book about his life that was given to me as a Birth Day gift by my mother on my tenth Birth Day. I read it many times and developed emotional attachment with Gandhiji.

Later, when I deeply studied Gandhiji for my M.Ed. dissertation I developed intellectual attachment with him and devoted myself to deep study of his philosophy. I continued to pursue intensive study of Gandhiji and published my first book on Gandhiji during Gandhi Centenary Year. The book 'Gandhian Philosophy—A Critical and Comprehensive Study', with a foreword by Dr. R.R. Diwakar, Chairman, Gandhi Peace Foundation, New Delhi got appreciative comments from several authorities on the subject in India and abroad.

When I was fifteen year old Gandhiji was assassinated. I can never forget that saddest and most shocking day of my life when the whole nation, rather the whole world, irrespective of caste, colour, creed and race was shocked. I kept crying for two days and I had seen tears in the eyes of million of people from every corner of the world. A National mourning was observed for twenty one days.

Rich tributes were paid to Gandhiji and pledges were made by our leaders to follow his principles. But after his death we gradually started deviating from his teachings and ultimately bid adieu to his philsophy. We Indians, especially the Congressmen, have not only forgotten him, rather betrayed him by adopting principles and actions that are antagonistic to Gandhiji's principles and actions.

I have travelled the whole of India and Europe and have discussed Gandhian Philosophy with thousands of Indians and foreigners and found that our people know little of Gandhiji's Philosophy whereas the foreigners have studied him deeply and have developed a great respect for him.

I found it rather surprising that many Russians too, though they believe in the teachings of 'Karl Marx', whose philosophy is the antitheses of Gandhian Philosophy, have now come around the view that Gandhian Philosophy is of great value to the entire mankind. Many Russians whom I talked to held Gandhiji in great esteem.

In India the younger generation hates Gandhiji and breaks his statues, burns his books and partraits, garlands his statues with shoes and blackens them with coal-tar.

Why is it so?

The so-called followers of Gandhiji are respensible for this. The younger generation has neither the stirring experience of actually seeing him and coming under the spell of his personality nor read the writings of Gandhiji. They see only his so-called followers who call themselves Gandhites, but have compromised with all the evils against which Gandhiji fought all his life. In a craze for power and pelf they have replaced his basic principle 'The means justify the end' by the Machiavellian principle 'Nothing succeeds like success.' Those who claim to be secular but are the most communal and engineer communal roits as a policy of vote bank.

Seeing these so-called followers of Gandhiji, the younger generation thinks that he must be like them. Moreover, many misunderstandings have been created against Gandhian Philosophy like 'Majboori Ka Nam Mahatma Gandhi'.

Gandhiji wrote in the Harijan on January 16, 1937, "...Out of my ashes a thousand Gandhi will arise". This has inspired me to take the message of Gandhiji to the present generation.

In the Prologue of this book I have discussed how the so-called followers of Gandhiji betray him and kill him every day rather every moment by their actions which are opposed to his teachings. In the Epilogue, I have tried to show how the problems of the present world can be solved by following Gandhian Philosophy.

Besides Prologue and Epilogue the book has been divided into eleven comprehensive but comprehensible chapters—The Theory of Reality, The Nature of God, The Nature of Man, The End and The Means, The Nature and Structure of Social Order, The Nature of State, The Structure of State. The Nature and Structure of Economic Order, Religion and Morality, The Philosophy of Education, The Ideal Man.

In one of his publications, Louis Fischer declares : "If man is to survive, if civilization is to survive and flower in freedom, truth and democracy, the remainder of the 20th century and what lies beyond must belong not to Lenin or Trotsky not to Marx or Mao or *Ho or Che*, but to Mahatma Gandhi." I too believe that we need to inculcate Gandhian ideas in our minds, if we wish to solve the problems of the present day world.

This compact book is an endeavour to enlighten the readers about various aspects of Gandhian Philosophy and its relevance in the present time. It is an effort to present Gandhian Philosophy in its proper prospective.

It has been authored to enlighten the readers about Gandhian Philosophy. It is especially important for the so-called followers of Gandhiji and the younger generation, who have neither seen Gandhiji nor read his writings, and have developed many misunderstandings about him.

I would make an humble request to readers, especially the younger generation, on whose shoulders the future rests to do justice to that great soul by studying his philosophy deeply and by trying to adopt it in their life. We should not betray him.

O.P. Dhiman

ASHIANA
49, Raghbir Nagar
Patiala–147001
India

Acknowledgements

ANY accomplishment requires inspiration, help and guidance of many people and this book is not an exception. During its preparation, I have been inspired, helped and guided by a number of well wishers.

I cannot but remember with performed feeling of piety and gratitude my mother, Late Mrs. Maya Dhiman, my first teacher, friend and philosopher, a staunch democrat who created in me a burning passion for democratic ideals and critical objective thinking.

Formal though it may look, I must acknowledge my grateful appreciation to my wife, Mrs. Manorma Dhiman, former Head, Department of Home Science, Government College for Women, Patiala for her inspiration and devotion but for which the present work would have been well-nigh impossible.

I must appreciate my 15 year old grandson Anish Dhiman who helped me a lot working hard at his Computer.

I acknowledge the cooperation extended to me by several friends and collegues especially Dr. Swaraj Walia, Head, Department of English, Govt. Mohindra College, Patiala; Prof. V.M. Kapur, Former Head Department of English, Multani Mal Modi Post-Graduate College Patiala.

I extend my deep sense of gratitude to my friends and colleagues of Multain Mal Modi Post Graduate College, Patiala–

Dr. C.P. Sharma, former Head, Department of Economics and Dr. Harcharan Singh senior lecturer for reading the manuscript and proofs of this book and giving me valuable suggestions.

I take this opportunity to put on record my deep sense of gratitude to late Dr. R.R. Diwakar, Chairman, Gandhi Peace Foundation New Delhi, who wrote a Foreword to my first book 'Gandhian Philosophy—A Critical and Comprehensive Study", published during Gandhi Centenary year and inspired me to do more work on Gandhian Philosophy.

I must be thankful to all the authors on whose work I have drawn freely.

I express my thanks to Kalpaz Publications, Delhi for extending me full co-operation to print this book in an elegant manner.

O.P. Dhiman

1

Prologue

"Twelve months have passed away since the assasination of Mahatma Gandhi. The first death anniversary is going to be observed on the 30th of January. We Hindus observe the death anniversary of our ancestors, but it has become only a form except perhaps in some rare cases. It will be a tragedy greater than the one which was enacted on 30th. January 1948, if we also are to reduce this observance to mere form or ceremony. We must utilize this occasion for bringing to our minds the great virtues which the Mahatma embodied and for strengthening our resolve to adopt them in our individual and national life.

–Dr. Rajendra Prasad,
on the first death anniversary of Gandhiji

JANUARY 30, 1948 was the most tragic and shameful day in the history of India, when an Indian fundamentalist assasinated our beloved leader Mahatma Gandhi—the Father of the Nation, a votary of Truth and Non-violence and an embodiment of Absolute Love and Forgiveness.

Only five and a half month earlier India, under his leadership, won freedom on August 15, 1947. On that auspecious day, when people all over the country were celebrating the dawn of indepence, the man who more than any one else, was intrumental for making India free from the foreign yoke, did not share the rejoicings. He was busy in his unending attempt to mitigate the mutual bitterness between Hindus and Muslims. His residence in Baliaghata had become a place of piligrimage for the citizens of Calcutta. The whole day continuous stream of visiters trudged their way to his residence and offered their obeisance to him. There were moving scenes of Hindu-Muslims fraternization in front on his residence. In response to a journalist's demand for independence day message, Gandhiji said that he had run dry. Journalist's peristent demand evoked the reply, "there is no message at all."[1] He himself celebrated the day by fasting, prayer, and spinning, as preached by him.

The penance undertaken by the Mahatma, the tremendous self-suffering and torture imposed by the Messiah of Peace on himself and the act of putting his life at stake reveal his utmost anxiety for uniting the two communities, i.e. the Hindus and the Muslims, to enable them to live like brothers. What a great man he was!

After getting freedom, reconstructing India was Gandhiji's next dream. Gandhiji dreamt of making new society and new man who will not be interested in exploiting others and will not allow others to expoit him. His goal of life will be to promote his own happiness and to keep others in becoming happier. The mad craze for material progress beyond all reasonable limits will no longer attract this new man. This man, Gandhiji thought, can be produced with the help of education and new surroundings. He, therefore, came out with a scheme of socio-politico-economic set up and a new educational system.

Gandhiji wanted to reconstruct new India based on high moral values and free from illiteracy, poverty, inequality, untouchability, communalism, exploitation, corruption and other ills which our country was facing at that time. But in order to achieve this goal, he did not assume any government office as that of President or Prime Minister.

How ungrateful we are! We never allowed him to make his dream come true and assassinated him just five and a half months after India won freedom.

WORLD-WIDE HOMAGE TO GANDHI JI

As the news of Mahatma Gandhi's martyrdom reached the United Nations, the Security Council suspended its activities in order to enable its members to pay their tributes to the departed leader. The United Nations lowered its flag to half-mast. Philip Noel-Bakar, the British representative, praised Gandhiji as the "friend of the poorest and the loneliest and the lost." He further declared "Gandhi's greatest achievements are still to come." Other members of the Security Council lauded the Mahatma's spiritual qualities and praised his devotion to peace and non-violence. The

Soviet Union representative, Mr. Gromyko called Gandhiji "One of the outstanding political leaders of India whose name will always be linked with the struggle of Indian people for the national liberation."

Although Gandhiji died as a private citizen without wealth, property, official designation or academic distinction, governments of the several countries all over the world paid high compliments to this 'little brown man of seventy eight in a lion cloth.' The government of India received about three thousand five hundred messages of sympathy from almost all the foreign countries. It was a spontaneous gesture on the part of the world to a true 'World-Citizen'. The British Prime Minister Clement Attlee described him as "the greatest citizen" who "seemed to belong to a different period of history". Sir Stafford Cripps maintained, "There has been no greater spiritual leader in the world in our time". Lord Halifax observed. "I suppose there can be few men in all history who, by personal character and example, have been able so deeply to influence the thought of their generation". Lord Penthie stated : "He is no longer with us in the flesh, but his spirit endures." *The London Times* commented in an editorial : "No country but India and no religion but Hinduism could have given birth to a Gandhi." President Truman of America observed : "His life and his work will be through the years to come the greatest monument to him. ... Another giant among men has fallen in the cause of brotherhood and peace." The New York Times wrote : "A light has gone out. ... His undying spirit speaks now to all India and all the world. He has left as his heritage a spiritual force that must in God's good time prevail over arms and armaments and dark doctrines of violence. ... Now he belongs to ages." General Mac-Arthur described Mahatma Gandhi as "One of those prophets who lived far ahead of time." General Harshall called the Mahatma 'the spokesman for the conscience of all mankind.' Mr. Eamon De Valera said

"The loss is not India's alone—the world has lost a great leader, whose influence will long survive his death."

Leon Blum, the French socialist, who had never seen Gandhiji himself, wrote : "The whole world has been plunged into mourning by the death of this extraordinary man." But, perhaps the richest tribute was paid by Albert Einstein : "Generations to come, it may be, will scarce believe that such a one as this ever in flesh and blood walked upon this earth."

TRIBUTES AND PLEDGES BY INDIAN LEADERS

Great Indian leaders and statesmen also paid rich tributes to Mahatma Gandhi. They pledged to dedicate their lives to his principles and to follow his footsteps. Pandit Jawahar Lal Nehru grieved over the death of Gandhiji, said "Our beloved leader Bapu, as we called him, the Father of the Nation, is no more. Perhaps I am wrong to say that; nevertheless, we will not see him again as we have seen him for these many years. We will not run to him for advice and seek solace from him, and that is terrible blow not to me only but to millions and millions in this country ... the light has gone out, I said and yet I was wrong. For the light that shone in this country was no ordinary light. The light that has illuminated this country for these many years will illuminate this country for many years will illuminate this country for many more years and a thousand years later that light will still be seen in this country and the world will see it and it will give solace to innumerable hearts. For that light represented the living truth and the eternal man was with us with his eternal truth reminding us of the right path, drawing us from error, taking this ancient country to freedom. ... All this has happened. There is much more to do. There was so much for him to do. We could never think that he was unnecessary or that he has done his task. But now, particularly, when we are faced with so many difficulties, his not being with us is a blow most terrible to bear."[2]

After paying these tributes, Nehru added : "And while we pray, the greatest prayer we can offer is to pledge to dedicate ourselves to the truth, and the cause this great countryman of ours lived and for which he died. That is the best prayer we can offer him and his memory. That is the best prayer we can offer to India and ourselves."[3]

Just after Nehru, Sardar Vallabhbhai Patel in his speech said : "Just now my dear brother, Pandit Jawahar Lal Nehru has spoken to you. My heart is aching. What shall I say to you? My tongue is tied. This is a day of sorrow, shame and agony for India. ... The occasion demands not anger, but earnest heart-searching from us all. If we give vent to our understandable anger, it would mean that we have forgotten our beloved master's teaching so soon after his death. ... I am sure Gandhiji's supreme sacrifice will wake up the conscience of our countrymen and evoke a higher response in the heart of every Indian. I hope and pray that it may be given to us to complete Gandhiji's mission. At this solemn moment no one of us can afford to waver or lose his heart. Let us all stand united and bravely face the national disaster that has overtaken us. Let us all solemnly pledge ourselves afresh to Gandhiji's teaching and ideals."[4]

Paying his tribute to Gandhiji, Dr. Rajendra Prasad said, "We are sad. We are stunned. Must we need be despodent? The body will not be seen. The voice will not be heard. But has he not left us an invaluable heritage? Has he not given us enough of guidance and inspiration to lead us on and to sustain us in our onward march? In the face of this awful tragedy let his clarion call once more rouse us to our sense of duty. He made heroes out of clay. He made consummate use of indifferent instruments in the life long struggle he carried on against injustice, against oppression, against slavery. India needs the same heroism, the same disregard of dangers, the same recklessness of consequences for establishing righteousness. Gandhiji has given away his life for it. Shall we not follow him after death as we did when he was walking on this earth?"[5]

He continued, "If India is to live, grow and prosper, then she shall have to go on the path of truth and non-violence blazed by Gandhiji. It is the same path which brought us to the temple of freedom, but surajy is yet to be attained."[6]

Sarojini Naidu paid rich tributes to Gandhiji, "... I feel that sorrow is out of place and tears become blasphemy. How can he die, who through his life and conduct and sacrifice, who through his love and courage and faith has taught the world that the spirit matters, not the flesh, that the spirit has the power greater than the powers of the combined armies of the earth, combined armies of the ages? He was small, frail, without money, without even the full complement of garment to cover his body, not owning even as much earth as might be held on the point of a needle, how was he so much stronger than the forces of violence, the might of empires and the grandeur of embattled forces in the world? Why was it that this little man, this tiny man, this man with a child's body, this man so ascetic, living on the verge of starvation by choice so as to be more in harmony with the life of the poor, how was it that he exercised over the entire world, of those who revered him and those who hated him, such power as emperors could never wield. It was because he did not care for applause, he did not care for censure. He only cared for the path of righteousness. He cared only for the ideals that he preached and practised."[7]

Our leaders, especially Congressmen took many pledges to follow Gandhiji's principles and teachings. Pandit Jawahar Lal Nehru stated : "Bapu has done giant's work for India and the world and even for our poor selves, and he has done it astonishingly well. And now it is our turn not to fail him or his memory but to carry on the work to the best of our ability and to fulfil the pledge we have so often taken".[8]

Sardar Vallabhbhai Patel also said the samething : "Let us all solemnly pledge ourselves afresh to Gandhiji's teachings and ideals."[9]

Dr. Rajendra Prasad lamented that even during Gandhiji's life many Congressmen had forgotten his teachings. He said, "Let all Congressmen who used to pride on following Gandhiji fully understand that the moment of their severest test has arrived. Today every Congressman has to answer himself or herself as to how far covertly or overtly he can be held responsible for Gandhiji's tragic end. Only if Congressman had fully imbibed and lived upto Gandhiji's teachings, the present national calamity could not have overtaken us. Gandhiji has suffered because of our individual and collective sins."[10] It is implied by the above statement that Dr. Rajendra Prasad admitted that Gandhiji was killed by Congressmen who failed to follow Gandhiji's teachings.

After the demise of Gandhi, the whole nation was shattered. A national mourning was observed for twenty one days. Every one, irrespective of sex, caste, colour, creed lamented his death. On the first death anniversary of Gandhiji, Dr. Rajendra Prasad said, "Twelve months have passed away since the assassination of Mahatma Gandhi. The first death anniversary is going to be observed on 30th January 1949. We Hindus observe the death anniversary of our ancestors, but it has become only a form except perhaps in some rare cases. It will be a tragedy greater than the one which was enacted on 30th January 1948, if we also are to reduce this observance to a mere form or ceremony.

We must utilize this occasion for bringing to our mind the great virtues which the Mahatma embodied and for strengthening our resolve to adopt them in our individual and national life."[11]

BETRAYAL OF GANDHI

Though rich tributes were paid to Gandhiji on his martyrdom day and pledges were made by our leaders, especially Congressmen to follow his principles and action yet gradually we started deviating from his teachings and ultimately bid adieu to his philosophy. We Indians, especially the congressmen, have forgotten him, rather betrayed him.

Gandhiji Wanted Congress Should Dissolve Itself

November 1947, Gandhiji suggested that the political objective of the congress having been realised, the congress should voluntarily dissolve itself. What he wanted was that the progressive and patriotic elements in the congress should devote themselves to the task of nation-building "...Hitherto the fight with the British engaged all the energy of our people. That energy must now be mobilised to make the nation prosperous and strong, or else it will recoil upon us and breed discord and disruption."[12] The congress leaders, however, did not react fabourably to the proposal. They were afraid of dissolving the congress because they thought that the hard won freedom would be jeopardised if the organizational support of the Congress was lost on account of its dissolution.

Gandhiji had foreseen that the Congress would eventually degenerate into corrupt and timid organization and we felt worried over the "scramble for loaves and fishes in the congress, and discord and personal rivalries among members of the Congress High Command". Gandhiji, seeing a rapid deterioration among the Congress worker, advised the congress leaders to dissolve the Congress Party. After the meeting of All India Congress Committee in November 1947, Gandhiji repeatedly advised his Colleagues for dissolution, for that, according to him was the only way to save the Congress before the rot set to its own deteriment. But the wholly negative attitude of Nehru and others on this greatly disappointed Gandhiji, and in a painful but helpless tone he said, "I can carry no one with me in this."

Though Nehru said about Gandhiji more than once, "We were but small men. He picked us up, made us part of a great movement and something of its greatness passed into us", but he did not listen to his advice of dissolving the congress. The Congress was not dissolved and Gandhiji was betrayed.

Gandhiji Wanted a Broad-based National Government

After Independence Gandhiji felt that freedom had been achieved by the combined efforts of all nationalist forces in the Country and not by Congress alone. He wanted the first government of free India to be a national government capable of inspiring confidence and creating enthusiasm in the whole nation. He, therefore, insisted that the first cabinet should be broad-based. It was on his own insistence that a number of distinguished non-Congressmen were also invited to join the cabinet. They included Sir John Mathai, the noted economist and business magnate; Sir Shaumukham Chetty, the well-known financial expert; Dr. B.R. Ambedkar, a celebrated jurist and leader of the Scheduled Castes, Dr. Shyama Prasad Mookerji of the Hindu Mahasabha, Sardar Baldev Singh of Akali Dal. But the leaders of integrity—both Congress and Non-congress—soon left the government.

Congress not a Political Party, but a Movement

We all know that Congress was in reality not a Political Party, but a movement. People of all views, caste, colour, creed and religion participated in this movement for the freedom of our country. Had Congress been dissolved as advised by Gandhiji, automatically two new National Political Parties would have emerged and the fate of India would have been entirely different.

But it did not happen. Gongress became the only National Political Party unchallenged by any other Political Party, it befooled and exploited the Nation in the name of Gandhiji. Most of the ills which India is facing today are the result of mis-rule of Congress.

Degeneration of Congress

After the death of Gandhiji, the Congress as he warned, started degenerating into corrupt and timid organization. In March 1949, Dr. Pattabhai Sitaramaya wrote : "Two years of Congress rule had not yet passed when there came to the people the realization that they had neither food nor freedom. Gradually, their eyes opened to the great betrayal which was taking place and they realised that they were being made to live in a new fascist state which the Congress had built around them."

Topping the list of the misdeeds of the government is political corruption. If corruption in political life has achieved almost criminal proportion, it has to be admitted that it has ceased to provoke that amount of shock and disgust as it would have four decades ago. The virus of corruption has infested from the highest to the lowest in the hierarchy and most unfortunately it is salvaged by political bosses. The wide-spread corruption has eroded the entire administrative apparatus and daily people experience that their legistimate and lawful work cannot be done in any office without greasing the palms of the dealing persons. By 1953 there were several resignations and dissensions from it as some leaders were convinced that Congress has utterly failed and betrayed Gandhiji and the people of INDIA in founding and perpetuating a new religion, a new philosophy, a new faith built on strong and untarnished idealism out of the preachings of Mahatma Gandhi. People exepected the Congress to evolve a Gandhian Constitution, a Gandhian Government, a Gandhian Democracy and a Gandhian Way of Life based upon laws, economics, ethics, sociology, art, religion and philosophy. All the promises of the workers were only wordy but none of those was materialised.

The Condition in the Country during 1948-1953 Period

There was terrorism in Telangana and the Government was charged with having violated the principles of democracy by the enactment of the 'Preventive Detention Act' and the First Amendment Bill to the Constitution. The Government was also criticised for exercising executive control over the judiciary. Several policies of the Government were in opposition to the Congress creed which was violated on several occasions. To enforce their rule, the Party whip was raised against several staunch followers of Gandhiji, who bitterly criticised the Government and their policy and were forced to resign when they demanded an enquiry with a view to end the activities of those Congress workers, who were nose-deep in corruption, nepotism, vandalism and several other vices. Those who openly spoke about the misdeeds of Government, and were not members of the Congress, were put in jail for several months without a judicial trial. An eminent professor of Delhi quoted the following statistics of repression in free INDIA from 15th August 1947 to 15th August 1950.

"There were 1,782 Police and Military firings in support of the non-violent regime. These resulted in *3,784 killed and 9,342 injured*. Nearly 50,000 people including Communists, R.S.S. men, Socialists, Students and even Congressmen were detained for varying periods".

There were numerous problems like the Kashmir trouble, imperial and capitalist pressure, division within the Government and the Congress, failure of the production machine, the strike of capital on one hand and the increasing labour unrest on the other, resulting in economic insolvency, rampant corruption, black marketing, tax evasion and artificial shortages; an agrarian crisis, the refugee problem and general paralysis of action of the Government which was actually conscious of its unpopularity.

Several tirades against the Government and ministers of various States were delivered, and a good many invectives were published by the press charging the Government with inefficiency and other vices as mentioned above. Leaving margin for the hyperbolic statements of the criticizers, the common man believed that there was something radically wrong with the Congress and most of its leaders, and efforts must be made to purge it. Many remedial ways were suggested and people found the Congressites in general incorrigible, and the last attempt, made by Acharya Kriplani, the ex-president of the all India congress Committee, of forming the "Kisan Majdoor Praja Party" after severing his connections with the Congress was symbolic of the misrule in INDIA, which the *Free Press Journal*, in its issue of the 4th June 1951, had editorially published.

Degeneration of Congress Under Indira Gandhi

Though Congress started degenrating after the death of Gandhiji, but under the leadership of Shrimati Indira Gandhi it reached at lowest ebb. Her only purpose was to remain in power. She created a split in the Congress by adopting 'foul means, hypocricy, indiscipline, untruth and all other evils against which Gandhiji fought throughout his life. She, in a craze for power and pelf changed the basic Gandhian Principle, "The means justify the end" by the Machinavellian principle, " Nothing succeeds like success" and created a split in the Congress. She won elections by befooling the people by slogans like 'Bank Nationalization' 'Garibi Hatao' etc. and the moral and economic condition of the country became from bad to worse.

Declaration of Emergency

Declaration of Emergency by Indira Gandhi was the darkest day in the History of india. During 1975, the Opposition parties joined by local groups and NGOs staged regular demonstrations in almost all the states of the country protesting against the rising inflation and unchecked corruption in the government. The intensity of protest was increasing day by day. The government failed to pacify them and contain the movement. On June 12, 1975, Allahabad High Court, hearing a petition against Indira Gandhi ruled that she had used illegal practices during the election. The Court also ordered her to vocate the seat, immediately. The ruling helped in adding fuel to the ongoing political fire. The agitation and anger of the people amplified crowds surrounded Parliament demanding her resignation. Realizing the consequences, Indira Gandhi, on June 26, 1975, declared 'a state of emergency, due to the turbulent political situation in the country.'

India, the proud democracy, was transformed overnight into a tinpot dictatarship and was brought, in Indira's own words, to a grinding halt.

Now, the political baton came into the hands of Indira Gandhi, which she used very tactfully. All her political rivals were imprisoned, constitutional rights of the citizens were abrogated. Courts were gagged and the press was muzzled and placed under strict censorship. It was reported that the leaders of the Opposition parties were beaten and assaulted in the jails.

Even great National leader like Jayaprakash Narayan, Acharya Kripalani, Morarji Desai, Atal Bihari Vajpayee, Lal Krishan Advani, Chander Shekhar, Krishan Kant and Chaudhary Charan Singh were put behind bars. This Emergency was worse than the dictatorship of Hilter and Mussolini. It is shameful that this all was done by the one who claimed to be follower of Gandhiji and used his name to win votes in election. It was betrayal of Gandhiji.

Lack of Courage Among Congressmen

Most of the Congressmen did not have the courage to oppose Indira Gandhi for imposing Emergency and bent at the feet of Indira Gandhi and made her absolute dictator.

These congressmen who claim to be followers of Gandhiji lack a unique quality of courage that was in Gandhiji's character. He feared neither the British Government, nor political parties, neither friends not enemies, neither Indians nor foreigners. "He who wrongs no one fears no one". He says, "There is no bravery greater than refusal to bend the knee to an earthly power, no matter how great, and that without bitterness of spirit and in the fullness of faith that the spirit alone lives and nothing else does". With defiant courage, he challenged the British Government. A

Government that is evil has no room for good men and women except in its prison. For me, the whole of India is a prison, even as the master's house is to his slave. A slave to be free must continuously rise against his slavery and be locked up in his master's cell for his rebellion. The cell door is the door to freedom.

When in his famous trial at Ahmedabad he was charged with sedition and promoting disaffection against the Government, he bluntly told the judge that disaffection against such a Government is a virtue, for affection can not be regulated or manipulated by law.' We are challenging the right of this government 'because we consider its activities to be wholly evil. We want to overthrow the Government. We want to compell its submission to the peoples' will. We desire to show that Government exist to serve the people, not the people to serve the Government. Whether we are one or many, we must refuse to purchase freedom at the cost of our cherished convictions. He may well have pleaded justification for his actions in the words of an Arab poet who said, 'If the stand that I took was disobedience, then I desire by my disobedience obidence to God.' It was not only one man against the world but he made one feel that the world was in the dock and he was sitting in judgement on it.

Gandhiji displayed this courage, this supreme fearlessness of all earthly power, from the early years of his public life. It was evident not only his fight with the British Government but also when he saw his own people and his followers going astray, which is rarer form of courage. In 1916 when he was a comparatively young man, and not known all over India, he was invited to attend the opening ceremony of the Hindu University Central College. The meeting was presided over by Annie Besant and attended by the Viceroy, the Governors, the Maharajas and Maharanis as well as some of the foremost leaders of the day. When he stood up to speak, he gently refused the glittering specimens assembled there for flaunting their wealth and jewellery in a land of poverty and privation. This was a time when most persons did not dare to open their mouth even in the presence of a British Distric Collector. In the face of the Chairman's discouragement and the walking out of some dignitaries from the meeting, he firmly pointed out, 'There is no salvation for India unless (among other things) you strip yourself of jewellery and hold it in trust for your countrymen in India.'

What a unique courage and but a unique lesson for us!

It is painful that his so-called followers have forgotten his lesson and have betrayed him. Every leader in his declaration to contest Lok Sabha election has shown property, bank balances, jewellery and diamonds worth, crores of rupees. It is shameful that they call themselves Gandhite. They are responsible for killing Gandhiji every day rather every moment.

Gandhiji's Birth Day on Martyrdan Day observed only as rituals

Now January 30 is observed just as a ritual of observing silence for two minutes. Even this is done in a casual manner as nobody bothers about Gandhiji and his supreme sacrifice. With every passing day, we are getting away from the teachings of Gandhiji. The Mahatma is remembered when a foreign dignitary pays a visit to our country. Then he is escorted with a large wreath of flowers to Rajghat, the samadhi of Gandhiji. The next moment he is forgotten and the politicians get busy in materialistic pursuits. Whether it is Gandhi's birth day or martyrdom day the same types of rituals are observed and are highlighted through media, but actually the spirit of Gandhiji and his teachings are totally ignored by most Indians especially by the power hungry politicians. There is mere show of respect for the him and the next moment he is forgotten.

The Gandhi centenary was celebrated with great pomp and show, but the celebrations although widespread, made little impact on us. In India, we celebrated his centenary by displaying a naked dance of communal riots in Ahmedabad and burning his portraits in West Bengal. We swear in his name and his principles, but daily deny him and his teachings in our deeds. We have compromised with the evil against which Gandhiji fought all his life. In the craze for power and pelf, we have replaced his basic principle, "The means justify the end" by the Machiavellian principle "Nothing succeeds like success". The Congress Party which claims to be followers of Gandhiji is especially guilty in this regard. Thus, we have betrayed Gandhiji.

Congress Policies antagonous to Gandhian Principles

The Congressmen revive the name of Gandhiji at the time of elections and they beg for votes in his name. They use him as a very effective tool for their success. They still wear white cotton clothes as if they are the incarnations of Gandhiji's spirit. But actually most of them are wolves in lamb's clothing. They incite people to violence to have a dependable vote-bank. All political parties, especially the Congress party which claim to be followers of Gandhiji have said good bye to all the principles of Gandhiji.

"In his time Gandhi was the undisputed leader of India. But even after independence of the country he held no office in the government. But his followers can go to any extent to grab power. Now, even M.P.s. can be purchased to get confidence votes in the Parliament.

Gandhiji was loved, admired and respected, his so called followers are hated and despised. Gandhi was a saintly, simple, moral, straightforward man, but his followers are hypocrites, immoral and cunning. They exploit innocent and simple people and are bluff masters. Gandhi preached what he practised, whereas the new Gandhi clan pretend to be angels but are actually devilish fellows.

Gandhi belonged to a prosperous family, but he led a life of self-imposed poverty. To be in harmony with the poor, he lived by choice a life which was frugal and spartan. But those who pose to be the successors of Gandhiji are accumulating more and more property and bank balances. They remain busy in laundering their black money in safe foreign banks. They shed crocodile tears for the poor and give assurances through slogans such as "Garibi Hatao". After winning elections and gaining power, they consider it below their dignity to associate themselves with the poor.

Gandhi sacrificed his life for the communal harmony and unity of the nation, but his so called followers call themselves secular while they exploit people of different castes, creeds and religions as a policy of vote bank to remain in power. They are most communal.

Whenever there were communal riots Gandhiji used to go alone without any security. People of India worshipped him and obeyed him and used to shun violence when he used to go on a hunger strike to show his protest against the violence of the angry people of India. This was his way of bringing about communal harmony in the country. But now Gandhiji's followers engineer communal riots for vote bank. When they visit such riot-hit areas, they travel in bullet-proof vehicles and wear bullet-proof jackets and move around only under the protection of heavy security.

For Gandhiji, politics without religion was lame, politics and religion were inseparable, but his so called pseudo-secular followers are averse to religion in the name of secularism.

Gandhiji was proud to be a staunch Sanatinic Hindu and undoubtedly he was a great Hindu. But now if a Hindu claims to be such, he is branded as communal and anti-national. Such prcpaganda is done by the so called followers of Gandhiji who pose to be secular in order to get Muslim votes to remain in power. The adoration of Gandhiji is just a show off and a pretence. Actually the followers of Gandhiji are betraying the Father of the Nation by saying goodbye to all his principles.

Gandhiji was against conversion of religion. He used to say, "Instead of making me a Christian, make me a better Hindu." But Gandhiji's followers call such persons communal who are against conversion of religion.

Ram was so dear to Gandhiji that when he was assassionated he uttered 'Hey Ram'! and collapsed dying with Ram's name on his lips. Whereas Ram was in every breath of Gandhiji, his followers deny even the very existence of Ram and are determined to destroy Ram Setu with an eye on their vote Bank. The Indian Government even submitted an affidevit in the Suppreme Court to deny the existence of Ram.

Gandhiji dream was to establish Ram Rajya (Sarvodya Swaraj) in Inda, but his followers have established Ravan Raj where the gulf between the rich and the poor has been increasing with every passing day. Corruption is eating the very vital nerve of the Nation. All moral values have evaporated.

The work of national integration was initiated by Gandhiji and his final aim was to raise it to the level of 'Brotherhood of Mankind' in the whole world. But after Gandhiji's death India was divided into linguistic states and there came into existence several regional political parties. Which are trying to disintegrate our great Nation to achieve their political ends without having any national perspective.

Gandhiji favoured decentralization and making Panchayats self-sufficient and self-governing units, but his successors attempted to concentrate all powers at the centre. Even the Constitution of India was framed against Gandhiji's principles of decentralization.

The politicians in India wear a mask of peace but their real faces are fierce and diabolical. They are guided by a strong political instinct to safeguard their interests and for this they are even prepared to bow before the powerful blocks in the world even if their country's honour is at stake. Culturally they appear to be true Indians but their economic approach is completely occidental and materialistic. They are platform politicians who use the rhetoric with Gandhian terminology with a sense of reverence but they betray him because their language and actions do not coincide. In the hands of such politicians the explosive force of Gandhian revolution has misfired. They work under the harsh and obtuse rule of bureaucracy. Leaders of the calibre of Gandhi are nowhere to be found in India. The so called leaders now are men of limited vision. They are vain and behave like the kings of the past. They even accept crowns of gold and are weighed with coins and currency notes. Their perverse behaviour is disgusting and shameful. They work only for the corrupt and have no rapport with the majority of the common masses.

It is shameful that Shrimati Maya Devi, Chief Minister of Uttar Pradesh passed most derogatory remarks against Gandhiji, but there was not much protest by the people especially the Congress. Had she passed such remarks against Shrimati Sonia Gandhi or any other Congress leader, there would have been so much of hue and cry that she would have been compelled to apologise for her remarks.

Gandhiji was all for prohibition, but his so called followers consider drinking as status symbol. Today there are more shops of liquor in our country than of other items. Gandhiji was against earning income for the country by selling liquor, today most of the income of the states is from excise duty on liquor at the cost of health and moral values of their citizens.

Gandhiji was really great. When he left his earthly abode all the countries, all the religions, all the creeds, all the presidents and kings, all those who had understood him and all those who had always loved him, all his followers and all his opponents who had scoffed at him as a half-naked fakir, missed him badly. His cremation ground was a wasteland of burning hearts. The people of the entire world stood transfixed with tears in their eyes because the second Prince of Peace had been crucified. There was nothing apocryphal about him. He was simple and real, as perhaps no other great man in history had been real. He was a seeker and teacher of Truth.

Now the United Nations has announced that it will celebrate Gandhi Jayanti as "World Non-Violence Day." In a tribute to Gandhiji's philosophy of brotherhood and peace, the United Nations General Assembly declared Mahatma Gandhji's Birth Anniversary as the International Day of Non-violence and urged the member states to observe it each year in an appropriate manner.

But in India, it was celebrated to the accompaniment of riots and attacks on the poor Bhaias of Uttar Pradesh and Bihar in Maharashtra as if they were seeking employment in Kenya or Uganda. No action was taken as it was in the interest of the ruling party to ignore such unconstitutional activities as vote bank policy. Gandhi preached love and brotherhood between various communities belonging to the diverse states of India but now those Gandhian principles are openly flouted by certain violent organizations which are supported by some political parties. So now we find that India is no more a country which Gandhiji envisaged in his dreams – a nation of peace-loving and non-violent people.

Now the people of other countries seek solace from the philosophy of Gandhiji.

Whereas the people world over have started studying Gandhians principles and adopting them in their life, we in India have betrayed him and have said good bye to his teachings.

The author has travelled the whole of India & Europe and has discussed Gandhian principles and actions with thousands of Indians and foreigners and found that whereas our people, even the so called followers of Gandhiji know little about his principles and actions, the foreigners have studied him deeply and have developed a great respect for him.

The author found it rather surprising that many Russians too, though they believe in the teachings of 'Karl Marx', whose Philosophy is the antithesis of Gandhian Philosophy, have now come around the view that Gandhian Philosophy is of great value to the entire mankind. Many Russian the author talked to held Gandhiji in great esteem. We, especially the Congressmen have forgotten Gandhiji and have betrayed him.

But, now in India, the pedulum is swinging in the opposite direction. The younger generation hates Gandhiji and breaks his statues, burns his books and portraits, garlands his statues with shoes and blacken them with coal-tar.

Who is responsible for this?

For this the so-called followers of Gandhiji are responsible. The younger generation has neither the stirring experience of actually seeing him and coming under the spell of his personality nor read the writings of Gandhiji. They see only his so-called followers who call themselves Gandhites, but have compromised with all the evils against which Gandhiji fought all his life. In a craze for power and pelf who have replaced his basic principle. 'The means justify the end', by the Machiavalian principle, 'Nothing succeeds like success.' Who claim to be secular but are most communal and engineer communal riots as a policy of vote bank. Who are corrupt, hypocrite and what not.

Seeing these so-called followers of Gandhiji, the young generation thinks that he must be like them. However, many misunderstandings have also been created against Gandhian Philosophy like, 'Majboori Ka Nam Mahatma Gandhi'.

The saddest part has been the fall in character which has been more responsible for the impression of disillusionment than inadequacy of policy. The major share of the blame is that of the Congress both as an orgaization and as a collection of political and social workers. Corruption would not seem as unredeemable as it is, if Congressmen at least bore the imprint of Gandhi's character as they had borne the brunt of the suffering he prescribed for them. The common man whose welfare was always Gandhi's objective has been forgotten.

If Gandhiji were alive today, he would be nearly one hundred twenty years old and would find that he was near godhood. The world has not changed much since his death, and people talk of him as if he were as remote as saints in calendars. he has lent himself to caricature not only in appearance. Congressmen use him as their talisman without practising either truthfulness or a sense of non-possession to which he attached great value. Opposition parties use Gandhiji to criticize Congressmen. Conservative parties twist his theory of trusteeship and use it to support the principle of predatory self-interest. The consequences of Gandhiji are yet to be critically assessed and given a historical perspective. The devotion which he evoked and the mass discipline which he inspired led to an unintellectual atmosphere. Many ceased to think; they lost the habit of thinking for themselves. In invoking the forces of freedom, he invoked much that was good and much that was bad. His direct action has been imitated in many crude forms of direct action; his satyagraha has been carricatured into all kinds of violent demonstrations, destroying public property and false hunger strikes. His influence on Indian national evolution will require study. He is a submerged part of the national consciousness, as broad as the nation, and all the good and the bad go with it.

"Today India's greatest need is that her people should have faith in the bonafide and the integrity of their Government. They should not be alienated from the government. It is no exaggeration to say that Congress has lost the confidence of the people. The reason is simple.Congressmen are no longer selfless, there is scramble among them for the prestige and spolils of office. Congressmen have lost contact with the people, the contacts are limited to Congressmen out of office; and to Congressmen in office within their narrow self interest. Congress should not be monoply of one family. There should be real internal democracy in the congress. All corrupt congressmen should be shunted out of the party and the congress party, being the oldest should set examples before other political parties by strictly following Gandhian Principles and actions. All political parties should adopt atleast one Gandhian principle, 'The means justify the end' and stop following the policy of Vote Bank.

Gandhiji wrote in Harijan on January 15, 1937, "..... Out of my ashes a thousand Gandhi will arise. This has inspired me to take the message of Gandhiji to the present generation. In the next chapters of this book, I have tried to give the socio-politics-economic, educational & moral philosophy of Gandhiji. I would make an humble request to the reader to study his philosophy deeply and adopt is in his life.

References

1. D.G. Tendulkar, Mahatma, vol. VIII, p. 0.
2. From the text of Pandit Jawahar Lal Nehru's broadcast speech announcing Gandhiji's death on the evening of January 30, 1948.
3. Homage to Mahatma Gandhi, p. 10.
4. Broadcast from Delhi Station on Jaunary 30, 1948.
5. Harijan 8-2-' 48, p. 17.
6. Broad cast from Delhi Station on February 9, 1948.
7. Broad cast from Delhi Station on February 1, 1948.
8. Harijan, 15-2-' 48, p. 28.
9. Broad cast from Delhi Station an January, 30, 1948.
10. Broad cast from Delhi Station on February 9, 1948.
11. Harijan, 30-1-1949, pp. 405-406.
12. Gandhiji quoted in Pyarell, Mahatma Gandhi—The Last Phase, Vol. 2, Ahmedabad Navajivan Publishing House, 1958, p. 675.

2

The Theory of Reality and Knowledge

"I believe in the absolute oneness of God and therefore also of humanity. What though, we have many bodies ? We have one soul. The rays of the sun are many through refraction. But they have the same source."

–Young India, 25-9-1925

IN order to understand and appreciate Gandhiji as a philosopher, it is essential for us to understand the meaning and the concept of philosophy. Philosophy not only means the knowledge or wisdom about reality, but also implies the application of such knowledge to all walks of life. Mere theoretical knowledge is barren as action bereft of knowledge is futile.

The fundamental problem of philosophy is undoubtedly problem of reality. If reality is considered as one spiritual principle underlying, evolving and sustaining the Universe, then our view will be Monistic Idealism. If, on the other hand, we suppose that there are two opposite ultimate realities, one physical and the other spiritual, and one acting and reacting upon the other and therefore, one limiting the other, then it will be Dualistic Realism. If, again, on the other hand, we conceive of an infinity of ultimate existences, each independent and outside the other, our view of reality will be Pluralistic, which again will be Spiritualistic or Materialistic as we conceive of these realities, conscious or un-conscious respectively. But since philosophy has for its aim the explanation of the Universe, and since explanation means unification of our knowledge, the purpose of philosophy is best served, if it can trace all the diversities of things and relations to one ultimate principle, that is, if it is monistic in its conception of the Universe.

Dualistic conception of reality labours under the fundamental difficulty of explaining how two independent realities will at all co-operate with each other. If this difficulty of cooperation be merely ignored by assuming the fact of cooperation, the difficulty of one limiting the other and that of explaining knowledge, which involves appropriation of the object by the subject, remains unobviated. And in the case of the supposition of a plurality of realities the metaphysical and epistemological difficulties are no less serious than the difficulties in the way of the dualistic conception of reality. It follows then, the view of reality, which can steer clear of the above difficulties, will only be monistic. Now, whether this one reality should be material or spiritual can be decided if we take into account the metaphysical and epistemological questions that are involved here.

Metaphysically the conception of one material reality will be ruled out of court in view of the fact that life and mind exhibit features which are qualitatively different, and cannot really be shown to be mere complex developments out of the features of the physical reality. Conscious and vital powers cannot be satisfactorily shown to be out-growths by way of increasing complexity from the features of physical reality. Again, as physical reality for its very conception as such requires mind or spirit the latter must, therefore, be foundational to all knowledge and existence. It follows then that the ultimate principle of reality which must at once be explanation of minds and things and of knowledge which involves a relation between them, cannot but be spiritual. Now, if the ultimate reality be Thought or Spirit, then minds and things of the universe will only be relative realities deriving their existence from it and such a conception of reality will have the advantage of explaining the nature of mind and the world and the relations between them, while establishing the possibility of knowledge. Such a fundamental spiritual reality will be a creative and synthetic principle, accordingly relative reality and function to minds and things, and serving as foundation for knowledge and other relations between minds and things; and those between minds and things on the one side and its own nature on the other. We see then that Reality in its absolute and ultimate sense must be One and Spiritual and that if we are to concede reality to minds and things, they can only be relative realities deriving their existence and function and mutual relation from the One Absolute Spiritual Reality. Gandhiji agrees with this view point.

GANDHIAN THEORY OF REALITY

Gandhiji's view on the nature of Reality is monistic. "I believe", says he, "in the absolute oneness of God and therefore also of humanity. What though, we have many bodies ? We have but one soul. The rays of the sun are many through refraction. But they have the same source."[1] He again says, "I believe in advaita. I believe in the essential unity of man and for that matter of all that lives."[2] Gandhiji further says in unequivocal terms, "I subscribe to the belief or philosophy that all life in its essence is one, and that men are working consciously or unconsciously towards the realization of that identity. This belief requires a living faith in living God who is the ultimate arbiter of our faith."[3]

Gandhiji is an idealist. For him God is the ultimate reality behind the Universe which is always in a state of flux. God alone is real, the world is illusion. He alone persists in the midst of change. That God does not need any proof. It is an undefinable, mysterious power and pervades everything. "God is Life, Truth, Light. He is Love. He is Supreme Good."[4] In Gandhiji's view there is no other God than Truth.

Thus, Gandhiji uses the term Truth to mean reality, i.e. Truth in the Platonian sense of absolute, universal, infinite Truth. Truth is the 'Ultimate Reality', the 'Real Existent', and so synonymous with God. Gandhiji would say "Truth is God" rather than "God is Truth,"[5] because the atheists in their passion for discovering truth do not hesitate to deny the very existence of God. God transcends the senses and the intellect. If realization must be outside the senses and the intellect, it can be possible only through a living faith. Gandhiji says that faith "acts like a sixth sense to unravel that which is beyond the purview of reason."[6]

Gandhiji's idea of reality, thus, partakes of the Socratic theory of the existence of permanent natures—'forms' or 'ideas'—beyond the world of sensible things and not knowable by the senses. Like Socrates, Gandhiji also believes that man must naturally seek liberation from material world if he is to find perfection. But unlike Socrates, he does not believe that 'perfection' or 'wisdom' is attainable by mere contemplation when once the soul can free itself from the bonds of flesh. He wants to mortify the flesh to gain control over animal passions, but it does not mean a disparagement of the body or of manual activities. He looks upon a life of active social service as the true way to know God, and in this life of service he gives a prominent place to manual labour. He holds that God is made known in His works and truth is to be found in action. In thinking of God as ever active, asserting in and through the turmoil of social and political events, and of Truth as something to which one cannot think one's way but has to live one way, Gandhiji testifies to an incarnate notion of Truth, and the Biblical view of reality as both transcendent and immanent.

Gandhiji considers that God is Satyam, Sivam, Sundaram i.e. true, good and beautiful. Truth, Beauty and Goodness are, thus, objective values recognised, but not constituted by human mind, and they have to be realized actively by living a true, beautiful and good life. He holds that the true end of all contemplation must be action; intellectual activity is justifiable only in so far as it interprets the world of experience and aids action.

Gandhian view of reality, thus, shares the classical and Biblical, both of which agree in affirming "the existence of absolute values which are neither the projection of individual minds, nor the product of social process."[7] Gandhiji echoes with the classical and biblical thinkers when he condemns modern relativism as disintegrating intellectual coherence. A philosophy which considers reality as wholly immanent could result also in an erosion of moral and personal values as it rules out all abiding norms by which human conduct is governed. Gandhiji wants positively to guard against this tendency to depersonalize human beings.

GANDHIAN THEORY OF KNOWLEDGE

We have already discussed Gandhian Theory of Reality. For Gandhiji, "Truth is the ultimate reality, rather the only reality." Connected with this metaphysical problem is epistemological problem. How is this reality apprehended ? How does knowledge originate and what are its sources ? Here, as elsewhere, philosophers differ. Thinkers of the empirical school have traced knowledge to sensations and feelings alone, those of rational schools to reason. According to rationalists, sense perception cannot go beyond the external qualities of objects. Many Western philosophers e.g., Hegel, Bosanquet, etc. hold that the ultimate nature of the universe can be grasped by thought or reason. According to them the real is rational. Thus Bosanquet defines reality as the object affirmed by thought. Kant traces to a combination of sensation and reason. He founded the empirio-rational school which received different developments at the hands of later rationalist philosophers.

But intellect cannot grasp the self, the known, the condition and the presupposition of all knowledge. Thus, 'I am' does not depend upon 'I think' for then the latter will have to be proved and so on to an infinite regress. Consciousness of self cannot come by reasoning. Even as regards external objects discursive intellect confines itself to the discernible aspects. Thus, conceptual knowledge about a thing is only the appearance of a thing, it is not the reality.

Gandhiji also considers the senses and reasoning as inadequate media of apprehending the Absolute Reality. "God" says he, "is indescribable, inconceivable and immeasurable". God transcends the senses and the intellect. "We must ever fail to perceive Him through the senses because He is beyond them. We can feel Him, if we will, but withdraw ourselves from the senses. The divine music is incessantly going on within ourselves, but the loud senses drown the delicate music."[8] "The intellect, if anything, acts as a barrier."[9] So realization must be outside the senses and intellect, it must have for its basis a living faith. The source of faith is the heart. "God cannot be realized through intellect. Intellect can only lead to a certain extent and no further. It is a matter of faith and experience derived from that faith...Full faith does not feel the want of experience."[10]

"... That which is beyond reason is surely not unreasonable...To ask anybody to believe without proof what is capable of proof would be unreasonable...But for an experienced person to ask another to believe, without being able to prove, that there is God, is humbly to confess his limitations and to ask another to accept in faith the statement of his experience. Without faith this world come to naught in moment. True faith is appropriation of the reasoned experience of people whom we believe to have lived a life purified by prayer and penance. Belief, therefore, in prophets or incarnations who have lived in remote ages is not an idle superstition, but a satisfaction of an inmost spiritual want. The formula for guidance is rejection of every demand for faith where a matter is capable of present proof and unquestioned acceptance through personal experience."[11] Soul or God is not the object of knowledge. He is Himself the knower and so He is beyond the intellect. There are two stages in knowing God. The first is faith and the second and the ultimate stage is experience—knowledge arising from it (faith).[12] Thus, 'faith' does not contradict reason but transcends it. "Faith is a kind of sixth sense which works in cases which are without the purview of reason".[13] "Faith is nothing but a living wide awake consciousness of God within."[14]

Thus, for Gandhiji, logical reasoning and sense perception are not the only source of knowledge. He supplements them by intuition. Intuition is "a mode of consciousness which is distinct from the perceptual, imaginative or intellectual, and thus, carries with it self-evidence and completeness. Religious men of all ages have won their certainty of God through this direct way of approach to the apprehension of reality". Gandhiji refers to it as faith whose source is heart.

References

1. Young India, 25-9-25.
2. *Ibid.*, 4-12-24.
3. Bose, N.K., Selections from Gandhi, p. 27.
4. Young India, 11-20-28.
5. *Ibid.*, 31-12-31.
6. Harijan, 6-3-27.
7. Jeffreys, Education, Christian or Pagan, p. 97.
8. Young India, 21-1-26.
9. Harijan, 18-6-38.
10. *Ibid.*, 4-8-46.
11. Young India, III, p. 143.
12. Gandhiji's Letter quoted in Diary, I, p. 135.
13. Harijan, 6-3-27, p. 26.
14. Young India, II, p. 1116.

3

The Nature of God

"I believe Him to be creative as well as non-creative... From the platform of the Jainas I prove the non-creative aespect of God, and from that of Ramanuj the creative aspect. As a matter of fact we are to know the unknown, and this is why our speech flatters, is inadequate and even often contradictory. That is why Vedas describe Brahman as 'not this, not this'. But if He or It is not this, He or It is...He is one and yet many; He is smaller than an atom, and yet bigger than the Himalayas."

–YOUNG INDIA, 21-1-1926

WE have already discussed Gandhian Theory of Reality and Knowledge in the preceding chapter. Here, we propose to discuss his views on the Nature of God. Gandhiji does not claim to have known reality in its entirety. Nor does he indulge in such metaphysical conundrums as proof for the existence of God, creation, evolution, immortality or objectivity of values. He wanted to lead the life of a non-attached man. "Non-attached to his bodily sensations and busts. Non-attached to his craving for power and possessions. Non-attached to the objects of these various desires. Non-attached to his anger and hatred; non-attached to his exclusive loves. Non-attached to wealth, fame, social position."[1] Such an ideal life presupposes an unshakable faith in God.

Gandhiji has a living, unshakable faith in God. So immovable is his faith that he feels that he may live without air and water, but not without God[2], and even if he were cut to pieces, God would give him strength not to deny Him[3]. The nuclear element of Gandhian philosophy is the idea of God. All other elements ranged around this centre in a peculiar way to form a new pattern. It will, therefore, be convenient to begin with his views on the nature of God.

THE NATURE OF GOD

Gandhiji does not mind how one defines God; for he is conscious that "there are innumerable definitions of God because his manifestations are innumerable."[4] "God is indescribable and impenetrable, because he is in every body and in everything...He is in everything...so no description of Him is adequate."[5]

Gandhiji was greatly influenced by the Vaishnava family in which he was born. A series of Vaishnava teachers like Ramanuj, Nimbarka, Madhva and Vallabha, who succeeded Shankra, tried to refute Shankra's interpretation of God and establish the conception of God as a concrete person, possessed of all suspicious qualities and perfections like Omnipotence, Omniscience and All-merciful. Whereas, Shankra looks upon the world as a mere appearance resting on the ignorance of the individual (and, therefore, God's creatorship of the world also is, for him, no more real than the magician's creation of a show). All the Vaishnava teachers accept the world and, therefore, God's creatorship, as real. Gandhiji, influenced by the Vaishnava teachers believes that "God is the Creator, the Ruler and the Lord of the Universe and not a blade of grass moves but by His will."[6] Again, whereas Shankra regards knowledge of God as the ultimate, attributeless reality, as the path to liberation, all the Vaishnava teachers on the contrary, agree that liberation can be obtained only by the mercy of God propitiated by devotion and self-surrender. Gandhiji, though opposed to fatalism on the one hand, and a firm believer in the theory that man can shape his destiny by his own action, on the other, believes that man's perfection and liberation can come only by self-surrender and grace. He says, "For perfection or freedom from error comes only from grace...without an unreserved surrender to this grace, complete mastery over thought is impossible."[7] This is typical of a Thiest, a Vaishnava. Shankara and his orthodox followers, the Advaitins or monistic Vedantins, do not believe in grace, but in knowledge as the path to liberation.

Moreover, Gandhiji being a true Vaishnava, was conscious of God every minute of his life whether asleep or awake.[8] He pined "to see God face to face" and often "had faint glimpses of the Absolute Truth, God."[9] It was an unbroken torture to him that he was far from Him.[10] He felt the sense of entire dependence on Him, humbly sought His guidance and found that His voice had been increasingly audible as the year rolled by.[11] In the darkest despair, in the most terrible trial, at the last moment His help never failed Gandhiji and this help was to him "the visible finger of visible God."[12] Often in the name of God, in answer to His voice, he undertook fasts. And he had real mystic experiences. Here is one of these in his own words:

"It relates to my 21 days' fast for the removal of untouchability. I had gone to sleep...at about 12 O'clock in the night, something wake me up suddenly and some voice whispers :

'Thou must go on a fast.'

'How many days ?' I ask.

The voice again says, 'Twenty-one days'.

'When does it begin ?' I ask.

It says, 'You begin tomorrow.'

...That kind of experience has never happened in my life before or after that date."[13] "...My mind was unprepared for it, disinclined for it. But this came to me as clearly as anything could be."[14] On another occasion he described the experience in these words, "I saw no form... but what I did hear was like a Voice from a far and yet quite near. It was as unmistakable as some human voice definitely speaking to me, and irresistible. I was not dreaming at the time I heard the voice. The hearing of the Voice was preceded by a terrific struggle within me. Suddenly, the Voice came upon me. I listened, made certain it was the voice and the struggle ceased. I was calm...The determination was made accordingly, the date and the hour of the fast was fixed"[15]

From this experience of Gandhiji, it appears he was a mystic, but it is not so. Once, in an answer to a question if he had any mystical experience, he said, "If by mystical experience you mean vision, no...But, I am very sure of the voice which guides me."[16]

Such uncommon spiritual experiences may be ruled out by the short-sightedness of modern scientific outlook as mere delusion. But according to Indian tradition, if a seeker has integrated his personality and risen to the level of what the Gita describes as 'Budhi-yoga',[17] he can have an insight into reality and can discern Truth. Undoubtedly, for the last 60 years of his life the one constant endevour of Gandhiji had been progressive self-integration and steadfast pursuit of spiritual discipline essential for 'Sthithprajna'.

Looking at Gandhiji in this background, little doubt is left about the fact that Gandhiji was a Theist rather than an Advaitin; that is, he was not a follower of Shankra—a believer in an Inderminate, Attributeless, Impersonal Absolute i.e. Nirguna Brahman (निर्गुण ब्रह्मः). Yet we are sometimes embarrassed by the occasional expressions which seem to go against his real beliefs. It may be that he sometimes uses some of the Indian philosophical terms which having passed into common parlance, have lost their precise technical significance, of which he seems to be not so particular. For instance, he says in reply to a friend's question, "I am an advaitist and yet I can support dvaitism (dualism). The world is changing every moment, and is therefore unreal, it has no permanent existence. But though it is constantly changing, it has something about it which persists and it is therefore to that extent real. I have therefore no objection to calling it real and unreal and thus, being called an anekantavadi or syadvadi. But my syadvada is not the syadvada of the learned, it is peculiarly my own."[18]

Thus, it is clear that Gandhiji is using the words advaitist, dvaitism and similarly anekantavadi and syadvadi without being so particular about the technically philosophical meanings of these terms which he admits by saying that he has been using the words in his own sense, not like the learned. Gandhiji's own words clearly show that he is not the advaitist in the sense of a shankarite who would neither support dualism nor the logic of syadvada. On the contrary, his attempt to do justice to the unity and diversity of the world would strongly remind one of the theistic Vedantist. Nimbarka, who tries to reconcile Dvaita with Advaita. Nimbarka is the founder of one of the four schools of Vaishnava Theism who, though rejecting the Advaita of Shankra, his monism that tolerates no plurality and change, advocates, some kind of monism that tolerates them. It appears that Gandhiji uses Advaita for this kind of monism.

Sometimes Gandhiji speaks like the Shankarite, and calls the world unreal. But reading between the lines it is found that he perhaps means by the word "unreal" only "impermanent" or "transitory" (as in the paragraph cited above). His strong sense of duty towards suffering fellow-beings stood in the way of his dismissing the world as wholly unreal). He writes, "Joy or what men call happiness may be, as it really is, a dream in a fleeting and transitory world...But we cannot dismiss the suffering of our fellow creatures as unreal and thereby provide a moral alibi for ourselves. Even dreams are true while they last, and to the sufferer his suffering is a grim reality."[19]

But it should be noted that even the non-Shankarite theists, though affirming, unlike Shankara, the reality of the world, attach to it a lower value and aesthetically describe it as a sport of God. Gandhiji echoes this theistic sentiment when he says, "Let us dance to the tune of his Bansi—flute, and all would be well."[20] In this sense he calls the world an illusion, Maya. But this word is also used by him, like the Vaishnavas, in the sense of Lila or sport. So he says, "Therefore, it is that Hinduism calls it all His sport—Lila, or calls it an illusion—Maya."[21] It is taking this sportive view of God that he describes God as "the greatest tyrant...(who)...dashes the cup from our lips...to provide only mirth for Himself at our expense."[22]

Again, though he sometimes says like a Shankarite that he does not believe in the personality of God, closer scrutiny shows that he does not believe in the possibility of God assuming the form of human being. "God" he says, "is not a person. To affirm that he descends to earth every now and again in the form of human being is a partial truth which merely signifies that such a person lives near to God."[23]

Even Western philosophers differ over exact meaning of personality. If personality implies self-consciousness plus will, Gandhiji may be said to believe in the personality of God whom he regards as the Omniscient, Omnipotent creator, and just Governor of the world. On the whole, therefore, it will be reasonable to think that Gandhiji was a theist—a Vaishnava, rather than an Advaitist—a follower of Shankara.

True, we find Gandhiji sometimes speaking in an Advaita langauage. But these ideas float loosely on his mind. His theistic attitude and outlook dominate his thoughts as well as his practical life.

God, for him, is the all-pervasive Reality, immanent in man and also in the world, which he regards as His manifestation and creation. But, unlike an ordinary pantheist, he believes that God is also transcendent. He is in the world as well as beyond it. He is not expressed fully by His creation just as a poet is not by his poems. Gandhiji has thus a comprehensive conception of God, like that of the Western pantheists. Like Whitehead, in more recent times, who describes God from both the primordial and the consequent aspects and tries thereby to comprehend the diverse religious concepts of God, Gandhiji also tries hard to comprehend the diverse elements of current religious traditions and to understand them as the different aspects of one Reality whose infinite richness surpasses our full comprehension. He says, "I believe Him to be creative as well as non-creative...From the platform of the Jainas I prove the non-creative aspect of God, and from that of Ramanuj the creative aspect. As a matter of fact we are to know the Unknown, and this is why our speech flatters, is inadequate and even often contradictory. That is why the Vedas describe Brahaman as 'not this, not this'. But if He or It is not this, He or It is...He is one and yet many; He is smaller than an atom, and yet bigger than the Himalayas."[24]

The logic of the many foldness of truth consequent on the many and inexhaustible possible aspects of Reality is particularly emphasized by the Jainas in India in their doctrine of syadvada[25] and anekantavada[26]. Gandhiji accepted this logic, for it enabled him to reconcile apparent contradictions in all fields of life and to have respect for other's views and humility about his own. It cannot be said whether he had any knowledge of the technical arguments in support of Jaina logic. He knew however, the often quoted Indian parable which favours this point of view. He says, "It has been my experience that I am always true from my point of view, and often wrong from the point of view of my honest critics. I know that we are both right from our respective points of view. And this knowledge saves me from attributing motives to my opponents or critics. The seven blind men who gave seven different descriptions of the elephant were all right from their respective points of view. I very much like this doctrine of the manyness of reality. It is this doctrine that has taught me to judge a Mussulman from his own stand point and a Christian from his. Formerly, I used to resent the ignorance of my opponents. Today, I can love them because I am gifted with the eye to see myself as others see me and vice versa. I want to take the whole world in the embrace of my love. My anekantavada is the result of the twin doctrine of Satya (i.e. Truth) and Ahimsa (i.e. Love)."

Gandhiji finds further confirmation of this all inclusive attitude in the teachings of Jesus, "In my father's house there are many mansions...I have not come to destroy but to fulfill."

It is with this Catholic and all-round outlook that he described his conception of God, on different occasions, from different points of view; and his basic idea of God as the all-pervasive reality underlying all phenomena, concrete and abstract, sometimes inspired him to ecstatic raptures that momentarily overflowed the well-disciplined measures of his habitual thought and speech. As one of the rare specimens of such a comprehensive and eloquent description we may take the following paragraph :

"God is that indefinable something which we all feel, but which we do not know. To me God is Truth and Love. God is Ethics and Morality. God is fearlessness. God is the source of light and life and yet he is above and beyond all these. God is conscience. He is even the atheism of the atheist. He transcends speech and reason. He is personal God to those who need His touch. He is the purest essence. He simply is to those who have faith. He is long suffering. He is patient, but he is also terrible. He is the greatest democrat the world knows, for he leaves us unfettered to make our own choice between evil and good. He is the greatest tyrant èver known for he often dashes the cup from our lips and under the cover of free will leaves us a margin so wholly inadequate as to provide only mirth for himself at our expense. Therefore, it is that Hinduism calls all this sport—Lila, or calls it an illusion—Maya."[27]

Students of philosophy may find in this description a very similar parallel to the famous description of God by the great scientist, mathematician and philosopher of the century, Whitehead. He says, "It is true to say that God is permanent, and the world is fluent, as that the world is permanent and God is fluent. It is as true that God is one and the world many, as that the world is one and God many" and so on.

The similarity between the two lies in their attempts to comprehend in one synthetic sweep the divergent aspects of God-head and the different religious traditions representing different points of view. Both descriptions appear, to superficial view, as jumbles of contradictions which can, however, be reconcilled by recognising the possibility of divergent aspects and view points. Even Whitehead has been misunderstood and severely criticized by philosophers, and more so may be Gandhiji. For they impose too great a strain on the customary moulds of thought. Yet, when the world is fast shrinking towards one community under the pressure of the scientific devices for overcoming space and time, and the people and ideas so long inhabiting isolated areas are running into one another, the necessity of synthetic outlook is being more and more felt by the greatest men of the world in different spheres. It is no wonder, therefore, Whitehead and Gandhiji would think alike.

GOD AND EVIL

In some respects, however, the paragraph cited above shows Gandhiji moving faster than Whitehead. For he takes our breath away when he stretches his idea of God not only to include the good and the benign aspects of the world, but even its terror, tyranny and atheism. These points make us pause to think what Gandhiji really means by God.

Even in our casual survey of the history of the religions of the world, we find two general types of conceptions about God. God is either conceived as a benign power struggling against an opposite principle or principles responsible for the world's evils, or God is regarded as the only and all-inclusive reality. Though in accordance with the first conception, God may be and often is conceived as ultimately capable of over coming the evils or Satan, yet it makes God subject to partial limitation by an opposite principle. The religious sentiments want an unfailing source of help, and nothing but the second conception of God fully satisfies it. Moreover, religious belief is encouraged to posit the idea of an all-inclusive God by the monistic tendency of science which also tries, so far as possible, to explain the diverse phenomena of the world by bringing them under as few principles as possible. But as soon as God is made all-inclusive, evils, also necessarily come to be lodged in Him. Developed Christianity and Monistic Indian thought with which Gandhiji is in deepest sympathy, face the problem of evil rather than sacrifice the infinite and sole reality of God. Trying to describe this all-inclusive idea of God, Gandhiji is realistic enough to include His aspects of suffering, terror and tyranny.

The question naturally arises, does Gandhiji accept the position that God—this total reality—is both good and bad—as the above description seems to suggest ? Or does he hold that the evil is only apparent, or that though it is real, it is or can be ultimately overcome? By family tradition and temperament Gandhiji's heart remained captivated by the theistic romantic and benign conception of God as possessed of supreme grace, goodness, love, duty and harmony. The study of great religions also strengthened this disposition. Throughout his long life of struggle, he lived with such a God, courted His grace, took refuge in Him, "The Rock of Ages," prayed to Him, "Lead Kindly-Light", saw Him in the great harmonies of nature and in man's love of man, and tried "to dance to the tune of His flute." But his rational mind and moral nature led him to recognize also the grim realities of evils and imperfections in the world. They were, however, the greatest challenges to his theism. But his faith was too great a source of practical value to him to be sacrificed. He follows, therefore, the traditional ways of reconciling the existence of evil with his belief in God as the only and omnipotent and benevolent Reality. He tries to understand, like Christian theists, moral evils, sins and vices, as being due to the acts of man who has the freedom of will. To this he sometimes adds the Indian theory of Karma according to which actions of man are responsible not only for virtues and vices, but also for the physical conditions into which he is born. So Gandhiji sometimes speak of sins of men reacting on nature and creating catastrophies.

Gandhiji is sure that God could remove and prevent evils if He would. But God like a good democrat allows man full opportunity to remove evils by his own free effort and thus grow morally strong. As a stern and just educator God allows or directs by relentless laws the painful consequences of man's action so that he may learn to correct himself. But still, on the whole, he feels that the complete explanation of evil could be given only if man were able to know fully the motives of all actions of God. But that is not possible. So he confesses, "I cannot account for the existence of evils by a rational method. To want to do so is to be co-equal with God. I am, therefore, humble enough to recognise evil as such. And I call God long-suffering and patient precisely because He permits evil in the world. I know that He has no evil."[28] He further says, "He is the greatest democrat the world knows, for he leaves us 'unfettered' to make our own choice between evil and good."[29]

As a man is very unwilling to attribute bad motives to a tried friend and interprets even his apparently undesirable actions, of unknown motives, in the most charitable way and vaguely trusts that there must have been some good intention behind his curious behaviour, similarly a person who has enjoyed repeatedly the benefits of the belief in God tries to understand the evil of the world as being inspired by some unknown good motive. The over whelming force of the beneficial effects of faith in God enjoyed by him in life dispels from his mind doubts both about God's existence and His bonafides. Gandhiji could not find it in his heart to believe that the evils that we find in the world are due to any intention of God who has been his unfailing friend throughout his life, in personal and public struggles.

GOD IS TRUTH, TRUTH IS GOD

Having thus overcome the obstacle of evil, Gandhiji has little difficulty in conceiving God as the one, all-pervasive Reality in which everything—good and bad—lives, moves, and has its being. Even the atheist appears to him to be a work of the Divine. Perhaps a short spell of atheism and scepticism which Gandhiji experienced in early life convinced him of the healthy effects of rational doubt as a sound means to the generation of firm faith. Moreover, rational atheism appeared laudable as a fearless devotion to what the atheist regards as the truth. The spirit of the pursuit of truth, is, therefore, common to both rational theist and the rational atheist.

Gandhiji finds here a valuable clue for the expansion of his faith and his notion of God. He says, "I would say with those who say God is Love, God is Love. But deep down in me I used to say that though God may be God. God is truth above all...But two years ago, I went a step further and said Truth is God..., I then found that the nearest approach to truth was through love. But I also found that love has many meanings in English language atleast, and that human love in the sense of passion could become a degrading thing also. I found, too, that love in the sense of Ahimsa had only a limited number of votaries in the world. But I never found a double meaning in connection with truth and not even the atheists had demurred to the necessity or power of truth. But in their passion for discovering truth, the atheists have not hesitated to deny the very existence of God, from their own point of view, right. And it was because of this reason that I saw that rather than say God is truth, I should say Truth is God."[30]

To sum up, we may say that Gandhiji has a living faith in God. For him God is both—personal as well as impersonal, Absolute, Creative as well as Non-creative. It is an indefinable mysterious power that pervades everything. It transcends reason. But it is possible to reason out its existence to a limited extent. God is Truth and Love and the only way to realize it, is through Ahimsa. It is probably because of this belief that Gandhiji stuck to Ahimsa in the course of his struggles, political as well as others, because he firmly believed that this way alone he could reach truth, or even God, who would ultimately see him through.

References

1. Huxley, Ends and Means, pp. 3-4.
2. Harijan, 14-5-38, p. 109.
3. Young India, III, p. 504.
4. Autobiography, I, p. 7.
5. F. Mary Barr, Conversation and Correspondence with Gandhi, p. 100.
6. Harijan, 14-11-36, pp. 407 & 410.
7. Autobiography, p. 388.
8. Young India, II, p. 65.
9. Autobiography, I, pp. 4 & 8.
10. *Ibid.*, p. 11.
11. Harijan, 6-5-33.
12. Autobiography, II, p. 432.
13. Harijan, 10-12-38.
14. *Ibid.*, 14-5-38.
15. *Ibid.*, 6-5-33.
16. F. Mary Barr, p. 120.
17. Gita, II, 49 and 51 X, 10; XVIII, 67.
18. Young India, 21-1-26.
19. Harijan, 21-7-46.
20. Young India, 3-3-25
21. *Ibid.*
22. *Ibid.*
23. *Ibid.*
24. Young India, 21-1-26.

25. The Doctrine that many apparently conflicting judgements are possible about a subject taken in different aspects, and therefore, each judgement gives only a partial truth.

26. The Doctrine that everything has multiple characters.

27. Young India, 5-3-25.

28. *Ibid.*, 11-11-28.

29. *Ibid.*, 3-3-25.

30. *Ibid.*, 31-12-31.

4

The Nature of Man

Man must choose either of the two courses, the upward or the downward, but as he has the brute in him, he will more easily choose the downward course than the upward, especially when the downward is presented to him in a beautiful garb...the downward instinct embodied in them (Men).

—Harijan, February 1, 1935

MAN is a complex multi-dimensional being including within him different elements of matter, life, consciousness, intelligence and the divine spark."[1] At different times, because of different influences, the whole of human nature has been seen by the wise and the exalted from the point of view of this phase or that phase of Man, giving rise to different concepts of man.

Astronomical concept of Man looks at man as a tiny physical process lost in the vast encompassing spaces of a galactic universe. Biological concept of Man focuses him as a living being and regards him as the last stage of a protracted planetary evolution. Animalistic concept of Man concentrates upon his elementary appetites. Libertarian concept of man focuses his freedom of choice and sees him as the master of his history. Divine concept of man interprets the individual's whole being in terms of a relation to Eternal Spirit.

GANDHIAN CONCEPT OF MAN

Whereas Communism stresses on the economic aspect of human nature, and Democracy idealises the libertarian concept of man. Gandhiji idealises the spiritual aspect of man. Gandhiji believes that man is not merely a bundle of flesh and bones, but something more and beyond this.

Behind all this visible but ephemeral and unconscious matter, there is a spirit, a soul...indivisible, eternal, all-pervading and self conscious. It is a part and parcel of God. In other words, it is God-head within man. It is this belief of Gandhiji which made him hate the sin, not the sinner.

Gandhiji is of the considered view that man has two distinct inheritance—the biological and cultural—man as 'an animal' and as 'a bearer of culture.' These indicate his view of man's total self which may be separated as the 'biological inheritance, and the 'cultural inheritance'.

BIOLOGICAL INHERITANCE

Subscribing to the Hindu doctrine of rebirth, Gandhi declares that man's physical being is the result of his "sinful deeds" in the past.[2] He dubs human body as a "devilish" and a "perishable" force. Though he condemns it as "a filthy mass of bones, flesh and blood", he insists that it should be kept clean and pure, inside and outside, so that, by properly using it, man may in this very body "meet and recognize God".

His understanding of the structure of human body also led him to argue that man is so made by nature as to require him to restrict his locomotive ambition as far as his hands and feet will take him. In his *Hind Swaraj,* he observes : "God set a limit to a man's locomotive ambition in the construction of his body ... I am so constructed that I can only serve my immediate neighbours, but in my conceit I pretend to have discovered that I must, with my body, serve every individual in the Universe".[3] It is this basic plea which made him declare that service of God's creation, for the purpose of achieving self-realization, is possible only through the service of that part of God's creation which is nearest and best known to us".[4]

CULTURAL INHERITANCE

Gandhi thus attaches some importance to man's biological inheritance and drew a number of inferences from it. This aspect of man is, however, not his basic consideration. To him, man's cultural inheritance was of prime importance. He regards man as a consciously-divine, rational and social being.

His belief in the divinity of man and in the supremacy of his conscience is fundamental. He describes man as essentially a "creature of God striving to realize his divinity."[5] He equates God with Absolute Truth and declares this God of Truth to be the only Ultimate Reality.[7] He insists that man possesses the spark of this God in the form of his soul or atman,[8] which he variously describes as the Voice of God, of Conscience, of Truth, or the Inner Voice, or even as the "still small voice."[9]

He was fond of quoting the Mohammedan saying "Man is not God; but neither is he different from light (or spark) of God—adam Khuda nahin; lekin Khuda ke nur se adam juda nahin."[10] Gandhiji's position is clear from his statement, "We were perhaps all originally brutes, and I am prepared to believe we have become men by a slow process of evolution from the brute. We were thus born brute strength, but we were born in order to realize God who dwells in us. That indeed is the privilege of man, and it distinguishes him from the brute creation."[11]

In other words, man is beastial in origin, but he is human precisely because he is potentially and essentially divine. It, however, will be wrong to presume that by making these statements Gandhiji denies the presence of soul (*i.e.*, the spark of the God) in sub-human being. The only distinction he makes is that while man is capable of "conscious striving to realize the spirit within",[12] "in brute the soul lies ever dormant."[13] Hence, it is not the attribute of divinity as such that distinguishes man from the brute; it is rather his ability of its conscious cultivation, i.e. the faculty of "conscious-divinity".

His recognition of "conscious-Divinity" as the most important feature of human nature led him to attach to the soul (or *atman*) perhaps all those adjectives which are referred to it in the Gita.[14] He declars soul to be immortal, indestructible, intranscient, omnipotent, merciful, good and pure.[15] He attributes all these qualities to soul, obviously because he regards it to be the spark of Ultimate Reality of the God of Truth, which, in turn, is described by him as omnipresent, omnipotent, omniscient, timeless, formless, stainless, unfathomable, unknown, unknowable, indivisible, uncreate and most elusive.[16] He also states this Ultimate Reality to be the Summum Bonum of Life, Truth, Knowledge and Bliss, the Law-maker, the Law and the Executor, Upholder of justice, Lord and Master, Good, God of the poor and Protector of the faithful and Preserver of their honour.[17]

His belief in the monistic doctrine of the metaphysical unity between God and man enables him to describe the relationship between man and man as also divine. Believing that "all life in its essence is one", he declares that we are all children of the same God and that, therefore, potentially human nature is the same everywhere. This is to say that soul is one in all and that its possibilities are the same for everyone.

In the offshoots of man's attribute of "conscious-divinity". Gandhiji prominently includes the virtues of moral-progression, non-violence and benevolence. Subscribing to the view that there is nothing in this world which is not subject of change. He regards human nature also to be dynamic and not static. He declares that "Human nature either goes up or goes down."[18] And, this virtue of moral progression, he thinks, distinguishes man, both, from the God and the beast. He argues that the question of progression just does not arise, as God is already perfect and the beast is essentially dormant. Distinguishing man from God, in this respect, he observes that "No one can remain without eternal cycle unless it be God himself."[19] And about man's destinction from the beast he declares that "Progress is man's distinction, Man's alone, not beast's." This distinction enables him to regard man as "a special creature of God, precisely to the extent that he is distinct from the rest of His creation."[20]

Emphasizing the non-violent aspect of man's Divinity, he makes the following statement: "Man, as animal, is violent, but as spirit is non-violent. The moment he awakens to the spirit within, he cannot remain violent".[21] The belief in the essentially non-violent nature of soul led him to declare that "Not to believe in the possibility of permanent peace is to disbelieve in the godliness of human nature".[22] And about benevolence being an offshoot of man's divinity he says : "The chief difference between man and beast is that man is a beneviolent creature. All live happily where one feels happy in the happiness of others." The basis of this conviction is his belief that "there is something good in every man."[23]

Another distinction that Gandhi maintains between human and sub-human beings is that while the latter are merely feeling animals, the former have the faculty of reason by virtue of which they can think for their betterment. He declared that "unlike the animal, God has given man the faculty of reason"[24] and that it is by virtue of this faculty that "everyone can think for himself".[25] His most comprehensive statement in this respect is as under[26]:

... the essential distinction between man and brute... is man's special privilege and pride to be gifted with the faculties of head and heart both; that he is a thinking — no less than a feeling animal, as the very derivation of the word Manushya shows, and to renounce the sovereignty of reason over the blind instincts is therefore to renounce a man's estate. In man reason quickens and guides the feeling, in brute the soul lies ever dormant. To awaken the heart is to awaken the dormant soul, to awaken reason, and to inculcate discrimination between good and evil.

Translating Ruskin's *Unto This Last,* he observes that "God has endowed man with understanding, with a sense of justice", and with the authority of Milton (the English poet) he declares that the mind is the cause at once of bondage (hell) and moksha (heaven). He, thus, emphasizes the distinguishing human attribute of rationality, i.e. his capacity to be self-conscious, his capacity to judge between good and evil, between what will help him in his evolution to higher levels of being, and what will obstruct his path.

In man's cultural heritage, Gandhiji also includes the attribute of his sociability. He, no doubt, values individual freedom, but he regards man as "essentially a social being."[27] He believes that man had risen to the present status by learning to adjust his individualism to the requirements of social progress. He believes that unrestricted individualism is the law of the beast. He believes in "willing submission to social restraint for the sake of well being of the whole society enriches both, the individual and the society, of which one is a member."[28]

In Gandhiji's considered opinion the attributes of 'consciousness—divinity,' rationality and sociability culturally distinguish human beings from all other beings.

Gandhian concept of "The Nature of Man" will be further clear from the following points.

The Dignity of Personality

For Gandhiji, "the individual is the one supreme consideration."[29] Personality is sacred, because the soul in man is part of God. In fact, what is reality in man, is only the soul; he is nothing but Brahman. Gandhiji's belief in the advaita doctrine that there is but one Brahman in all, whether it be human or sub-human beings, means that all living beings are bound together inseparably to God. "It makes man the servant of God's creation and not its lord."[30] It also means that whatever happens to one body, must affect the whole of matter and the whole spirit[31]; this is why Gandhiji believes that "if one man gains spiritually, the whole world gains with him and if one man falls, the whole world falls to that extent."[32] This is a conclusion of great significance since we find in it a powerful plea for universal education and for oftenly observed fact that sometimes one great person exalts so many and sometimes one corrupt person corrupts so many.

Equality of Man

Gandhiji believes in equality between man and man. His concept of equality of man is also derived from the concept of the universal soul. He says, "In my opinion there is no such thing as inherited or acquired superiority. I believe in the rock-bottom doctrine of advaita and my interpretation of advaita excludes any idea of superiority, at any stage whatsoever. I believe implicitly that all men are born equal. All—whether in India or in England or America or in any circumstances whatever—have the same soul as any other... I consider that it is unmanly for any person to claim superiority over a fellow-being...He, who claims superiority, at once forfeits his claim to be called a man."[33] This is in line with the Christian belief that man's worth arises not from his civic status but from his being a child of God. "Because children of God, all men are brothers."[34] Gandhiji's letter to the Rev. Keithahn makes this concept of equality clearer still. "All men", he says, "are born equal, but one is much stronger or weaker than another physically and mentally. Therefore, superficially there is no equality between the two. But there is an essential equality. In our nakedness God is not going to think of me as Gandhi or you as Keithahn. And what are we in this mighty universe? We are less than atoms, and as between atoms there is no use asking which is bigger. Inherently we are equal. The difference of race and skin, of mind and body, and of climate and nature are transitory."[35] Gandhiji's disarming humility and his gross identification with the masses, the poor and the down-trodden stem from this kind of thinking.

Free Will Versus Pre-determinism

Gandhiji's notion of the presence of God in man amounts to another belief that man has free will, reason, conscience, and love. Man is the maker of his destiny. If he chooses to use his reason correctly and guides his life by listening to the dictates of his conscience (the inner voice of God), and lives with his fellow beings with love in his heart, he can realize God and bring heaven on earth.

Hindu philosophy attributes the inequality among men and Karma, the effect of ones' deeds in the lives one had lived in the past, and so, of one's own making. In line with Hindu tradition Gandhiji too believes in the doctrine of Karma and rebirth,[36] but he interprets both as favouring the spiritual growth of the individual instead of working to put him in chains. The doctrine of rebirth ensures that even a little effort in this life is not wasted[37], because it provides repeated opportunities for the man, who has not been able to fully realize himself in one birth, to work again and again for self-development. The law of Karma is the law of moral continuity; it lays down that our future will grow out of the present even as the latter is the outcome of our past. This is why Gandhiji declares: "The law of Karma is inexorable and impossible of evasion. There is thus hardly any need to interfere. He laid down the law and as it were retired?[38] Any breach of the divine law is sure to have its consequences. "We are the makers of our destiny. We can mend or mar the present and on that will depend the future,"[39] says Gandhiji.

Gandhiji's belief in the law of Karma does not imply that he considers man's life and activities to be completely determined. Freedom of will is considered by Gandhiji as a necessary postulate of morality. "The real question is not whether behaviour is free or determined since it is obvious that all behaviour, being a response to some 'given' stimulus, must be in some sense determined. The question is how it is determined, whether it is determined from within or from without the self. When we say that behaviour is 'free', what we really mean is, not that it is undetermined, but that the self acts as a whole, summoning all resources of knowledge and imagination, making the action his own, taking full responsibility for it—acting, that is to say, as a person. Such self-determined behaviour is to be contrasted with behaviour at the instinctive level, where action is determined in a quasi-reflex manner by immediate stimuli and the only unity is that represented by the groups of forces. In the first type of behaviour we recognize personal volition; in the other case we see a creature of impulse. Mere mechanical action, performed under the influence of blind impulse or custom, cannot therefore be moral. Morality implies conscious, deliberate volition. According to Gandhiji, "No action, which is not voluntary can be called moral. So long as we act like machines, there can be no question of morality. If we want to call an action moral, it should have been done consciously and as a matter of duty."[40] In fact, there is no antithesis between the law of Karma and freedom of will, if Gandhiji's line of thinking is adopted. The doctrine of Karma implies freedom, for it says that man is the architect of his own destiny. Continuity with the past implies creative freedom of the individual. No doubt, our previous Karma limits the range for the exercise of our free will. There are some other limitations too, which cannot entirely be overcome—the limitations with which one is born, the laws of nature to which man is subject and the hardened core of his own habits and tendencies, which begin to 'drive' him. Thus, Gandhiji recognizes that "the free-will, which we enjoy, is less than that of a passenger on a crowded deck."[41] But in spite of all these limiting influences, and within their own field, man has sufficient freedom for exercising his will and moulding his environment, body and mind. The freedom we have may be little, but it is real in the sense that we are left "unfettered"[42] to how we use that freedom. We can choose "to act at the level of decision instead of being acted upon at the level of cause and effect."[43] The freedom to experiment, to commit and rectify mistakes, is of course, a necessary condition of progress. If he wills, man may be able to change his habits or shape his destiny. Freedom of will, all limitations notwithstanding, determine his present state and in a way predermine his future wherewithal.

Gandhiji believes that, though our will is free, "we cannot command results; we can only strive."[44] Man can change temperament, can control it, but certainly not eradicate it. God has not given him so much liberty. If the leopard can change his spots, then only can man modify the peculiarities of his spiritual constitution."[45] Of course, he can counter-act the effects of past mistakes by attaining complete detachment[46]; but, "in spite of the greatest effort to be detached no man can altogether undo the effect of his environment or his "upbringing."[47] While conceding that people are controlled by their environment, Gandhiji would like them to live by self-direction and not by mere habit. In other words, he would like them live as 'persons' acting at the moral level. He does not believe in complete freedom which might enable man to sever himself from or transcend nature. Such freedom can mean only chaos. He does not favour freedom that detracts from the moral path.

The 'Self' in Self-expression

The abuse of free-will causes evil. Gandhiji believes that for God nothing is good or evil, but for "human purposes" good and evil are "from each other distinct and incompatible, being symbolic of light and darkness..."[48] Good is self-existent, but evil is not; evil flourishes only by the implication of the good that is in it, and dies when that support is withdrawn. Gandhiji points out that purity of means is, therefore, the only safe means to minimise evil. He further states, "...in order to overcome evil, one must stand wholly outside it i.e. on the solid ground of unadulterated good."[49]

Man's body is a product of nature and so, physical. But, consciousness, reason, will, emotion and such other qualities and powers which man has are the expressions of the spirit of soul. The true self is this spirit; not the finite self, with its lust and passion. When Gandhiji preaches self expression, the 'self is used in this restricted sense and not in the same sense in which the term is used by the Naturalists. The false self should not be allowed to express itself. "If man yields to the temptation," says Prof. Jeffreys, "to subside on to the 'natural' level, he makes a beast of himself; and the beastliness of man is something quite different from the naturalness of the beast."[50] But if he wills, man can follow the spiritual path and become more and more like God in love, goodness, and abiding joy; for the divine powers within us are infinite.

The Progress of Man

As a believer in the theory of evolution, Gandhiji is conscious of man's animal origin, and so, he does not subscribe to the Wordsworthian view that the child comes from heaven "trailing clouds of glory"—that man is born all good, an angel. "We were perhaps all originally brutes. I am prepared to believe that we have become men by a slow process of evolution from the brute".[51] Again, "Man must choose either of two courses, the upward or the downward, but as he has brute in him, he will more easily choose the downward course than the upward, especially if the downward course is presented to him in a beautiful garb...the downward instinct is embodied in them (men)".[52]

Thus, Gandhiji contends that every one of us is a mixture of good and evil, the difference between the cultured and brute being only a question of degree. So long as man is in the flesh, even the greatest man can only be imperfect. "There is no one without faults, not even men of God. They are men of God not because they are faultless, but because they know their own faults...and are ever ready to correct themselves."[53] The glory is that man is not mere brute. He is, above all, the soul and so, even the more brutal of men has potentiality for goodness. It is this self-conscious impulse to realize the God inherent in him that distinguishes man from the beast. As Gandhiji says that "We were born with brute strength, but we were born in order to realize God who dwells in us. That is the privilege of man and it distinguishes him from the brute creation."[54] There is, thus, goodness inherent in human nature. That man has godliness in him implies that it is more natural for man to be good than to be evil.

When Gandhiji is in a mood to philosophize on the course of History, he takes a longsighted view and judges things as a whole in the light of dominant trends. Viewing human history in this way he feels confident that humanity is on the whole progressing. He says, therefore, "I believe that sum total of energy of mankind is not to bring us down but to lift us up, and that is the result of the definite, if unconscious, working of the law of love."[55]

But though it means, for him, that God, as love and reason, is working through man to help man raise himself, he does not forget that God has given man freedom to play the game in his own way, only trusting that man would learn to improve himself by his failures, making them the pillars of success. So Gandhiji speaks in a balanced tone, "If we believe that mankind has steadily progressed towards ahimsa (i.e. love), it follows that it has to progress towards it still further. Nothing in this world is static, everything is kinetic. If there is no progression, then there is inevitable retrogression. No one can remain without the eternal cycle, unless it be God Himself."[56]

The Summum Bonum of Life

According to Gandhiji, "There is no contradiction between God and men, as well as in the lower order of creation. Soul transcends time and space and unifies all apparently separate existence."[57] Gandhiji also believes that "human beings are working consciously or unconsciously towards the realization of spiritual identity." "Life,"[58] he says, "is an inspiration. Its mission is to strive after perfection, which is self realization. What I want to achieve—what I have been striving and pining to achieve these thirty years, is self realization—to see God face to face, to attain Moksha. I live and move and have my belief in pursuit of this goal."[59]

This is an Ideal which he prescribes for all and sundry. Because "the soul is one in all, its possibilities are, therefore, the same for every one."[60] Gandhiji says, "I wear the same corruptible flesh that the weakest of my fellows wear and am, therefore, as liable to err as any."[61] Therefore, "the ideals that regulate my life are presented for acceptance by mankind in general. I have arrived at them by gradual evolution...I have not the shadow of a doubt that any man or woman cannot achieve what I have, if he or she would make the same effort and cultivate the same hope and faith."[62] "And I claim that what I practise, is capable of being practised by all, because I am very ordinary mortal open to the same temptations and liable to the same weaknesses as the least among us."[63]

Thus, to Gandhiji, the aim of human life is nothing different from that of Hindu Seers. But, unlike most of the latter he does not believe that the aspirant after self-realization must keep himself aloof from all which is mundane. Unlike the Sadhakas who dwelt in caves and were oblivious of worldly affairs, and who engrossed themselves all the twenty-four hours in something which is known as higher, Gandhiji looks at samsar as real and hence reveals, "to attain my end it is not necessary for me to seek the shelter of a cave."[64] He says, "A cave dweller can build castles in the air whereas a dweller in a palace like Janaka has no castles to built. The cave dweller who hovers round the world on the wings of thought has no peace. A Janaka though living in the midst of pomp and circumstance may have peace that passeth understanding."[65]

Thus, Gandhiji believes that self-realization is possible in and through society, because he believes in "the absolute oneness of humanity"[66] and, therefore, to him there is complete identity between him and humanity. So, the goal of life—self realization cannot be attained unless 'greatest good of all'—Sarvodya is materialized.

To sum up, we can say that Gandhiji emphasizes the spiritual nature of man and he believes in the exercise of freewill as well as the effect of environment. According to him the summum bonum of man's life is self-realization.

References

1. Dr. Radhakrishnan, The Bhagwat Gita, Introduction Essay, p. 46.
2. Collected works of Mahatma Gandhi (Delhi : The Publication Division, Ministry of Information and Broadcasting, Govt. of India 1964), XII, p. 375.
3. M.K. Gandhi, Hind Swaraj or Indian Home Rule (II Edn., III Imp.; Ahmedabad : Navajivan Publishing House 1958), p. 48, *ibid.,* 61-62.
4. *Ibid.,* 22-8-1936, p. 217.
5. *Ibid.,* 21-4-1946, p. 94, *ibid.,* 3-6-1939, p. 150.
6. Harijan 8-6-1940, p. 156, "Wherein he declared that Truth is known only to God". Indian opinion (Phoenix), 8-2-1908 wherein the following lines appear." Truth is God, or God is nothing but Truth".
7. Yervada Mandir, p. 9.
8. Harijan 26-9-1936, p. 260; *Ibid.,* 12-11-1938, p. 326, *Ibid.,* 11-3-1939, p. 44; *Ibid.,* 18-8-1946, p. 267.
9. *Ibid.,* 8-7-1933.
10. Young India 6-8-1931, p. 205. Wherein he state : There is an Urdu saying which means Adam is not God but he is spark of divine.
11. Harijan, 2-4-1938, p. 65.
12. *Ibid.,* 7-4-1946, p. 74.
13. *Ibid.,* 21-11-1936.
14. The Gita according to Gandhi (I Edn.; IV Imp.; (Ahmedabad : Navajivan Publishing House 1956), p. 152-55.
15. Harijan, 12-11-1938, p. 327; *Ibid.,* 3-3-1946, p. 32 wherein Gandhi categorically stated that "Immortality is an attribute of the some".
16. Harijan, 25-8-1940, p. 263; *Ibid.,* 29-9-1946, p. 332 and *Ibid.,* 20-4-1947, wherein he stated that God is knowable "only to the extent that our limited intellect allows."
17. Harijan, 20-2-1937, p. 9; *ibid.,* 16-9-1939, p. 276, *ibid.,*

23-9-1940, p. 55.

18. Harijan, 8-6-1947, 1977.
19. *Ibid.,* 11-8-1940, p. 245, *ibid.,* 9-11-1947, p. 406.
20. Young India, 13-2-1930, p. 56.
21. Harijan, 11-8-1940, p. 245, *ibid.,* 26-11-1938, p. 356.
22. *Ibid.,* 16-5-1936, p. 109, *ibid.,* 12-10-1935, p. 277.
23. Harijan 29-9-1940, p. 304. Wherein he observed : "I...picture the world as full of good human beings—not goody goody human beings."
24. Harijan 5-5-1946, p. 123.
25. Harijan 11-8-1940, p. 244.
26. Harijan 21-11-1936, p. 322.
27. Harijan, 27-5-1939, p. 144, *ibid.,* 14-12-1947, p. 468.
28. *Ibid.,* 27-5-1939, p. 144.
29. Young India, 13-11-1944.
30. Harijan, 26-12-36.
31. *Ibid.,* 12-11-1938.
32. Young India, 4-12-1924.
33. *Ibid.,* 29-9-1927.
34. Jeffreys, Education, *Christian a Pagan*, p. 148.
35. Harijan, 13-3-1937.
36. Young India 5-6-1924, wherein Gandhiji said "I believe in rebirth as much as I believe in the existence of my body".
37. *Ibid.*
38. Autobiography, I, p. 563.
39. Ethical Religion, p. 8.
40. *Ibid.,* p. 8.
41. Harijan, 23-3-1940.
42. Young India, 5-3-1925.
43. Jeffreys, p. 123.
44. Harijan, 6-5-1939.

45. Satyagraha in South Africa, p. 219.
46. Harijan, 17-9-1946.
47. Young India, 30-1-1930.
48. Harijan, 20-2-1937.
49. Young India, 25-2-1921.
50. Jeffreys, p. 5.
51. Harijan, 2-4-1938.
52. *Ibid.,* 1-2-1935.
53. *Ibid.,* 23-1-1939.
54. *Ibid.,* 2-4-1938.
55. Bose N.K., Selections from Gandhi, pp. 22-23.
56. *Ibid.,* p. 23.
57. Dhawan, Gopinath, Political Philosophy of Mahatma Gandhi, p. 45.
58. Gandhiji's Correspondence with the Govt., p. 82.
59. Autobiography, p. 4.
60. Harijan, 18-5-1940.
61. Young India, III, p. 517.
62. *Ibid.,* II, p. 204.
63. *Ibid.,* III, p. 517.
64. *Ibid.,* 3-4-1924.
65. *Ibid.*
66. *Ibid.,* III, p. 79.

5

The End and The Means

(Truth and Non-Violence)

Ahimsa and Truth are so intertwined that it is practically impossible to disentangle and separate them. They are like the two sides of a coin, or rather a smooth unstapled metallic disc. Who can say, which is observe, and which the reverse ? Nevertheless, ahimsa is the means; Truth is the end. Means to be means must always be within our reach, and so ahimsa is our supreme duty. If we take care of the means, we are bound to reach the end sooner or later.

—From Yeravda Mandir, p. 13

THE ultimate end, as discussed in the preceding chapter, according to Gandhiji is self-realization—seeing God face to face, realizing absolute truth. Closely connected with the ultimate aim is the problem of means. Communists, Fascists as well as most of the politicians believe in the Machiavellian maxim, "the end justifies the means" that is, if the end is desirable, even means, like cunningness, deceit and violence, are justified.

In Gandhian philosophy means and ends are convertible.[1] The two are inseparable and should be equally pure. That the end is high and laudable is not enough for him, the means too must be moral. In fact, the means are to him everything.[2] He says, "The clearest possible definition of the goal and its appreciation would fail to take us there, if we do not know and utilise the means of achieving it. I have, therefore, concerned myself principally with the conservation of the means and their progressive use."[3]

Why this emphasis on the means ? This emphasis on the means is partly due to the fact that man can only strive, he cannot command results. We can control the means, but not the end. Besides, the end grows out of the means. As Gandhiji says, "As the means so the end."[4] "The means may be likened to a seed, the end to a tree, and there is just the same inviolable connection between the means and the end as there is between the seeds and the tree."[5] Gandhiji agrees with Gita's doctrine of nishkam karma (action without attachment) that teaches us that a good deed produces only a good result.[6] Gandhiji believes "If one takes care of the means, the end will take care of itself,[7] and that realization of goal is in exact proportion to that of means."[8] To him, the attempt made to win Swaraj is Swaraj itself.[9]

Moreover, if we believe in the ultimate aim stated above and in the fundamental unity of life, good ends will mean, in the words of Huxley, "a state of greatest possible unification." This can obviously be achieved by intrinsically unifying, that is good means and not by separative or divisive, that is, bad means.[10] According to Tolstoy "All that tend to disunite are Evil and Ugly."[11] So, to achieve the good end only good means should be used.

Gandhiji's emphasis on the importance of means should not be misconstrued as implying that the end with him is, only a secondary consideration. Gandhiji believes that the end is primary and the means is contributory, and because it is contributory it must be good and pure. He believes that the means used should in no way detract from the moral character of our end. Hence, his repeated insistence on the purity of means and his effort to give concrete expression, in the form of Satyagraha, to the principle of moral approximation of the end and the means is, perhaps, the most unique contribution of our time to the philosophy and technique of revolution.

What then is the means that Gandhiji prescribed for the realization of the ultimate end ? The answer is— Ahimsa or Non violence. As Gandhiji says, "Ahimsa is means; Truth is the end."[12]

Let us now discuss the concept of Truth and Nonviolence.

TRUTH

Truth is the pole star of Gandhiji's life and philosophy. To Gandhiji Truth is the sovereign principle which includes numerous principles and his whole life is an experiment with Truth.[13] Gandhiji agrees with Mahabharata that Truth is the ultimate reality, rather the only reality. Mahabharata says

सत्यं ब्रह्म सनातनम्
सर्वं सत्ये प्रतिष्ठितम्।

(Truth is the eternal Brahamn. Everything rests on Truth.)[14]

Gandhiji distinguishes between absolute truth and relative truth as perceived by finite individuals in relation to a particular set of thought and circumstance.

Absolute Truth

In the sense of Absolute truth Gandhiji indentifies truth with God. He says, "The word Satya (Truth) is derived from Sat, which means 'being', nothing is or exists in reality except truth. That is why Satya or truth is perhaps the most important name of God. In fact, it is more correct to say that truth is God, than to say that God is truth. And where there is truth there also is knowledge which is true. Where there is no truth, there can be no true knowledge. That is why the word Chit or knowledge is associated with the name of God. And where there is true knowledge, there is always bliss (Ananda). There sorrow has no place. And even as truth is eternal, so is the bliss derived from it. Hence we know God as Sat-Chit Ananda, one who combines in Himself truth, knowledge and bliss."[15] Thus Gandhiji worships God as Truth only; he is devoted to none but Truth."[16]

Truth in a Wider Sense

Gandhiji understands the word truth in a wider sense. He says, "Generally speaking, observation of the law of truth is understood merely to mean that we must speak the truth.

But we should understand the word Satya or Truth in a much wider sense. There should be truth in thought, truth in speech and truth in action. To the man who has realized this truth in its fullness, nothing else to be known, because all knowledge is necessarily included in it. What is not included in it, is not truth, and so not true knowledge; and there can be no inward peace without true knowledge."[17]

Truth Alone can be Victorious

The entire philosophy of Satyagraha is based on the fact that truth alone can be victorious and not untruth (सत्यमेव जयते नानृतम्). It is because truth is 'that which is', while untruth means 'that which is not'. "If untruth does not so much as exist, its victory is out of question. And truth being that which is, can never (being that which is) be distroyed."[18] Thus, Gandhiji agrees with Vedanta that truth can never be destroyed, it is beyond the limitations of time, space and causality, Vedanta says :—

सत्यं त्रिकालावधिराहित्यम्।

(Truth is beyond the three limitations of time, space and causality).

Relative Truth

For Gandhiji the aim of man's life is to realize absolute truth. But man, even if he is a great soul like Gandhiji can have but faint, fleeting glimpses of absolute truth. He says, "We cannot through the instrumentality of this ephemeral body see face to face truth which is eternal."[19]

How then to realize absolute truth ? According to Gandhiji, to advance towards absolute truth, we should hold by the relative truth, that is, what we consider to be truth.[20] He says, "But as long as I have not realized this absolute truth as I conceive it, that relative truth must meanwhile be my shield and buckler."[21] This means that in Gandhian philosophy, truth is static and absolute, but its knowledge is dynamic. Through intuition and experiments. Gandhiji discovered the technique of Satyagraha or as he calls it soul force to realize truth. Satyagraha is a very good illustration of practicing truth even in political battles.

Truth as a Social Principle

As regards truth as a social principle, Gandhiji says, "...devotion to this truth is the sole justification for our existence. All our activities should be centred in truth. Truth should be the very breath of our life."[22] Because "without truth it is impossible to observe any principles or rules in life."[23] Thus, truth should be practised in all walks of life—even in politics. There is no place for prejudice, evasion, secrecy, deception, or distortion when practising truth. Man should be bold enough to hold truth, to suffer for truth and lastly to die for truth. But the practice of truth implies tolerance, liberty and politeness in behaviour. While one should never forsake his truth, he should not be dogmatic to impose it on others. Gandhiji says, "while it is good guide for individual conduct, imposition of that conduct upon all will be an insufferable interference with every body's freedom of conscience."[24] Gandhiji observed that bitterness blurs our version and to that extent disables one from seeing even the limited truth."[25] Bitterness or harshness also offends the principle of the fundamental unity of soul; it makes us forget the unity and is divisive and separative. According to Gandhiji, therefore "One had better not to speak it (truth) if one cannot do so in a gentle way...Truth without non-violence is not truth but untruth."[26] But non-violent truth or gentle speech does not mean hypocrisy or circumlocutory speech. "Harsh truth may be uttered courteously and gently, but the words would read hard. To be truthfull you must call a liar a liar—harsh words perhaps, but the use is inevitable."[27] To illustrate the point Gandhiji gives the instance of Jesus, "Jesus knew the generation of vipers, minced no words in describing them, but pleaded for mercy for them."[28] The thing which is important is that the intention behind the words must not be to do harm to the opponent."[29] As a matter of fact truths of different thinking men are sure to differ. Mind is not a standardized product. Its characteristic is to differ. Therefore, Gandhiji says, "What may appear as truth to one person will often appear as untruth to another."[30] So the seeker after truth or the holder of truth needs not, rather should not, be bitter to another who does not accept the former's truth. Thus, we can say that to Gandhiji truth is God.

NON-VIOLENCE

To Gandhiji, Non-violence i.e. Ahimsa, is a logical corrolary to the principle of truth. To him "Ahimsa and truth are so intertwined that it is practically impossible to disentangle and separate them. They are like the two sides of a coin, or rather of a smooth unstamped metalic disc."[31] "who can say" he asks, "which is the obverse and which is reverse."[32] To Gandhiji "Ahimsa is the means; truth is the end."[33] He says, "Means to be means must always be within our reach, and so ahimsa is our supreme duty. If we take care of the means, we are bound to reach the end sooner or later. When once we have grasped this point, final victory is beyond question."[34] Gandhiji has a living and unshakeable faith that truth can be realized only by means of ahimsa. Violence, which has its roots in divisive propensities like anger, selfishness, lust etc., cannot take us to the goal. Violence arises out of ignorance. If untruth endures and nothing were true to itself and to others, if all laws of life and nature were uncertain and undependable, the universe would turn into chaos. Thus, violence is untruth.

Violence is Untruth

But why is violence untruth ? For one thing, truth, as known to man, is relative and never absolute. People look at a thing from different angles, and conscience, is not the same thing for all. No man can claim to be absolutely in the right. Pursuit of truth, therefore, does not admit of violence inflicted on one's opponent who must be weaned from error by patience and sympathy that is by self-suffering.[35]

Besides, violence attacks not only the sin and the evil, but also the sinner and the evil-doer. This is offending against the great truth, the unity and sacredness of all being.[36] Pursuit of truth means realization of this unity through love and service of all i.e. willingness to suffer for all. Violence interferes with the realization of this unity, both—in the case of the violent man and his victim—by arousing in them feelings of anger, hatred, fear etc.

Moreover truth which is the object of our quest is not outside ourselves but within. The more we take to violence in dealing with these who create difficulties the more we recede from truth. For in fighting imagined enemy without, we neglect the real enemy within.[37] Ahimsa is thus the practical application of the great truth of spiritual unity, or as Gregg terms it, "the spiritual democracy of all life." In the words of Gandhiji, "the basic principle on which the practice of non-violence rests is that what holds good in respect of oneself, equally applies to the whole universe."[38] Gandhiji differs from those Darwinians who swear by a ruthless struggle for existence as the determinant in evolution. Like Plato, Gandhiji holds that universe is governed by Ahimsa or love, for the life persists in midst of destruction. He writes, "Though there is repulsion enough in nature, she lives by attraction. Mutual love enables nature to persist. Man does not live by destruction. Self love compels regard for others."[39] Psychologically also love for others succeed self-love. "We all are bound by the tie of love. There is in every thing a centripetal force without which nothing could have existed...even as there is cohesive force in blind matter, so must there be in all things animate and the name of that cohesive among animate being is love...Where there is love there is life; hatred leads to destruction."[40] Psycho-analytically too life is the off-shoot of love instinct, while hatred is that of Death instinct. Therefore, Violence is untruth and Non-violence or Ahimsa is our supreme duty.

Ahimsa is an All-pervasive Eternal Principle

Ahimsa is thus an all pervasive eternal principle applicable to every situation in life without any exception. That is why Gandhiji insists, as a condition of complete success of non-violence, that when it is accepted as the law of life, it must pervade the whole being and must not be applied to isolated acts.[41] To Gandhiji "Ahimsa is the Kingdom of Heaven, and if we seek it first, every thing else shall be added unto us."[42] He writes, "For me...ahimsa comes before swaraj...ahimsa must be placed before everything else while it is professed. Then alone it becomes irresistible."[43] Ahimsa is, according to him, at the root of every one of his activities.

Ahimsa in the Negative Sense

But, what is Ahimsa ? The words 'Ahimsa' and Nonviolence are seemingly negative in form on account of negative prefixes 'a' and 'non' respectively. Gandhiji suggests the reason why this highest religion has been defined negatively. Himsa is an inherent necessity for life in body. Life lives upon life.[44] According to Gandhiji, the negative aspect of ahimsa consists in refraining from causing pain or killing any life out of anger or for selfish purpose, or with intention of injuring it. Thus, ahimsa means avoiding injury to any thing on earth in thought, word or deed.[45] Ahimsa in its negative sense does not mean merely non-killing. Other and more insidious forms of himsa, Gandhiji points out, are harsh words and harsh judgements (that is those intended to hurt), ill-will, anger, spite, cruelty, the torture of men and animals, the starvation, wanton humiliation and oppression of the weak, the killing of their self-respect etc.[46] "Exploitation" according to Gandhiji, "is the essence of violence."[47] Thus, ahimsa in the negative sense requires that we may not harbour an uncharitable thought even in connection with one who may consider himself our enemy.[48]

Ahimsa in the Positive Sense

Ahimsa is usually mistaken for a purely negative doctrine. To Gandhiji ahimsa is essentially a positive and dynamic force. In its positive and active aspect non-violence means benevolence or love in more comprehensive than Pauline sense, for ahimsa includes the whole creation and not merely human-beings. St. Paul's definition is good enough for all practical purposes.[49] "Ahimsa embraces sub-human life, not excluding plants or flowers, noxious insects or beasts. Nonviolence is, therefore, in its active form goodwill towards all life."[50] Refraining from ahimsa is, the only form of ahimsa, love is its soul. But the love, that is ahimsa, is not the mercenary affair which is based on the goodness of the object of love. It is true love that is self-effacing and demands no consideration.[51] "True love", says Gandhiji, "consists in transferring itself from the body to the dweller within, and then, necessarily realizing the oneness of all life inhabiting numberless bodies.[52] The real love is to love them that hate you, to love your neighbour even though you distrust him... of what avail is my love, if it is only as I trust my friend ? Even thieves do that."[53] Ahimsa thus means the largest love, love even for evil doer. "Love", says Gandhiji, "does not burn others, it burns itself.[54] Tha non-violent man continues to suffer till the evil-doer understands his mistake and repents for his misdeeds. It is in this sense that Ahimsa can be used as a corrective device.

In short, "ahimsa consists in allowing others the maximum of convenience at the maximum of inconvenience to us."[55] Every act of injury to a living creature and endorsement of such act by refraining from non-violent effort, whenever possible, to prevent it, is a breach of himsa."[56] "Absolute ahimsa means perfect freedom from ahimsa, that is; freedom from ill-will, anger and hate rooted in ignorance and an over flowing understanding love for all. From the point of view of complete ahimsa, all violence in whatever form, must be eschewed. But such non-violence is a perfect state and is reached only when mind, body, and speech are in perfect coordination."[57]

Non-Violence not a Policy of Helpless Persons

Generally it is taunted that Gandhian Non-violence is a policy of helpless persons. But Gandhiji says, "Non-violence is not a cover for cowardice, but it is the supreme virtue of the brave."[58] It does not mean meek submission to the will of the tyrant.[59] Non-violence, therefore, presupposes ability to strike. It is a conscious, deliberate restraint put upon one's desire for vengeance.[60] If one cannot do so he must take the vengeance as he can. Because, "vengeance" says Gandhiji, "is any way superior to passive, effeminate and helpless submission."[61] "Between cowardice and violence he would prefer violence."[62]

Non-Violence Both for the Individual and the Society

Is non-violence meant for the 'individual' alone or for the society too ? To Gandhiji, "Non-violence is not any individual virtue, but a course of spiritual and political conduct, both, for the individual and the community."[63] For a democratic social order non-violence is but necessary. He observes, "True democracy of the Swaraj of the masses can never come through untruth and violent means, for the simple reason that the natural corollary to their use would be to remove all opposition through the suspension or extermination of the antagonists. That does not make for individual freedom. Individual freedom can have the fullest play only under a regime of unadulterated Ahimsa."[64]

Need of Truth and Non-violence in the Modern Age

To sum up, we can say that Gandhiji believes that Truth is God. Truth is the Summum Bonum of life. Truth is the end and non-violence is the means. Truth and Non-violence are like the opposite sides of the same coin and therefore, inseparable. Truth can be realized only through Non-violence. Therefore, Gandhiji lays great emphasis on Non-violence. Self-realization, seeing God face to face, realizing Absolute Truth, to Gandhiji is possible only through Non-violence.

References

1. Young India, II, p. 956.
2. *Ibid.*, p. 364.
3. Amrit Bazar Patrika, 17-9-33.
4. Young India, II, p. 364.
5. Hind Swaraj, p. 60.
6. Young India, I, p. 714.
7. Harijan, 11-2-39, p. 8.
8. Young India, II, p. 364.
9. Speeches, p. 720.
10. Huxley, Ends and Means, pp. 320-21.
11. A letter of Tolstoy to Romain Rolland, translated from French by Dr. Kalidas Nag. Modern Review, January, 1927.
12. From Yeravda Mandir, p. 13.
13. Note the title of his autobiography styled as "The Story of my Experiments with Truth."
14. Mahabharata, Shantiparvan, Ch. XII, V, 5.
15. From Yeravda Mandir, pp. 1-2.
16. Harijan, 25-5-35. p. 115.
17. From Yeravda Mandir, p. 2.
18. Satyagraha in South Africa, p. 433.
19. From Yeravda Mandir, p. 9.
20. Harijan, 25-5-35, p. 114.
21. Autobiography, 1, p. 6.
22. From Yeravda Mandir, p. 2.
23. *Ibid.*
24. Young India, II, p. 1182.
25. *Ibid.*, p. 1286.

20\. *Ibid.*, p. 1295.

27. Harijan, 6-2-37, p. 414.
28. *Ibid.,* 19-12-36, p. 362.
29. *Ibid.*
30. From Yeravda Mandir, p. 3.
31. *Ibid.,* p. 13.
32. *Ibid.*
33. *Ibid.*
34. *Ibid.*
35. Young India, I, p. 36.
36. Autobiography, II, pp. 53-54.
37. From Yeravda Mandir, p. 10.
38. Harijan, 12-11-38, p. 327.
39. Young India, I, p. 284.
40. *Ibid.,* p. 734.
41. Harijan, 5-9-36, p. 327.
42. *Ibid.,* 14-3-36, p. 37.
43. *Ibid.,* 24-6-39, p. 174.
44. *Ibid.,* 1-9-40, p. 271.
45. *Ibid.,* 7-9-35, p. 234.
46. Young India, III, p. 860.
47. Harijan, 4-11-39, p. 331.
48. Speeches, p. 320.
49. Harijan, 14-3-36, p. 39.
50. Young India, II, p. 286,
51. *Ibid.,* II, p. 651.
52. Bapu's Letters to Mira, p. 167.
53. Harijan, 3-3-46.
54. Young India, 2-2-30, p. 60.
55. *Ibid.,* II, p. 984.
56. *Ibid.,* III, p. 812.

57. *Ibid.*, 1-10-31.
58. *Ibid.*, 12-8-26.
59. *Ibid.*, 11-8-20.
60. *Ibid.*, 12-8-26.
61. *Ibid.*
62. *Ibid.*, 11-8-20.
63. Harijan, 29-9-40, p. 299.
64. *Ibid.*, 27-5-38, p. 143.

6

The Nature and Structure of Social Order

In this structure composed of innumerable villages, there will be ever-widening, never ascending circles. Life will not be a pyramid with the apex sustained by the bottom. But it will be an oceanic circle whose centre will be the individual, always ready to perish for the village, the latter ready to perish for the circle of villages, till at last the whole becomes one life composed of individuals, never aggressive in their arrogance but ever humble, sharing the majesty of oceanic circle of which they are integral units. Therefore, the outermost circumference will not wield power to crush the innermost circle but give strength to all within and derive its own strength from it.

—HARIJAN, JULY 28, 1946

GANDHIJI, as it has been already discussed, firmly believes that summum bonum of man's life is realization of God. Man is a part and parcel of the social structure through which alone he can realize this highest aim of self-realization. So, we propose to discuss, in this Chapter, the nature and structure of Gandhian social order which depends upon the relationship between the individual and the society.

Let us first discuss this basic problem of the relationship between the individual and the society.

THE INDIVIDUAL AND THE SOCIETY : THEIR INTER-RELATION

It has been universally admitted that man is born alone, but it seems as if it were natural with him to live in society. This is why Aristotle, the father of all social sciences, called him a 'social animal.' Even a cursory glance over his progress or evolution is enough to reveal that whatever qualities, characteristics and powers man has developed, in short, in whatever way he has evolved, would have been impossible had he isolated himself from society. Nay, it would have been hardly possible for him to survive as a man. In fact, individual and society are so interdependent and complementary to each other that it is difficult to imagine the existence of one without the other. What an 'Individual' is, he is because of the society. An isolated individual is a figment of imagination, and society without the individual is absurd and meaningless.

Gandhiji also admitted this inter-relationship between the individual and the society. He says, "I value individual freedom, but you must not forget that man is essentially a social animal. He has risen to his present status by learning to adjust his individualism to the requirements of social progress. Unrestricted individualism is the law of the beast of the jungle. We have to learn to strike the mean between individual freedom and social restraints. Willing submission to social restraints for the sake of well-being of the whole society, enriches the individual and the society of which one is a member."[1]

Thus, it has been universally admitted that plural individuals make singular society which in return is expected to make their existence comfortable and realization of aim of life possible.

But, it is pertinent to note that in order to realize the aim of his life, a particular type of social order is necessary. Because, as Hobhouse says, "In society it is possible that individuals of the very same potentialities may, with good organization, produce good results, and with bad organization, results which are greatly inferior."[2] Since the days of Plato in the West and Vedic Seers in the East, many thinkers gave their solution to the problem of 'how to strike a balance between individual freedom and social obligation', and visualized different social orders. But these solutions either failed or merged themselves into more complex ones.

The modern age is witnessing two major and comprehensive social orders. Democracy and Communism each trying to solve these problems, but making them more and more complex. Gandhiji also faced with these problems. He gave his own solution and visualized an Ideal Social Order. But before discussing the nature and structure of Gandhian Ideal Social Order, it seems necessary to discuss his views about the existing social orders.

GANDHIJI AND DEMOCRACY

Gandhiji was a born democrat, perhaps the greatest democrat of all times, because he saw God in humanity and humanity in God. The one saved him from the dilemma which sometimes confronts humanists when demos turn into chaos; the other saved him from the fallacy of Individualism which leads men to seek peace and personal salvation in the retirement of the cave. However, there are two approaches to democracy.

One involves the elimination of the weakest for 'the good of the greatest number', as may be the case with some of the Western Democracies today. States in the West tend to ignore the vital requirements regarding non-violence and purificatory discipline. Hence they made race for armaments, imperialism, exploitation, capitalism and world leadership. According to Gandhiji, "Capitalism has, by making state intervention necessary in economic affairs, contributed to the emergence of all powerful state which makes individual freedom impossible and is the greatest danger the world faces. The real problem today is to devise checks and balances on such a state and to prevent its rise."[3]

In Hind Swaraj Gandhiji criticizes the mother of parliaments comparing to a "sterile women." It has not yet of its own accord done a single good thing. If Parliament consists of the best men elected by enlightened voters, it "should not need the sour of petitions or any other pressure.

Its work should be so smooth that its effect should be more apparent day by day. But as a matter of fact, it is generally acknowledged that the members are hypocritical and selfish. Each thinks of his own little interest. It is fear that is the guiding motive."[4] Besides, Parliament is mercurial and unsteady in its fidelity to ministers. "Today it is under Mr. Asquith tomorrow it may be under Mr. Balfour."[5] Another instance of parliaments' fickleness is that there is no certainty about its decision. "What is done today may be undone tomorrow."

"It is not possible to recall a single instance in which finality can be predicted for its work."[6] The members of the parliament are seen to stretch themselves and doze when the greatest questions are debated. "Sometimes they talk away until listeners are disgusted. Carlyle called it the talking shop of the world. Members vote for their party without a thought."[7] "The Prime Minister is more concerned about his powers than about the welfare of the parliament. His energy is concentrated upon securing the success of his party. It is never his constant care that parliament shall do the right. Prime Ministers are known to have made parliament to do things merely for party advantages."[8] They cannot be really considered to be patriotic, and though they do not take bribes, they are open to subtler influences. "In order to gain this end, they certainly bribe people with honours...They have neither real honesty nor a living conscience."[9] "The voters are as changeable and fickle as their parliament. Their views swing like the pendulam of a clock and are never steadfast."[10] The people would follow a powerful orator or a man who gives them parties, receptions etc. Due to these defects democracies in the west are undemocratic. Masses, instead of ruling themselves, are exploited by the ruling classes. Parliaments are the emblems of slavery and costly toys of the nations—costly because they are a waste of time and money.

Gandhiji describes Western Democracy as it functions today, as "diluted Nazism or Fascism. At best...merely a cloak to hide the Nazi and the Fascist tendencies of imperialism."[11] Under it "the weakest...goes to the wall." Gandhiji regarded this as an insult to man and God, a travesty of true democracy. "No country in this world today shows any but patronising regard for the weak...My notion of democracy is that under it the weakest should have the same opportunity as the strongest."[12] "The rule of the people by the people, for the people" means the rule of 'unadulterated Ahimsa', for the simple reason that the natural corollary to the use of violent means would be 'to remove all opposition through the suppression and extermination of the antagonists.' That does not make for individual freedom."[13] This is the violent approach.

The other is the non-violent approach based on the principle of 'Unto This Last', which is Gandhian approach. "A votary of Ahimsa" says Gandhiji, "cannot subscribe to the utilitarian formula (of the greatest good of the greatest number). He will strive for the greatest good of all and die in the attempt to realize the ideal. He will, therefore, be willing to die, so that the other may live. He will serve himself with the rest, by himself dying. The greatest good of all inevitably includes the good of the greatest number, and there Gandhiji and the utilitarian will converge in many points in their outlook, but there does come a point when they must part, and even work in the opposite directions. The utilitarian, to be logical, will never sacrifice himself. The absolutist will even sacrifice himself."[14] Being a born democrat Gandhiji's concept of democracy was based not on the utilitarian principle of 'the greatest happiness of greatest number' but rather on the greatest happiness of all. He was the greatest lover of individual freedom. He says, "If the individual ceases to count, what is left of society? Individual freedom alone can make a man voluntarily surrender himself completely to the service of society. If it is wrested from him, he becomes an automation and society is ruined. No society can possibly be built on a denial of individual freedom."[15]

GANDHIJI AND MARXISM

It has been often said that Gandhiji was a communist minus violence. The common points between Gandhiji and Marx is extreme concern of both for the suppressed, the resourceless and the ignorant, the dumb and the starving section of humanity.

Both, Gandhiji and Marx wanted to establish an order, which would make the masses co-sharers in the gifts of nature and fruits of human labour and human genius. Gandhiji was never against communism if it is true communism, because he says, "what does communism in the last analysis mean? It means a classless society, an ideal that is worth striving for."[16] "But he would never support the communism of the Russian type. Because he observes, "communism of Russian type, that is communism which is imposed on the people, would be repugnant to India."[17] To Gandhiji, communism minus violence is welcome. He says,

"If communism came without violence, it would be welcome. For then, no property will be held by anybody except on behalf of the people and for the people. A millionnaire may have his millions, but he will hold them for the people. The State could take charge of them for the common cause."[18] These and many others are the innumerable instances which evince that Gandhiji favoured socialism, nay communism, provided it did not come through violence and we may say that Gandhiji was a communist minus violence.

No doubt, "Gandhiji has often claimed in the course of his discussions with communist and socialist friends that he is a better communist or socialist than they. Their goal is identical. The difference in regard to means and technique employed is however fundamental."[19] Gandhiji himself says, "socialism and communism of the West are based on certain conceptions which are fundamentally different from ours. One such conception is their belief in the essential selfishness of human nature. I do not subscribe to it, for I know that the essential difference between the man and brute is that the former can respond to the call of the spirit in him, can rise superior to the passions that he owns in common with the brute, and therefore, superior to selfishness and violence, which belong to the brute nature and not to the immortal spirit of man. That is the fundamental concept of Hinduism, which has years of penance and austerity at the back of discovery of this truth. That is why, whilst we have had saints who had worn out their bodies and laid down their lives in order to explore the secret of the soul, we have had none in the West, who laid down their lives in exploring the remotest or the highest regions of the earth. Our socialism or communism should, therefore, be based on non-violence and on harmonious cooperation of labour and capital, landlord and tenant."[20]

Thus, Gandhian philosophy is an antithesis of Marxian philosophy, and it is wrong to say that Gandhiji was a communist minus violence. These two ideologies are irreconcilable; the difference between them being fundamental. "The fundamental difference between Gandhiji and Marx lies in their different approaches towards life and the universe. All other differences, whether of ends and means or of ideas of political, social, economic or religious order arise from this basic differences."[21]

Gandhiji has a living faith in living God, whereas Marx emphatically denies the existence of God, rather treat Him 'as an opium for the Masses'. For Gandhiji spirit or soul is the ultimate, rather the only reality, whereas Marx believes that the matter is the only reality. Gandhiji's Man is Spiritual Man, whereas Marx Man is Economic Man. Gandhiji believes in detachment (आसक्ति), whereas Marxism is an ideology of attachment (अनासक्ति). Because of this fundamental difference Vinoba Bhave calls Gandhiji a great soul and Marx a great thinker.[22]

TWO FUNDAMENTAL CREEDS OF SOCIAL CHANGE

Thus, there were two fundamental creeds—construction of social order and development of virtue, which have exercised for so long man's mind, regarding the end and aim of man's activities. Communists' creed believes in the construction of social order. They hold that development of moral virtues, is a set of phenomena, which though becomes manifest in the mind, are not however the creation of the mind, but are the result of environment. The mind itself is the product of its natural environment. Bhautikam Chittam (Mind is the product of matter)...Mind is not a substance independent of matter. It is just a reflection of the world outside—an image. An image cannot govern the former. If we bring about a change in the substance, the mind will reflect the change, that is, will seem to have changed in character. If we create the right conditions that will inevitably give rise to right set of qualities. "Hence change the natural environment as rapidly as you can and by whatever means available, and do not waste your time vainly in weaving fantasies. The mind of man will remain, what it is. Do what you will, it will neither become like that of a lower animal, nor like that of your imaginary God. It is set within a limited structure. With the improvement in the environment, it shows a little development,.with its deterioration, slight retrogression. Do not worry about it. If violence is necessary for the reformation of society, do not scream out with alarm, 'Alas'! goodness is dead." Take it easy, since it puts an end to a bad system of society. The violence employed in order to gain that end cannot be classed as on par with ordinary violence. It is violence on a high level. Nay, it is really a virtue. If you can understand this, the proper development of character, which you worry about, will also follow."[23]

The exponents of the second creed who believes in development of virtue maintain that "life and the welfare of society depend upon man's character, his moral qualities, and his efforts at self improvement. An individual life is driven under the force of his moral nature. The social structure changes its form along with the development of human character. Hence, all lovers of good should concentrate their attention on the development of moral qualities. Laborious activity for constructing society (externally) serves no useful purpose. It leads merely to egoism. Jagad-Vyapara-Varjam (control of world forces excepted) is well known Sutra (Maxim) of Vedanta, and it marks the limit to which a devotee might aspire to rise. All that we must do is to ever strengthen our faith in the rules of spiritual and moral discipline, such as non-violence, truth, self-control, contentment, co-operation etc.; and try to incessantly translate these in our day to day life. Let us do this, and all else will be added unto it. No child need to be told that it should cry, if it is hurt. Given the necessary parental love the child will be fed, given the hurt crying will follow.

This creed manifests spontaneously in the hearts of the godly. The Gita gives a list of the moral qualities and characteristics indicative of the Jnana (knowledge) and Janadeva has given a beautiful elucidation of these in his masterly commentary."[24]

GANDHIAN APPROACH TO SOCIAL CHANGE

We have discussed above two extreme doctrines—the doctrine of the communists and that of the saints. Gandhian approach is in between these two. His approach is ethical. "He does not deny the importance of changing the social structure, but it should be brought about only through the development of particular moral attributes. After all, it is the people, who make a society. Hence a society will be as the individual making it. Hence any scheme of changing the society must be not only subject to preservation—indeed, enhancement—of standards of character and moral values, but the change must be brought about by the means and strength of character and moral values. We must not worry if it takes place gradually and at a seemingly lower pace."[25] Gandhiji does not subscribe to the communists' doctrine that the end justifies the means. Contrary to it, Gandhiji believes that means justify the end as the end grows out of the means. He says, "The clearest possible definition of the goal and its appreciation would fail to take us there, if we do not know and utilize the means of achieving it. I have, therefore, concerned myself principally with the conservation of the means and their progressive use. I know if we can take care of them attainment of the goal is assured. I feel too that our progress towards the goal will be in exact proportion to the purity of our means. This method may appear to be long, perhaps too long, but I am convinced that it is the shortest."[26]

Gandhiji agrees with Mahabharata that a social order cannot be established by violence or laws, it can be established only if the people observe moral law. Mahabharata says :

नैव राज्यम् न राजासीत्, न च दण्डो न डाण्डिका ।
धर्मेणैव प्रजाः सर्वाः रक्षन्ति स्म परस्परम ।।

(A people flourish not because of a constitution or coercion or a law giver, but because they are guided by Dharma and keep each other in cooperation.[27])

Gandhiji was greatly influenced by John Ruskin's 'Unto This Last'. Ruskin in his book says, "Men can be happy only if they obey the moral law." "Morality" says Gandhiji, "is an essential ingredient in all the faiths of the world, but apart from religion, our common sense indicates the necessity of observing the moral law. Only by observing it can we be happy." Thus Gandhiji believes that no social order can be stable, if the individual does not observe the moral law. He believes that "a small body of determined spirited, fired by an unquenchable faith in their mission, can alter the course of history."[28] With this end in view, he visualises a picture of an Ideal Social Order. He formulates a complete ethics for remaking the man.

GANDHIAN IDEAL SOCIAL ORDER

Gandhian social order includes in it the good points of Marxism and Democracy, but it is fundamentally different from the both. It is a case-sui-generous. Unlike Communism and Western Democracy it is based on spiritual foundations. The ideal social order as visualised by Gandhiji is a classless, casteless, and stateless society based on non-violence, non-cooperation (with evils), and non-centralization (decentralization). He calls it Sarvodya Samaj in which 'the greatest good of all' is the end.

This ideal society, according to Gandhiji, is the stateless democracy, the state of enlightened anarchy where social life has become so perfect as to be self-regulated. "In such a state (of enlightened anarchy)" says Gandhiji, "every one is his own ruler. He rules himself in such a manner that he is never a hindrance to his neighbour. In the Ideal State, there is no political power because there is no state."[29] Freedom to the individual is, therefore, implied in such a state.

As regards its structure, the Ideal society will be a federation of more or less self-sufficing and self-governing Satyagrahi Village Communities. As Gandhiji says, "Society based on non-violence can only consist of groups settled in villages in which voluntary cooperation is the condition of dignified peaceful existence."[30] The federation like the groups will obviously be organized on a voluntary basis. In such a community almost every individual will have developed a high level of non-violence and acquired almost complete self-control. The individual, continuously aware of Spiritual Reality, will live a life of simplicity and renunciation and live for social service.

Referring to the democratic Satyagrahi Rural Communities, he says, "...every village will be a republic or panchayat having full powers... In this structure composed of innumerable villages, there will be ever-widening, never ascending circles. Life will not be a pyramid with the apex sustained by the bottom. But it will be an oceanic circle whose centre will be the individual always ready to perish for the village, the latter ready to perish for the circle of villages, till at last the whole becomes one life composed of individuals, never aggressive in their arrogance, but ever humble, sharing the majesty of oceanic circle of which they are integral units. Therefore the outermost circumference will not wield power to crush the innermost circle but give strength to all within and derive its own strength from it."[31]

Gandhiji did not believe in drawing up a futile Utopia. The goal did not interest him more than as a pole star which was to steer his course through the storms which life presented. He did not give a detailed blue print of the ideal social order. His concern was much rather with the means i.e. with shaping the present in the light of the goal. He was certain that if we could work for our ideal in terms of the immediate present, the end was bound to follow. He says, "I may be taunted with the retort that this is all Utopian and therefore, not worth a single thought. If Ecluids' point, though incapable of being drawn by human agency, has an imperishable value, my picture has its own for mankind to live. Let India live for this true picture, though never realisable in its completeness. We must have a proper picture of what we want, before we can have something approaching it. If there ever is to be a republic of every village in India, then I claim verily for my picture in which the last is equal to the first or, in other words, no one is to be the first none the last."[32]

To sum up what has been said in this chapter, we can say that for Gandhiji the end is "the greatest good of all." He is a Philosophical Anarchist because he believes that end can be realized only in the classless and stateless democracy of autonomous village communities, based on non-violence instead of coercion, on service instead of exploitation, on renunciation instead of acquisitiveness and on the largest measure of local and individual initiative instead of centralization. Non-violent nationalism will be cooperative and constructive and will be an integral part of universal humanity instead of being exclusive, competitive and militant; and conflicts will be resolved not on the physical plane of brute force but on the spiritual plane of love.

For the realization of such social order, Gandhiji starts with the 'Individual' who will live and die for this 'Ideal Social Order'.

References

1. Harijan, 27-5-38.
2. Hobhouse, L.T. Social Evolution and Political Theory (1911), p. 30.
3. Louis Fischer, A week with Gandhi, pp. 82-83.
4. Hind Swaraj, pp. 15-16.
5. *Ibid.,* p. 15.
6. *Ibid.,* p. 16.
7. *Ibid.*
8. *Ibid.*
9. *Ibid.,* p. 17
10. *Ibid.*
11. Harijan, 18-5-40, p. 129.
12. *Ibid.*
13. Harijan, 27-5-39, p. 143.
14. Young India, 12-12-26.
15. Harijan, 1-2-42.
16. *Ibid.,* 10-12-38.
17. *Ibid.*
18. *Ibid.*
19. Payara Lal, Gandhiji and Communism.
20. Amrit Bazar Patrika, 2-8-34.
21. Mashruwala, K.G., Gandhi and Marx, p. 40.
22. *Ibid.,* Introductory Chapter by Vinoba Bhave, p. 15.
23. *Ibid.,* pp. 9-10.
24. *Ibid.,* pp. 8-9.
25. *Ibid.,* p. 11.

26. Amrit Bazar Patrika, 17-9-33.
27. Mahabharata, Santiparvan.
28. Harijan, 19-11-33.
29. Young India, 2-7-31, p. 62.
30. Harijan, 13-1-40, p. 411.
31. Harijan, 28-7-46, p. 236.
32. *Ibid.*

7

The Nature of the State

I look upon an increase of power of the state with greatest fear, because, although while apparently doing good by minimising exploitation, it does the greatest harm to mankind by destroying individuality which lies at the root of all progress.

THE MODERN REVIEW, OCT. 1935, P. 413.

IT has been already discussed that Gandhiji is a philosophical anarchist who, ideally speaking, repudiates the state as such, whatever its form. This repudiation has an ethical, historical as well as an economic basis. The compulsive nature of state authority damages the moral value of the individual's action; for an action is moral only when it is voluntary. "No action which is not voluntary can be called moral...so long as we act like machines, there can be no question of morality. If we want to call an action moral it should have been done consciously, and as a matter of duty."[1] Besides, the state, even though its machinery be most democratic, is rooted in violence. Violence implies exploitation and every state exploits the poor. "The state represents violence in a concentrated and organized form. The individual has a soul, but as the state is soul-less machine, it can never be weaned from violence to which it owes its very existence."[2] Once while discussing his theory of trusteeship in relation to private property he remarked, "I look upon an increase in the power of the state with the greatest fear, because although while apparently doing good by minimizing exploitation, it does the greatest harm to mankind by destroying individuality, which lies at the root of all progress. We know of so many cases where men have adopted trusteeship but none where the state has really lived for the poor."[3]

The ideal society is, according to Gandhiji, the stateless democracy, the state of enlightened anarchy where social life has become so perfect as to be self regulated. "In such a state (of enlightened anarchy) every one is his own ruler. He rules himself in such a manner that he is never a hindrance to his neighbour. In the ideal state, there is no political power because there is no state."[4]

THE SECOND BEST IDEAL : THE NON-VIOLENT STATE

But the stateless non-violent society in which there will be no police and military, no law-courts, doctors, heavy transport and centralized production, is an inspiring ideal rather than the goal to be soon realized.[5] Society can become stateless only when the individuals have acquired sufficient self control and are able to observe social obligation without the operation of the state. Gandhiji believes that the ideal society will always remain an Ideal unrealized and unrealizable in its entirety. Referring to the stateless society he says. "But the ideal is never fully realized in life."[6] Again in an answer to the question, "Can a state carry on strictly according to the principle of non-violence?" Gandhiji replied, "A Government cannot succeed in becoming entirely non-violent, because it represents all the people. I do not conceive of such a golden age. But I do believe in the possibility of predominently non-violent society. And I am working for it."[7]

The ideal non-violent society of Gandhiji, unattainable due to human imperfection, indicates the direction rather than the destination, the process rather than the consummation. The structure of the state that will emerge as a result of the non-violent revolution will be a compromise, a via media, between the ideal non-violent society and the facts of human nature. It will be the attainable "middle way"[8] of Gandhiji, the first step, after the revolution, towards the ideal. This predominently non-violent state is Gandhiji's second best Ideal. The state will no doubt continue to exist, for there will be some individuals or groups with anti-social tendencies and the absence of external restraint will lead to anarchy. Here the political life and institutions are moulded to the principles of non-violence consistent with practical facts of life; and police, military or law courts are not altogether abolished. We should remember that Gandhiji's ideal is not a static but a dynamic ideal. This is the best represented by what he calls 'Swaraj'. Thus, in 'Swaraj' the state continues to exist.

Let us now discuss Gandhian views on the nature of state.

THE NATURE OF STATE

To Gandhiji state is not an end in itself but "one of the means of enabling people to better their condition in every department of life."[9] Thus, he does not accept the Hegelian view of the state as the final goal of human organization, its own end and object, the ultimate end which has the highest right against the individual and is itself above morality, or the Mussolinian dictum, "Outside the state there is nothing." Gandhiji does not consider the state even the group of groups or the community of communities as the idealist thinkers like Green and Bosanquet do. To him, the state is only "one of the means" to secure the greatest good of all. There is nothing sacrosanct about the state. It is concession to human weakness and the more man can do without it, the more real is his freedom. He distrusts the state and seeks to develop in the people, through Satyagraha, the capacity to resist the state authority when it is abused. In fact, he expects every member of a democratic state to be "capable of defending his liberty against the whole world." According to him, "...real Swaraj will come not by the acquisition of authority by a few, but by the acquisition of the capacity by all to resist authority when abused. In other words, Swaraj is to be obtained by educating the masses to a sense of their capacity to regulate and control authority."[10] Again, "Real home-rule is possible only where passive resistance (Satyagraha) is the guiding force of the people. Any other rule is foreign rule."[11] It is because of this belief that Gandhiji has been severely critical of the Indian rule after independence. Gandhiji wanted 'Swaraj' no matter who brings it or who runs it.

Like pluralists and anarchists, Gandhiji is against the theory of absolute sovereignty of state which lays upon the individual the duty of absolute unquestioning obedience to the laws of the state. He believes in the sovereignty of the people based on moral authority.[12] A man, according to him, owes only a limited and relative loyalty to the state as to other associations. This loyalty is conditional on the decision of the state or any other association appealing to the individual's conscience. This is no doubt perpetual threat of anarchy. But this is the only adequate safeguard against the abuse of political power. Though Gandhiji makes the disobedience of laws, which offend the moral sense, a right as well as duty of the citizen and considers such disobedience the key to democracy.[13]

THE BASIS OF STATE

As regards the basis of state, Gandhiji agrees with T. H. Green when he says, "Will, not force is the basis of state." The moral conception of common good rather than physical force, is the central feature of Green's state. If the individuals obey the state, they do so not because the state is the embodiment of force, but because it maintains a system of rights necessary for the realization of common good. It is because of the presence of the idea of common good in the individual that the institutions have a constraining power over him, "a power which is not that of mere fear, still less of a physical compulsion, but which leads him to do what he is not inclined to because there is law that he should."[14] To represent it (fear) as the basis of civil subjection is to confound the citizen with the slave, and to represent the motive which is needed for the restraint of those in whom the civil sense is lacking, and for the occasional reinforcements of the law abiding principle in others, as if it were the normal influence in habits of life of which the essential value lies in their being independent of it."[15] The fulfilment of the moral obligation through the use of force or the legal enforcement of morality is the very denial of it. That is why when criticising Locke's conception of the state of nature, Green says, "In fact, the condition of society in which it could properly be said to be governed by a law of nature, i.e. by an obligation...of which the breach is not punished by a political superior, is not antecedent to political society, but one which it gradually tends to produce."[16] The state of nature in which force and law are quite dispensed with, is the very consummation of educational processes involved in the history of civil Government. Gandhiji, however, is more explicit in adopting the ideal of non-violence which follows from his metaphysics.

But, if force plays no part in the ideal, it does not mean that it can be eliminated from actual conditions of life. For Gandhiji and Green an ideal ceases to be an ideal if it is fully realized. Both recognize the necessity of the use of force in practical politics and refer to it as unavoidable or inevitable because of human imperfections. Thus according to Gandhiji, force is inevitable in actual politics because our very existence involves violence. The question arises whether this unavoidable use of force has the same significance as the utilitarians' use of force to prevent greater evil. In the latter case, the use of force when used to prevent a greater evil, acquires the character of goodness, but that is not so in the former case. According to Gandhiji, force does not change its moral character according to the circumstances of its use. If it is used in practical politics it is used in the sense of lesser evil—evil all the same. This description of force is not inconsistent with an ideal in which its use has been completely eliminated. The value of this recognition lies in the fact that if we are conscious of force as evil and are also conscious that its use is unavoidable because of practical imperfections, then it makes us strive to overcome the imperfections and thereby avoid the use of force.

True, that it does not make any difference in practical politics whether force is used in the utilitarian sense 'of avoiding greater evil' or in the sense of Green and Gandhiji as 'necessary evil,' but the latter position does avoid the inconsistency with an ultimate ideal which was inherent in the utilitarian position. Thus, Gandhiji referring to his position in the national state says, "If there were a national government, whilst I should not take any direct part in any war, I can conceive occasions when it would be my duty to vote for the military training of those who wish to take it. For I know that all its members do not believe in non-violence to the extent I do. It is not possible to make a person or society non-violent by compulsion."[17] To impose non-violence from above is against the very spirit of non-violence. It has to evolve on a voluntary basis from individuals. And to the extent the individuals have cultivated it, it will be reflected in their institutions including the state. Thus Gandhiji expects the evolution of the state to come with the moral evolution of the individuals.

FUNCTIONS OF THE STATE

The state, according to Gandhiji, is a mere means and not an end. The ultimate end or purpose of the non-violent state will be to advance "the greatest good of all." To that end it will give to the individual maximum opportunity for growth. The state is rooted in violence, exploits the poor and by enforcing action restricts the scope for self rule on the part of the individual. So, in a predominantly non-violent society the state will govern the least and use the least amount of force."[18] As regards the state governing the least, Gandhiji says, "Our capacity for Swaraj depends upon our capacity for solving without reference to or intervention of, the Government, all the varied and complex problems that must arise in the affairs of one of the biggest and the most ancient nations like ours."[19] "Swaraj Government will be a sorry affair if people look up to it for the regulation of every detail of life."[20] Again, "I admit that there are certain things which cannot be done without political power but there are numerous other things which do not at all depend upon political power. That is why a thinker like Thoreau said, "that that Government is the best which governs the least."[21]

If freedom is based on the non-violence of the brave, "least government will be practicable, for that freedom will be an organic inward growth. People will acquire capacity for voluntary co-operation and concerted action, and will learn to regulate most of their social life through voluntary organizations. Thus, the village units will be self-sufficient in regard to production and defence. "A village unit", says Gandhiji, "conceived by me is as strong as the strongest"[22] The bewildering multiplicity of functions which the modern state performs will also become unnecessary in the non-violent state due to the simplicity of life, decentralization and absence of violent class conflict and militarism. Besides, the justification and the extent of state activity depends on whether people attach greater value to security against the invasive acts of others, i.e. to peace and order imposed by law, than to freedom of action. In the non-violent state such invasive acts will be infrequent. People will have acquired the technique of dealing with them non-violently. This will also narrow the province of state action.

The functions of the state will be gradually reduced and transferred to voluntary associations. Gandhiji is, however, not a doctrinaire. He would decide every case on its own merits, and where state action is likely to advance the welfare of the people he would welcome it in spite of his distrust of the state. In performing its functions the object of the state will be to serve the masses. The interest of the classes, so long as these continue, will be its concern to the extent that this interest subserves and does not conflict with the interest of the masses. Gandhiji insists that every interest that is hostile to that of masses must be revised or must subside if it is incapable of revision."[23] Thus, Gandhiji looks with disfavour at every increase in the power of the state. He says, "I look upon an increase of the power of the state with the greatest fear, because although while apparently doing good by minimizing exploitation, it does the greatest harm to mankind by destroying individuality which lie at the root of all progress."[24] He devises the method of 'Satyagraha' which is based on individual initiative. It is here that he goes beyond Green by providing a positive moral method for dispensing with force and thus affect a speedier revolution towards the ideal.

POLITICAL OBLIGATION AND RIGHT TO RESIST

Why should we obey the state ? The exponents of the theory of absolute sovereignty hold that laws of the state are the highest arbiter of the conduct of the citizen irrespective of the conformity of the laws to the general interests of the community. They inculcate an absolute obligation of submission to the state and consider as unconstitutional any claim of moral right against its laws. The validity of the absolutist view is questioned by pluralists and others. To many of these thinkers the problem of political obligation is essentially moral; the state possesses no peculiar merit; and its right to the allegiance of the citizen is dependent on the moral adequacy of its laws. "Our first duty", says Laski, "is to be true to our conscience."[25]

Thus, the concept of political obligation involves some ethical standard by which political actions could be appraised or criticized. The question, why do we obey the state ? is not the question of explanation, but of justification i.e. an ethical question. The question of political obligation carries the implication of an ideal which alone can justify one's obedience to the state. The principles of political obligation, therefore, will depend on the nature of this ideal. Our obligation to the state is derivatory, being a means to the ideal.

The ideal of Gandhiji is the ideal of self-realization. The justification of the state, and for that matter of any institution, depends on the contribution which it makes to this ideal. That is to say, the reason for respecting the rights and duties as enforced by the state exist in so far as they facilitate the realization of this ideal. But this ideal being ethical in nature, cannot be enforced by the state but, must be realized through the individual initiative; and for this end, liberty is an essential condition. Hence, there is a conspicuous emphasis on individual liberty in Gandhian philosophy. According to Gandhiji, liberty consists in acting according to the dictates of good will and carries the implication of Kant's 'categorical imperative'. The individual again is not the isolated individual of Bentham, but is looked at in the totality of his relations with society. Hence the good of the individual is closely bound up with the good of society. The purpose of Government is to safeguard and foster all those relations which enable man to be himself at his best and which constitute for Gandhiji the liberty of the individual.

To Gandhiji, the question of political obligation is, thus, essentially moral and "disobedience to the law of the state becomes a peremptory duty when it comes in conflict with the law of God."[26] According to him, satyagraha will be unconstitutional "when truth and its fellow self-sacrifice become unlawful."[27] He holds that "It is contrary to our manhood, if we obey laws contrary to our conscience...So long as the superstition that man should obey unjust laws exists, so long will their slavery exist."[28] "Submission to a state law, wholly or largely unjust, is an immoral barter for liberty."[29]

Gandhiji would consider the government machinery itself as unconstitutional if it is undemocratic and rooted in injustice and exploitation. Civil resistance is the most constitutional and sacred duty of the people towards such a government.[30]

Even from the point of view of absolutists persuation to educate public opinion is everywhere considered constitutional, and non-violent direct action (i.e. Satyagraha) is the most effective form of persuation, being the appeal of the suffering love to the head through the heart. In the words of Gandhiji, "Satyagraha is the greatest means of educating the public and awakening the people."[31] Even if the satyagrahi is mistaken, his resistance harms none but himself, for he proceeds by self-suffering. His opposition to the established order is moral and not physical. It is an effort to convince the opponent rather than destroy him.

Further, every law gives the individual the option, either to obey the law or in the alternative to suffer the penalty for disobedience. In the case of immoral laws or if the Government is corrupt the Satyagrahi chooses the second alternative and willingly accepts the punishment imposed by the state.[32]

As is well known the Magna Charta and the Declaration of the Rights of Man legalized the right to resist the state under certain circumstances. Chapter 61 of the Magna Charta, which is still, in the words of Hallam, the keystone of English liberty, appointed a committee of 25 barons with the recognized right of resistence to the king as a means of enforcing the provisions of the charter.[33]

Thus, for Gandhiji, the grounds of political obligation reside ultimately in the duty of self-realization and for this individual liberty is essential.

RIGHTS AND DUTIES OF CITIZENS

Rights, according to Gandhiji, are the opportunities necessary for self-realization which, for him, is the highest duty. They are innate in the sense in which moral values are innate. As Green puts it, "They (rights) are innate or natural in the sense in which according to Aristotle state is natural; not in the sense that they actually exist when a man is born and that they have actually existed as long as the human race, but that they arise out of, and are necessary for the fulfilment of, a moral capacity without which a man would not be a man. There cannot be innate rights in any other sense than that in which there are innate duties, of which, however, much less has been heard." Indeed, for Gandhiji, social good has even in a sense primary importance; and every right really comes to be a right to perform one's duties. "...the right to perform one's duties," says Gandhiji, "is the only right that is worth living for and dying for. It covers all legitimate rights."[34] In this respect Gandhiji is following teachings of Gita.

Thus for Gandhiji, "The true source of rights is duty."[35] Gandhiji's position is quite in contrast to that of the utilitarians e.g., to that of Bentham for whom the assertion of rights is more fundamental than the performance of duty.

Gandhiji holds that the rights need only be recognised by the state for the purpose of enforcement. The state does not create rights, but, in the words of Green, gives fuller reality to rights already existing. Such a theory of rights stands in contrast to that of Bentham for whom "Rights properly so-called are the creatures of law properly so-called." For Gandhiji, rights are not the creatures of law, but its condition precedent. They are the conditions which law seeks to realize. Indeed, in the ideal society Gandhiji explicitly recognises the needlessness of the state for the enforcement of rights. People would simply grow accustomed spontaneously to observe their social obligations without the operation of the state. But the necessity of enforcement of rights through the machinery of the state arises because of the imperfections of individuals and consequent conflicts of rights.

LAW AND MORALITY

In the light of above discussion, the question arises, how can the law of the state serve a moral purpose ? Law is concerned with external acts which it enforces through external compulsion. Morality, on the other hand, is concerned with internal motives as well as external acts. The demands of law are fully satisfied if the external actions as required are performed irrespective of the internal motives; but that is not so in the case of morality. The performance of moral duties often implies a certain disposition and motive and does not admit of being legally enforced. Indeed, such legal enforcement may even make it impossible at all to perform actions with such motives and disposition.

Thus, there is a clear distinction between the nature of morality and that of law. But it does not mean that such a distinction abolishes any relation between the two. The relation exists not in the sense that law represents the minimum of morality, because that would ultimately lead to the denial of the distinction of law and morality and might even eliminate morality altogether; it rather consists in the fact that law seeks or should seek to secure external condition necessary for the realization of the moral ideal. Law cannot make men moral; but it does help to make morality possible. As such, law at its best represents not the minimum morality, but a system of conditions necessary for moral activity. In so far as law provides these external conditions by removing hindrances, it makes morality possible and thus serves a moral end.

Such a distinction and relation of law and morality is recognised by Gandhiji. A good act is good only when it is done "from a sense of duty" in the doer. State action, on the other hand, cannot ensure the doing of acts from this sense of duty. That is why Gandhiji would find no place for the state in his ideal society. But in actual conditions he concedes the necessity of state regulation for creating conditions which make morality possible.

There is complete duty to obey any state which enforces such laws, and there should be no conflict between our obligation to moral values and to the state; because by fulfilling our obligation to the state we are also fulfilling a moral purpose. Even when the state forces us to obey its laws, we obey the state not as an external power impinging on our will, but as upholder of a system of rights which as a system we approve, even though we may have failed to see its application at a particular point.

Such a distinction of law and morality enables one to draw the proper limits to state activity. When Gandhiji advocates prohibition, he does so not because it constitutes morality in itself, but because its opposite is a hindrance to good life. The prohibition of the sale of intoxicated drinks aim at removing from the environment such detrimental factors which stand in the way of well-being of its citizens. Prohibition is not a case of compelling to be moral. It is merely a case of removing hindrances. "Drink" says Gandhiji, "is more a disease than a vice."[36] Again, "Diseased persons have got to be helped against themselves.[37] In the case of non-drinker there is obviously no compulsion. "The State", says Gandhiji, "does not cater for the vices of its people. We do not regulate or license houses of ill fame. We do not provide facilities for thieves to indulge their propensity for thieving." It is only in the case of drink addicts that compulsion is felt. But then the state must interfere in such cases in order to prevent anti-social consequences.

It may, however, he asked, "how can the state interfere in the private life of an individual?" That is to say, the individual is sovereign in his conduct which does not affect others. But such separation of individual conduct into self-regarding and other-regarding spheres cannot provide a satisfactory principle. Whatever a man does, affects others in greater or less degree and with more or less directness of impact.

At the same time, Gandhiji, insists on the importance of educating public opinion. Legal prohibition is but the negative part of Gandhiji's temperance movement; the positive part being 'a type of adult education of the nation'. Green, whose approach is similar to that of Gandhiji admits that "to attempt a restraining law in advance of the social sentiments necessary to give real effect to it, is always mistake." He suggests not a national law of prohibition but one to promote some form of local option. Gandhiji, however, proposed a national prohibition for India. But this cannot be considered a dictatorial step, because Gandhiji represents in himself the will of the vast majority.

To sum up, we may say that according to Gandhiji the basis of the state is non-violence and not force. The non-violent state will not be end in itself, but one of the means for the achievement of the greatest good of all. It will perform limited functions using the minimum coercion. The allegiance to the state is derived from the allegiance to an ethical ideal. The performance of duties to achieve the ethical is more fundamental than the rights of the individual. The laws of the state cannot directly promote morality, their function being removal of hindrances to a better life.

References

1. Ethical Religion, p. 40.
2. Bose, N.K., Studies in Gandhism, pp. 202-04. Every anarchist thinker emphasizes the violent character of the State.
3. *Ibid.*
4. Young India, 2-7-31, p. 162.
5. Among anarchist thinkers, Godwin, Thomas Hodgskin and Proudhon did not look forward to the establishment of a society from which state would be completely eliminated. On the other hand Bakumin, Josiah Warren, Bengamin Tucker and Kropotkin, besides many other anarchist thinkers, held that it was possible to evolve a stateless society. Marx and Lenin also believe that the proletarian state would wither away and people will grow accustomed to observe conditions of social existence with force and without subjection.
6. Young India, 2-7-31, p. 162.
7. Harijan, 9-3-40, p. 31.
8. Gandhiji once said, "Having ascertained the law of our being, we must set about reducing it to practice to the extent of our capacity and no further. That is the middle way." Young India, II, p. 659.
9. Young India, 2-7-31.
10. *Ibid.,* II, p. 491.
11. Hind Swaraj, p. 74.
12. Harijan, 2-1-37, p. 374. The above is his definition of the term Ramaraj which he frequently used to convey to the people the content of a democratic state. Ramaraj is "the Kingdom of Righteousness." "By Ramaraj I do not mean Hindu Raj. I mean by Ramaraj Divine Raj, the Kingdom of God...the ancient ideal of Ramaraj is undoubtedly one of true democracy." Young India, 28-6-31, p. 126; 19-9-29, p. 305.

13. Hind Swaraj, p. 71.
14. Green Lectures on the Principles of Political Obligation, para, 116.
15. *Ibid.*, para, 118.
16. *Ibid.*, para 55.
17. Young India, 13-9-28.
18. *Ibid.*, 111: p. 560.
19. *Ibid.*, 1, p. 742.
20. *Ibid.*, 11, p. 290.
21. Harijan, 11-1-36, p. 380.
22. *Ibid.*, 4-8-46, p. 251.
23. Young India, 17-9-31.
24. Modern Review, 1935, p. 252.
25. Laski, H. J., The Grammar of Politics, p. 239.
26. Ethical Religion, p. 47.
27. Young India, III, p. 1043.
28. Hind Swaraj, pp. 70-71.
29. Young India, p. 10-21.
30. Speeches, p. 532; Young India, p. 938.
31. Harijan, 30-10-49, p. 293.
32. Hind Swaraj, pp. 70-71.

    It may be pointed out that General Smuts, Gandhiji's adversary in South Africa, considered the Satyagraha movement there as constitutional movement (Speeches p. 480). Lord Hardings, the then Viceroy of India, also approved of Gandhiji's Satyagraha in South Africa. Charles E. Merriam describes Gandhiji's system of Civil Disobedience as being "within the boarder of legality." (see his Political Power, p. 174). Sir Stafford Cripps considers as legitimate the use of general strike by the working class in a democracy under certain conditions, C R. Attlee holds that in the absence of democratic means of redress resort to unconstitutional, even violent means to bring about fundamental changes is inevitable. (Richard Actland (ed.), Why I am a Democrat, contributed by C.R. Attlee and Sir Stafford Cripps).

33. Gniest holds that the resistance conceded in Chapter 61 was in harmony with the legal conceptions of the feudal states of Middle Ages based on compact (Hudolph Gniest, History of the English Constitution, 2nd ed., Vol. I, pp. 306-07).

    The Magna Charta, according to Adams, lays down two fundamental principles which lie at the present day, as clearly as in 1215, at the foundation of the English Constitution, and of all constitutions derived from it. First, that "There is a body of law in the state, of rights belonging to the subjects or to the community which the King is bound to regard" and second, that "if the King will not regard these rights he may be compelled by force, by insurrection against him, to do." (G.B. Adams, Constitutional History of England, pp. 129-30 and 137-39).

34. Harijan, 27-5-39.

35. Young India, II, p. 479.

36. *Ibid.,* 12-1-28.

37. India of My Dreams, p. 70.

8

The Structure of the State

I have purposely refrained from dealing with the nature of Government in a society based on non-violence...When society is deliberately constructed in accordance with the law of non-violence, its structure will be different in material particulars from what is today. But I cannot say in advance what Government based wholly on non-violence will be like.

—HARIJAN, FEBRUARY 11, 1939

IN the previous chapter we have discussed the nature of the state—its basis and functions, the problem of political obligation and the right to resist, the relation of rights and duties and law and morality. Connected with the problem of the nature of the state is that of the structure of the state.

What is the structure of the ideal state? Gandhiji refrains from painting its picture. He says, "I have purposely refrained from dealing with the nature of Government in a society based on non-violence...When society is deliberately constructed in accordance with the law of non-violence, its structure will be different in material particulars from what it is today. But I cannot say in advance what the government based wholly on non-violence will be like."[1] His attitude here is determined by his philosophy of ends and means. That is, if one takes care of the means, the end will take care of itself. That is, why he puts non-violence before Swaraj—because for him "the attempt made to win Swaraj is Swaraj itself." However, he does give broad indications of his ideal society at several places. Such a society is in sharp contrast to the modern notions of Western society. Indeed, Gandhiji's "Hind Swaraj" is a great indictment of Western civilization. While referring to it, he says, "...what is written there was reference to an ideal state."

Gandhiji's social ideal, as it has been already discussed, is a classless and a stateless society, a state of self-regulated enlightened "anarchy," in which social cohesion will be maintained by internal and non-coercive external sanctions. But as this ideal is not realizable, he has an attainable middle ideal also—the predominantly non-violent state.

Now let us discuss the political constitution of the non-violent state, the administration of justice and place of crimes and jails in it.

THE POLITICAL CONSTITUTION OF THE NON-VIOLENT STATE

It may be pointed out that from 1909 onward Gandhiji subjected the parliamentary government as prevailing in England to severe criticism. In 1917 in his presidential address to the first Gujarat political conference he demanded parliamentary Government. In 1920 he said, "My Swaraj" is the parliamentary government of India in the modern sense of the term for the time being..."[2] In 1942 he told Louis Fischer that he did not believe in the accepted Western form of democracy with its universal voting for parliamentary representatives.[3] This seems to be confusing, but it should be borne in mind that he attaches far more importance to the spirit behind a constitution than to its external form. His criticism of parliamentary democracy is due more to the spirit in which it is actually worked than to the constitutional machinery. Gandhiji does not believe that representative institutions are something new or unsuitable to India, though he is against a wholesale copying of the West.[4]

In Hind Swaraj, Gandhiji severely criticises the mother of parliament comparing it to a "sterile woman," and "a prostitute." It is like the former, because "the parliament has not yet, of its own accord, done a single good thing... without outside pressure; it is like the latter because it is under the control of ministers who change from time to time."

The Prime Minister is more concerned about his powers than about the welfare of the parliament. "In order to gain their ends, they certainly bribe people with honours...they have neither real honesty nor a living conscience."[5] To the voters their newspapers are their Bible. They take their cue from their newspapers which are often dishonest. The same fact is differently interpreted by different newspapers, according to the party in whose interest they are edited.[6] The voters are as changeable as their parliament. Their views "swing like the pendulum of a clock and are never steadfast."[7] The people would follow a powerful orator or a man who gives them parties, receptions etc. Due to these defects democracies in the West are undemocratic. Masses, instead of ruling themselves, are exploited by the ruling classes. Parliaments are the emblems of slavery and costly toys of nations—costly because they are a waste of time and money.

In recent years, parliamentary government has been subjected to severe criticism. Thus the system of elections; the slow-moving procedure; the incapacity of the system, due to centralization and congestion of business, for the creative work of social and economic regeneration; the dictatorship of the cabinet; the increasing power of permanent officials; the failure of the system to induce the citizen to participate actively in political life; the absence of approximate economic equality—all these points have been assailed by critics. To Gandhiji democracy remains unachieved more on account of the prevailing belief in the efficacy of violence and untruth than on account of mere institutional inadequacy. If people accept the way of non-violence, the democratic state that emerge will be inspired by the ideal of truth and non-violence. Corruption and hypocricy that characterise the modern democracies will be minimized.

In a statement issued in 1934 Gandhiji remarked, "Western democracy is on its trial. If it has already proved a failure, may it be reserved to India to evolve the true science of democracy by giving a visible demonstration of its buttress. Corruption and hypocricy ought not to be the inevitable products of democracy, as they undoubtedly are today. Nor is the bulk the true test of democracy. True democracy is not inconsistent with a few persons representing the spirit, the hope and aspirations of those whom they claim to represent. I hold that democracy cannot be evolved by forcible method. The spirit of democracy cannot be imposed from without. It has to come from within."[8]

Gandhiji is not against elections and representation. In 1925 he wrote, "By Swaraj I mean the government of India by the consent of the people as ascertained by the larger number of adult population, male or female, native born or domiciled, who have contributed by manual labour to the service of the state and who have taken the trouble of having their name registered as voters."[9] Again, "If independence is born non-violently all the component parts will be voluntarily interdependent working in perfect harmony under a representative central authority which will derive its sanction from the confidence reposed in it by the component parts." The central power, he goes on to add will be based on "Universal sufferage exercised by a disciplined and politically intelligent electorate."[10]

Thus, though Gandhiji, is highly critical of the moral qualities of the parliament, nonetheless he advocates to a considerable extent the kind of representative institutions which have been favoured by English Liberal thinkers and particularly by J.S. Mill.

There are, however, important points of difference, arising partly from the different kind of society envisaged by Gandhiji from the existing in England and partly from Gandhiji's preoccupation with the need for moral leadership. J. S. Mill also was anxious to improve the quality of elected representatives as well as the procedure of their election. It is interesting to compare the views of Gandhiji and Mill on these matters. This would enable us more fully to appreciate Gandhiji's ideas. Both Gandhiji and Mill are anxious to avoid the dangers of the tyranny of the majority. But while Mill suggests institutional safeguards, Gandhiji, emphasises moral considerations. Indeed, Gandhiji is somewhat indifferent to the problems of checks and balances.

Both Gandhiji and Mill are against payment of large sums to the elected representatives. But while Mill is anxious to avoid the 'sinister' interest of the representative, Gandhiji's anxiety is about the moral effect on the representative himself. Both advocate a wide franchise, but Gandhiji would not give extra weight to any section as Mill does. While Mill attaches importance to literacy as a qualification for the vote, Gandhiji insists on manual labour, which when voluntarily undertaken is also, for him, a training in moral discipline. It is interesting to note Gandhiji's proposal for age limits of voters. He proposes age limits between 18 and 50. Here he seems to be influenced by Hindu ideal of the four-fold succession of the stages of life (ashrams). He is thinking in terms of performance of duties and not in terms of adjustments of interests or of individual's as the utilitarians do.

ADMINISTRATION OF JUSTICE IN NON-VIOLENT STATE

The non-violent state will also perform the judicial function, though according to Gandhiji as much of judicial work as possible should be transferred to panchayats, i.e. ad hoc arbitration tribunals the personnel of which is usually determined by the parties to the case. He severely criticises lawyers and judges and calls them "first cousins," as Bentham calls them "Judges and Co." "The legal system," says Gandhiji, "teaches immorality...the lawyers...as a rule, advance quarrels, instead of repressing them...their interest exists in multiplying disputes."[11] He further says, "Those who know anything of the Hindu-Mohammadan quarrels know that they have been often due to the intervention of lawyers."[12] Their worst Crime was that they tightened the grip of the foreign government. "Without lawyers, courts could not have been established or conducted, without the latter the English could not rule."[13] The object of the court is the permanence of the authority of the government which they represent.[14] And in so far as they support the authority of an unrighteous government the courts are not "the palladium of a nation's liberty," but "crushing houses to crush a nation's spirit."[15]

Gandhiji's complaint is that justice administered is much expensive. He says, "...administration of justice should be cheapened...parties to civil suits must be compelled in the majority of cases to refer their disputes to arbitration, the decision of panchayats to be final except in cases of corruption or obvious misapplication of law. Multiplicity of intermediate courts should be avoided. Case law should be abolished and the general procedure should be simplified.[16] To the argument that the decisions of private Panchayats are not binding in law and hence ineffective, Gandhiji replies that "only those will seek the protection of the Panchayats who wish voluntarily to abide by their decisions, and therefore, no process of enforcement of Panchayat decrees... The only penalty that is at our disposal is the force of public opinion. There is not much danger of parties who voluntarily seek the protection of the panchayat disobeying the latter's verdicts. We must run the risk of some disobedience; we must not, in impatience, resort to force or intimidation for the purpose either of securing reference to panchayats or execution of their decrees."

Lawyers may remain, but must not claim any superiority for their profession. The true function of lawyers is to unite parties driven as under.[17] Ideally speaking, Gandhiji's doctrine of "Bread Labour" demands that judges and lawyers should perform their judicial functions without any payment. They must depend for their living on some form of bread-labour and serve people free. However, as a second best ideal "Bhangis, doctors, lawyers, teachers, merchants and others would get the same wages for an honest day's labour."[18]

CRIME AND JAILS IN NON-VIOLENT STATE

In the predominantly non-violent state of Gandhiji, although crimes will be considerably reduced, there will still be some anti-social elements who might due to lack of self-control, resort to violence and disobey laws. "Some of it," says Gandhiji, "will go on perhaps till dooms day as thieving will."[19] Punishment by itself is an evil, according to Gandhiji. It is justified only as "a necessary evil". Gandhiji says, "I am quite capable of recommending even punishment to wrong-doers, under conceivable circumstances; for instance, I would not hesitate under the present state of society to confine thieves and robbers, which is in itself a kind of punishment. But I would also admit that it is not Satyagraha, and that it is a fall from the pure doctrine. That would be an admission not of the weakness of the doctrine but the weakness of myself. I have no other remedy to suggest in such cases in the present state of society."[20]

No government worth its name can suffer anarchy to prevail.[21] Now the purpose of punishment is served (*i*) If the criminal is prevented from committing the crime again; and (*ii*) if others are deterred from committing a similar crime. Regarding the former, Gandhiji emphasises the reformation of the criminal. He says, "Crime is a disease like any other malady and is a product of the prevalent social system."[22] This gives the impression that Gandhiji is advocating a purely psychological or sociological theory of punishment, a view completely at odds with his fundamental philosophy. If we respect personality, we must respect responsibility. If we respect responsibility, we must respect the right of the offenders to be punished for their offences.[23]

Gandhiji does not deny the deterrent character of punishment. He says, "It will go hard with us, if we let the real criminals understand that they will be set free or be very much better treated when Swaraj is established. Even in reformatories, by which I would like to replace every jail under Swaraj, discipline will be extracted." But he would not extend this principle, as Green would, to provide a justification of the death sentences in cases of murder. "Under a state governed according to principles of ahimsa, therefore, a murderer would be sent to a penitentiary and there given a chance of reforming himself."[24] Between capital punishment and other punishments there is, to Gandhiji, a difference not merely of degree, but also of kind. Other punishments can be recalled and reparations can be made to the person wrongly punished. "But once a man is killed, the punishment is beyond recall or reparation. God alone can take life, because he alone gives it."[25]

Now the inherent imperfections of human knowledge, according to Green, as also to Gandhiji, would make it impossible to know whether the capacity of the criminal for contributing to social good was absolutely extinct, and consequently there would be no justification for imposing the death penalty on any one. Green himself, expresses his doubt when he says, "...it may be doubted whether the presumption of permanent incapacity for rights is one which in our ignorance we can ever be entitled to make."

That no-body is beyond moral redemption, is explicitly recognised by Green as also by Gandhiji. Green comes near to Gandhiji when he concludes, "If punishment then is to be just, in the sense that in its infliction due account is taken of all rights, including the suspended rights of the criminal himself, it must be, so far as public safety allows, reformatory. It must tend to qualify the criminal for the resumption of rights."[26]

Gandhiji emphasizes education and training for the reformation of the criminals. Accordingly, he suggests many prison reforms based on his personal experience of life in jails. For the reforms of the jails Gandhiji had prepared a plan in 1922 when he was a prisoner. The plan was that "all industries that were not paying, should be stopped. All the jails should be turned into hand-spinning and hand-weaving institutions. They should include (whenever possible) cotton-growing to producing the finest cloth.... Prisoners must be treated as defectors, not to be criminals to be looked down upon. Wardens should cease to be terrors for the prisoners, but the jail officials should be their friends and instructors. The one indispensible condition is that the state should buy all the Khadi that may be turned out by the prisons at cost price. And if there is a surplus, the public may get it at a trifling higher price to cover the expenses of running a sales depot."[27]

In this respect it is similar to Bentham's idea of 'Panopticon' which was designed "to employ convicts instead of steam, and thus to combine philanthropy with business." But the reform of criminals through educational influences was not the principle behind it. Bentham defined it as a "mill for grinding rogues honest, and idle men industrious." The humanistic approach of Gandhiji aiming at restoring the sharp initiative and self-respect of the prisoners is in sharp contrast to the principle behind Bentham's scheme.

POLICE AND MILITARY

The basis of the state, we have already discussed according to Gandhiji, is non-violence and not force. Therefore, under ideal conditions there is no room for police and military based on force. But he concedes that even in the non-violent state a police force will be necessary. "This," admits Gandhiji, "...is a sign of my imperfect 'ahimsa.' I have not the courage to declare that we can carry on without a police force. Of course, I can and do envisage a state where the police will not be necessary; but whether we shall succeed in realizing it, the future alone will show." While thus retaining the police force he would completely change its character. He would demand of the policemen of the satyagrahi state the qualifications that he has prescribed for the volunteers of Peace Brigades. Thus he writes, "The police of my conception will, however, be of a wholly different pattern from the present day force. Its rank will be composed of believers in non-violence. They will be servants, not masters of the people. The people will instinctively render them every help and through mutual co-operation they will easily deal with the ever-decreasing disturbances. The police force will have some kind of arms, but they will be rarely used, if at all. In fact, the policemen will be reformers. Their police work will be confined to robbers and dacoits. Quarrels between labour and capital, and strikes will be few and far between in a non-violent state, because the influence of the non-violent majority will be so great as to command the respect of the principal elements in society. Similarly there will be no room for communal disturbances."[28]

In 1940 the Congress Ministries in some of the provinces of India were taken to task by Gandhiji, for they failed to devise peaceful ways and means of preserving order and had to fall back upon the police and the military to suppress communal riots and labour trouble. "To the extent", says Gandhiji, "that the congress ministries have been obliged to make use of the police and the military to that extent, in my opinion, we must admit our failure."[29]

In November 1946, during Bihar riots, the Prime Minister said that the Government would use even aerial bombing to put down communal violence. Gandhiji considered it the British way which would result in the suppression of India's freedom. He wrote, "Democracy to be true should cease to rely upon the army for anything whatever... It will be a poor democracy that depends for its existence on military assistance. Military force interferes with the free growth of the mind. It smothers the soul of man."[30] In his post-prayer speech on December 2, 1947, he remarked, "Unless India developed her non-violent strength she had gained nothing either for herself or for the world. Militarization of India would mean her own destruction as of the whole world."[31] Gandhiji is opposed not to the police as such, but to its present day form and its out-and-out violent methods.

The same rule holds regarding the military. Under the Swaraj of Gandhiji's dream there would be no necessity for arms at all.[32] He is, however, in favour of a non-violent army whose character is described by him as, "A non-violent army acts unlike armed men, as well in times of peace as of disturbances. They would be constantly engaged in constructive activities that make riots impossible. Theirs will be the duty of seeking occasions for bringing warring communities together, carrying on peace propaganda, engaged in activities that would bring and keep them in touch with every single person, male and female, adult and child in their perish or division. Such an army should be ready to cope with any emergency, and in order to still be frenzy of mobs, should risk their lives in numbers sufficient for the purpose. A few hundred, may be a few thousand, such spotless deaths will once for all put an end to the riots. Surely, a few hundred young men and women giving themselves deliberately to mob fury will be any day a cheap and braver method of dealing with such madness than the display and use of the police and the military."[33]

Gandhiji also definitely declares against the military as the means of defence against foreign aggression. Indeed, "a non-violent man or society does not anticipate or provide for attacks from without. On the contrary, such a person or society firmly believes that nobody is going to disturb them. If the worst happens, there are two ways open to non-violence. To yield possession, but not to cooperate with the aggressor. Thus, supposing that a modern edition of Nero descended upon India, the representatives of the state will let him in, but tell him that he will get no assistance from the people. They will prefer death to submission. The second way would be non-violent resistance by the people who have been trained in the non-violent way. They would offer themselves unarmed as fodder for the aggressor's cannons. The underlying beliefs in either case is that even Nero is not devoid of a heart. The unexpected spectacle of endless rows upon rows of men and women simply dying rather than surrender to the will of an aggressor" must ultimately melt him and his soldiery. Practically speaking, there will be 'probably no greater loss in men than if forcibly resistance was offered; there will be no expenditure on armaments and fortifications. The non-violent training received by the people will add inconceivably to their moral height."[34]

It should be noted that Gandhiji never fails to emphasize that ideals of this sort will only evolve with the moral evolution of individuals. The ideal cannot be imposed from above, because that would be against the very spirit of non-violence. Though Gandhiji, himself, does not believe in the use of arms, he would not hesitate to advise their use by those who had no faith in non-violence. During the first World War he advised his countrymen that "so long as they believed in War and professed loyalty to the British Constitution they were in duty bound to support it (government) by enlistment."

Regarding the extent to which the principle of non-violence would be adopted by free India, Gandhiji says, "It is and will be a mixture...I would advise the adoption of non-violence to the utmost extent possible and that will be India's great contribution to the peace of the world and the establishment of a new world order. I expect that with the existence of so many martial races in India, all of whom have a voice in the government of the day, the national policy will incline towards militarism of a modified character. I shall certainly hope that all the efforts for the last twenty-two years to show the efficacy of non-violence as a political force will not have gone in vain and a strong party representing true non-violence will exist in the country."[35]

It is clear that though Gandhiji would not concede any place to the military in his ideal of Swaraj, he was prepared to recognise that the military will be retained as long as public opinion is not equal to renouncing its use. That is why he says, "Alas! In my Swaraj of today there is room for soldiers."[36] "I agree too that a sudden withdrawal of the military and the police will be a disaster if we have not acquired the ability to protect ourselves against robbers and thieves."[37] When Kashmir acceded to Indian Union, he did not object to the dispatch of Indian troops to Srinagar for the defence of Kashmir territory.[38]

To sum up, it can be said that Gandhiji designates his conception of state by 'Swaraj' which is a dynamic ideal-evolving with the evolution of the individuals, finding its consumption ultimately in the enlightened anarchy of his conception. Democracy is its fundamental requirement. Gandhiji is a spiritual democrat before he is a political democrat. Although he is critical of the moral qualities of the British Parliament, he accepts some forms of parliamentary government as the best obtainable. He applies his doctrine of non-violence to crime and emphasizes the reformative character of punishment while recognizing the necessity of some deterrence. He does not extend the scope of punishment as a deterrent to include death sentence as T.H. Green does. His scheme of reformation is essentially based on education and training.

References

1. Harijan, 11-2-39.
2. Young India, I, p. 873 and 85; Introduction to Hind Swaraj, p. VIII.
3. Louis Fischer, A Week With Gandhi, p. 55.
4. Young India, III, p. 285.
5. Hind Swaraj, p. 17.
6. *Ibid.*
7. *Ibid.*
8. History of Congress, pp. 981-82.
9. Young India, II, pp. 488-89.
10. Harijan, 13-10-40, p. 320.
11. Hind Swaraj, p. 42.
12. *Ibid.*, p. 43.
13. *Ibid.*
14. Young India, I, p. 351. For similar views of H. J. Laski see his essays on "Judicial Functions" in the Dangers of Being a Gentleman.
15. Young India, I, p. 350.
16. *Ibid.*, II, p. 436.
17. Autobiography, I, p. 315.
18. Harijan, 23-3-47, p. 78.
19. *Ibid.*, 31-7-37, p. 86.
20. Young India, II, p. 852.
21. Harijan, 9-3-40.
22. *Ibid.*, 5-5-46.
23. Barker, E., Principles of Social and Political Theory, p. 179.
24. Harijan, 27-7-40, p. 101.
25. Young India, II, p. 862.

26. Green, Lectures on the Principles of Political Obligation, para 206.
27. Harijan, 17-7-37, p. 180.
28. Harijan, 1-9-40, p. 265. According to K. G. Mashruwala, "The true function of the police ought to be the prevention of crime. At present it pratically consists in watching for criminals and detecting and arresting them after a crime has been committed." See his 'Practical Non-violence', p. 21.
29. *Ibid.,* 13-7-40, p. 197.
30. *Ibid.,* 9-6-46, p. 169.
31. *Ibid.,* 14-12-47, p. 471.
32. Young India, 17-11-21.
33. Harijan, 26-3-38.
34. *Ibid.,* 13-4-40.
35. *Ibid.,* 24-6-42.
36. *Ibid.,* II, p. 924 (italic mine)
37. *Ibid.,* p. 641 (italic mine)
38. Tendulkar, D.G., Mahatma, Vol. VIII, p. 204.

9

The Nature and Structure of Economic Order

Our ignorance or negligence of the Divine Law, which gives man from day-to-day his daily bread and no more, has given rise to inequalities with all the miseries attendant upon them. The rich have a surplus share of things which they do not need...while millions are starved to death for want of sustenance. If each retained possession only of what he needed, no one would be in want, and all would live in contentment. As it is, the rich are discontented no less than the poor.

—YERVADA MANDIR, P. 34

WE have already discussed in the preceding chapters the socio-political philosophy of Gandhiji. Connected with Gandhiji's socio-political philosophy is his economic philosophy—the nature and structure of economic order of a non-violent state.

Since the very beginning, man has been in search of answers to two questions, *viz.,* 'What is wrong with our present world'? and what should be done to improve matters?' The fore-runners of economic science, the Mercantilists believed that for human happiness it was essential that a nation should have ever increasing stock of gold and silver, because that represented strength. So, a philosophy of restrictions and emphasis on export followed. But, a trial of this philosophy for a century or so that the nations and the world could not be happier than what they had been.

As a reaction, a new philosophy, in the form of physiocracy, grew which advised peoples to seek for solace in mother nature and asked the people to revert back to agriculture. The people, in search of happiness, followed that philosophy but matters remained where they were.

Then came the Master, Adam Smith. He laid down the foundations of what is today known as Classical Economics or Laissez-faire Economics or Capitalistic Economics. The spell of the Master tempted people to believe that industrialization, free play of forces, private ownership and the minimum interference by the Government, would improve matters. For some time the countries which followed this advice seemed to prosper. It was felt that the key to happiness and a passport to heaven had been found out.

Next came a succession of giant followers, like Ricardo, Malthus, Mill and Marshall, to name only a few, to broaden the path laid by the Master and smoothen it out by trying to solve a few knotty problems left half-solved or not solved properly. But, alas ! The mass of people in general and the thinkers in particular again started asking the age-old question 'Are we happier than before?' The answer was certainly not in the affirmative.

The revolt was started by Sismondi who disagreed with the Classical School on the aims and methods of economic study and criticized the growing use of machines. St. Simon was also no believer. He wanted to build an industrial Society and reorganize the Government. Fedric List, for the first time, raised the slogan against the much repeated theory of Free Trade of Adam Smith and convincingly pleaded the case of Protective Trade. Robert Owen was also dissatisfied with the then prevailing society and was anxious to build up a new society on the basis of cooperation. P. J. Proudhan, J. K. Rodbertus and, to crown them all, Karl Marx, the father of Socialism, gave the greatest jolt to the capitalist world. Under these growing criticisms, the classical doctrines could not hold the fort for long and were substantially modified by Marshall, Keynes, Schumpeter and others.

However, it is to be noted here that all the economists of the West, whether the followers of the classical school and its critics, or the propounders and followers of socialism of different shades and colours, wanted material advancement of men, because they thought that human happiness and material progress go together. Hence, the emphasis on industrialization, large scale production, growing automation, ever increasing wants etc., is visible in all the existing systems. The only difference between socialist thinkers and classical school economists, it can safely be said, centres around the problem of distribution and ownership of means of production.

When the two so called rival systems were preparing themselves for a fight the, first Armageddon came as a bolt from the blue. The people were shocked by its destructive and calamitous effects, which it produced on the world. The people, however, led themselves into the delusion that it was a mere accident, an event occurring due to the careless handling of mutual differences among various countries. A world organization sprang up to decide and settle international issues by negotiations. A period of peace followed. Prosperity and progress appeared to march hand-in-hand.

But the reign of peace was suddenly thrown out of gear. The world organization seemed to crumble down. Destruction seemed to pervade all walks of life. Life was no more a pleasure-ride. Countries no longer seemed to march towards prosperity of the masses, the welfare of the common man. Everything was in turmoil. This was the beginning of the Second World War. It left men with intelligence gaping, thinking, brooding and retrospecting. Something fundamentally wrong seemed to be there in the thoughts, actions and behaviour of the politicians, economists and philosophers. It appeared that either the aims or the methods, or both were wrong. A review to find out the fault seemed essential. The result of all this thinking and brooding was the establishment of the United Nations with all its allied agencies. Yet the goal—human happiness, peace and prosperity—appears to be as distant as it used to be and the clouds of a third world war are gathering, which rain in local form sometimes in Korea, sometimes in Cuba, sometimes in Vietnam and sometimes in Indo-China or on Indo-Pakistan borders. Though material comforts are increasing, but with them are also increasing tensions, diseases, anxiety and unhappiness. The world has ceased to be a place worth living with so much misery all around.

One of the major problems of all modern societies which is directly linked with the question of Justice, is what Marx called the 'relations of production.' The classical economists believed that the law of demand and supply was a "natural law". Therefore, they argued in favour of perfect competition and laissez faire. The early socialists maintained that what was natural was not necessarily the ideal. They put forward a variety of schemes for the economic reorganization of society. Whereas Saint Simon advocated a state-controlled economy run by experts, Charles Fourier and Robert Owen advocated an economy based primarily on worker's productive associations and co-operatives.

The Marxists, rejecting the classical model on the ground that it inevitably led to the growth of monopolies and imperialism on the one hand, and perpetual immersion of the working class on the other, suggested the revolutionary over-throw of the entire classical politico-economic system, the statization of all means of production, and the total elimination of the 'bourgeoisie' through the dictatorship of the proletariate.

In the modern Western Capitalistic economies, where the worker has achieved a large measure of security through what Galbraith has called the "countervailing power" of the trade unions and the legislative measures of the state the "relations of production" are still characterized by periodic conflicts, taking different forms from collective bargaining to the general strike.

Gandhiji rejects the Marxist solution to the problem of economic relations, because he believes it to be based on violence and tyranny. He also rejects the Western Capitalistic solution, because he considers the western politico-economic system to be based on exploitation, competition and conflict.

Gandhiji believes that there is not much to choose between Capitalism and Marxism. The malady is not merely confined, as both the camps believe in the ownership of "means of production" and in the organization of "relations of production." It is more deep-rooted. The present day unrest, he believes, is due mainly to our laying too much emphasis on matter and material comforts to the complete neglect of moral values. Our misfortunes are mainly due to the following factors :

1. Multiplication of wants,
2. Growing use of complicated machines,
3. Pattern of production, and
4. Method of distribution

Let us try to analyse these factors from Gandhian point of view.

MULTIPLICATION OF WANTS

The first important factor responsible for driving the world away from peace, happiness and real prosperity is the idea that multiplicity of wants, even beyond a minimum, and happiness are directly related. The aim of life, according to an economist, is to get maximum satisfaction, i.e. happiness. But what is happiness ? An economist trained in the Western ideology believes that the person who consumes greater number of goods is necessarily a happy man. Gandhiji does not subscribe to this view. He feels that happiness relates not merely to bodily and material needs but also to all those innumerable items that go to enrich and ennoble life and raise it above the level of bare physical existence. Gandhiji, therefore, believes that beyond a limit, the multiplication of wants and their satisfaction do not promote happiness and certainly not in the same proportion.

Gandhiji admits that a certain degree of comfort, physical and cultural, is essential for the moral and spiritual advancement. But the satisfaction of these needs must not go beyond a certain level. The aim should be not the multipliers of material wants but their restrictions consistent with comfort. One should not choose to think of getting what he can. On the other hand, he should decline to receive what others cannot get.[1]

Multiplication of wants creates chaotic condition. It makes a few rich persons consume more things at the cost of majority of people that consists of the poor. As the factors of production are limited in a country, they can produce only a limited number of things. Hence, in a capitalistic set-up, only such things are produced as bring greatest amount of profits to the capitalist, irrespective of their utility or disutility. And when wants increase—and wants of the rich only, who have the means to satisfy them and can effectively increase them, more and more factors of production are transferred to satisfy these ever-increasing new wants of the rich and lesser and lesser of those things, which the poor consume, are produced. This naturally multiplies misery manifold. Gandhiji says, "Our ignorance or negligence of the Divine Law, which gives man from day-to-day his daily bread and no more, has given rise to inequalities with all the miseries attendant upon them. The rich have a surplus share of things which they do not need...while millions are starved to death for want of sustenance. If each retained possession only of what he needed, no one would be in want, and all would live in contentment. As it is, the rich are discontented no less than the poor."[2] Love for multiplicity of wants has released greater calamities on the people in the form of exploitation of one man by another, of one country by another. Imperialism, world wars, jealousy, hatred, ill-will, production of luxury goods at the cost of necessities badly needed by the majority and introduction of foolish fashion and vulgar tastes are the off-springs of this love.

Thus, Gandhiji holds that multiplication of wants, beyond a limit, does not promote human happiness rather it multiplies miseries.

GROWING USE OF MACHINES

Growing use of machines is another important cause of the miseries of the modern world. Europe and America felt that speedy mechanization and technological developments are a necessity for them. But even in America and other western countries machine has outlived its utility by being carried beyond legitimate limits. It has even grown into a menace and source of tragedy. The 'American Federal Society of Labour' also observed that the technological developments engendered a whole host of fears in the minds of workers—fear of change, fear of technology itself, fear of displacement, fear of unemployment, fear of machines, fear of science in general.

Gandhiji also opposes the use of machines beyond a certain limit. His objections were based on ethical as well as economic grounds.

Ethical Grounds

Gandhiji's arguments opposing machines on ethical grounds may be summarized as follows :

1. Labour is a value relative to Non-violence, and machinery tends to undermine it.

2. Machines are repugnant in his thinking to good life. In Hind Swaraj Gandhiji argues vigorously for a simple society characterized by high thinking and high moral values which, he thought, was represented by ancient India.[3] He further says "High thinking is inconsistent with complicated material life based on high speed imposed on us by Mammon worship. All the graces of life are possible only when we learn the art of living nobly."[4]

3. Machines tend to impart such characteristics to the men who operate them, as reduce them to machine-like personalities and undermine their creative and artistic faculties.[5]

4. Technological advancement has led to the growth of monetary exchange system which is characterized by inequality and exploitation. The barter system of economy is superior to a monetized economy in this respect, and barter could prevail only in a wholly labour-intensive, rather than mechanized economy. In this connection Gandhiji says, "Under my system, it is labour which is the current coin, not metal. And any person who can use his labour has that coin, has wealth. He converts his labour into cloth, he converts his labour into grain. If he wants paraffin oil, which he cannot himself produce, he uses his surplus grain for getting the oil. It is exchange of labour on free, fair and equal terms—hence it is no robbery."[6]

5. Machines lead to the growth of economic competition which undermines the process of co-operation on which the organization of human society ought to be based.[7]

Economic Grounds

Gandhiji's arguments opposing machines on economic grounds may be summarized as follows :

1. Displacement of human labour is an essential characteristic of a machine, and this is held out by Gandhiji as a great argument against it. He says, "Machines will only help in making all the thirty-five crores of people unemployed."[8] Gandhiji is afraid not only of the unemployment that machines might generate, but also of the undesirable moral consequences of non-performance of sufficient labour.

2. Machines lead to the concentration of wealth in the hands of a few and, therefore, great disparities in the distribution of income. "I want the concentration of wealth", says he, "not in the hands of a few, but in the hands of all. To-day machinery merely helps a few to ride on the backs of millions."[9]

3. Machinery inevitably leads to mass production. Mass production necessarily leads to over-production, in view of the limited character of demand, and hence to economic crisis. The great depression of the early thirties Gandhiji attributes to this evil consequence of the growth of machinery.[10] Gandhiji also believes that the effects of such over-production do not remain confined to the domestic market, but tend to lead to imperialism.

All these supposedly evil characteristics of machinery led Gandhiji to conclude in Hind Swaraj that machinery "represents a great sin"[11] and that he "cannot recall a single good point in connection with machinery."[12] He launched a particularly violent attack on the railways whose main function, he thought, was the proliferation of evil. And he maintained the view till the last days of his life that in an ideal society machinery should not exist at all.[13]

But as in the case of other socio-politico-economic questions, the ideal solution constitutes only the first half of the Gandhian system of thought, the second half, representing a serious compromise, consisting of an acceptance of reality to a considerable extent. While regarding machines, therefore as ideally undesirable and unnecessary, Gandhiji nevertheless accepts their inevitability.

He explains, "How can I be 'against machinery' when I know that even this body is a most delicate piece of machinery ? The spinning wheel itself is a machine; a little toothpick is a machine."[14] Gandhiji wants to impose limit on the use of machinery. As he declares, "My object is not to destroy the machine but to impose limitations to it."[15] He says, "I have no objection if all things required by my country could be produced with the labour of 30,000 instead of that of three crores. But those three crores must not be rendered idle or unemployed."[16]

Gandhiji will, therefore, protect and even encourage any machine which does not deprive masses of men of the opportunity of labour, but which helps the individual and adds to his efficiency and which a man can handle without being a slave.

PATTERN OF PRODUCTION

Multiplicity of wants has become the corner-stone of happiness in a Capitalist or Marxist society. Therefore, large scale mechanized production has become the automatic choice. In this respect, the only difference between Capitalism and Marxism centres around the ownership of the powerful means of production.

Capitalism believes in individual freedom and therefore leaves ownership in the hands of the individuals. The governments of many Capitalist countries want to control the private ownership with the help of monetary and fiscal policies, corrective legislation and establishment of public sectors. In other words, they feel that a mixed economy will be able to maintain all the virtues of private ownership and minimise its vices. In such an economy, where private and public sectors are working side by side, efficiency will be highest, imputation of prices will be possible; freedom of production, consumption and occupation will exist; production will be maximum at the minimum cost, and so on. At the same time, the weak will be protected by the state; differences in income will be scaled down; employment will increase, welfare schemes will ensure minimum standard; public interest will be safeguarded through the nationalization of key industries etc. Thus, modern democratic governments are attempting to introduce mixed economy in place of a purely capitalist one.

The communists object to this type of mixed economy. They feel that this control over private ownership will not be sufficient to correct the grave inequalities of wealth, check the exploitation of the poor by the rich, improve the employment position and ensure a minimum standard for all. They think that, the misnomer of a mixed economy is merely an 'eye wash', a make-shift, and, an appeal to the more fortunate ones to show a little more charity. In a capitalist set up, the rich are most powerful. They are at the helm of affairs, may it be state, religion, or society and, therefore, they will never do anything which may be against their interests.

The communists, after condemning the capitalistic system and all its forms, come forward with a new technique of socialization of all means of production and abolition of all private ownership. In this new set-up, they explain, production will not be guided by the profit motive, but will be directed by the State's Central Planning Authority to those channels where it will be of maximum social benefit. In such a communistic state, there will be no place for exploitation, unemployment, grave inequalities of income etc., and a minimum standard of living will be ensured to all.

Gandhiji does not belong to any of these groups. He gave a new plan according to which individual freedom would be ensured to the maximum, but at the same time misuse of it would not be permitted. It is a new type of mixed economy. It may be called, if a name is to be given to it, a Labour-Oriented-Economy. As he says, "Under my system it is labour which is the current coin, not metal."[17] In Gandhian ideal economy, agrarian civilization will be revived, emphasis will be laid on decentralization of power, economic as well as political, and regional self-sufficiency in matters of basic needs will be aimed at. Under this type of economy, there will be more emphasis on agriculture than industries. In this economy, three sectors will function side by side. They are :

1. Private sector where production will be carried on by small and independent producers with the help of useful machines.

2. Trusteeship sector where production will be under trust control and will be carried out with the help of useful machines.

3. Public sector where production will be under state control. Here the latest and most upto-date complicated machines shall be harnessed in production.

Private Sector

The production in private sector, which will be concentrated in self-sufficient localities will be carried out by two types of people :

1. Farmers whose primary work will be to cultivate the land and secondary will be to produce goods like cloth, paper, oil, paddy, husking, pottery, toy, cutlery, bamboo and cane work, rope making, tiles and brick making etc. in their spare time.

2. The persons whose main and only work will be to run the cottage industries and meet the needs of villagers.

Now let us discuss these two in details.

The peasantry's first concern will be to grow its own food crops. The farmers in growing these crops will use the recently invented machines sparingly, as they may oust many men and bullocks from the land. For several months in a year the farmer is completely idle and even in the remaining months, except during the sowing and harvesting time, he is partially unemployed. It is for this reason that production in private sector, will be shifted from cities to the villages where it will provide subsidiary work to the farmers in their idle time.

The other part of private sector will constitute the cottage industries which will be working all the year round and producing anything which the climate, supply of raw material, opportunity to dispose of the produce, technical skill etc., permit. Here some firms will be owned by individuals, some by a few persons and some by a number of persons. But in every case the size of the firm will not be large enough as to enable its owners to oust the other producers from the field. The owner will be permitted to employ few labourers, the number not exceeding a certain limit which shall be fixed by the government from time to time.

The production carried out in cities will also be on the same pattern but because of the existence of mental workers in the cities another type of subsidiary industries will grow up. These subsidiary cottage industries will be working all the year round and for only a few limited hours every day as their sole purpose will be to provide an opportunity to the mental workers to do some physical work so that they may recognize the importance of bread-labour.

The Panchayats in villages or cities will keep an eye over these small firms and will take strong action against the offenders of the rules laid down by them regarding the size of the firm, number of people employed, types of machines employed etc. But the action taken by Panchayats will be non-violent in nature.

This type of private sector will retain all the virtues of a capitalistic system—freedom of occupation, consumption and production; possibility of correct imputation of prices as factors will be purchased and sold in open market, maximization of production, profit incentive to reduce cost and improve efficiency etc. Besides this, it will have certain other advantages to its credit. As production will be carried out on a small scale and under Panchayat's observation, chances of exploitation will be minimum. This decentralized production will remove class conflict, increase the earning capacity of the poor people and reduce the power to amass wealth. This will also save time and the middle man's profit as it will establish a direct relation between producers and consumers.

Trusteeship Sector

But in spite of small scale, decentralized production and self sufficient units, it may be possible in some cases that one person may be able to exploit others and amass wealth. A few of such cases may be :

1. A few commodities, by their very nature, cannot be produced on a small scale. The production of these commodities will naturally place the ownership in a unique position. As he will not get sufficient amount of the competition and will be able to exploit the ownership for his personal ends.

2. The production of a few commodities requires special technical knowledge and training. The person who has this training and knowledge may be able to exploit people as it will not be possible for other producers to start production in a short period and compete with him.

3. The owners of small firms may combine and start enjoying the benefits of monopoly by keeping down the production and artificially raising prices.

4. Some producers, in spite of people's preference for small scale production, may carry on with production on large scale and exploit the public.

5. Some persons, due to their peculiar circumstances may be in a position to exploit others and may be using these circumstances for their benefit at the cost of others. For example, a landlord and a factory owner, with no hand in production, belong to this group.

6. Any other such reason which may place special power in the hands of a few to exploit others.

Gandhiji wants to check exploitation. But he does not believe that the capitalists and landlords are exploiters by any inherent necessity, or that there is a basic and unreconcilable antagonism between the interest of the former and those of the masses. In his opinion, "What is needed is not the extinction of landlords and capitalists, but a transformation of the existing relationship between them and the masses into something healthier and purer."[18] The tranformation in labour-capital relations, thinks Gandhiji, can be brought about by the institution of Trusteeship.

The basic idea underlying the doctrine of Trusteeship is very simple. "The rich man will be left in the possession of his wealth, of which he will use what he reasonably requires for his personal needs and will act as a trustee for the remainder to be used for the society."[19] Gandhiji seems to make a distinction between legal ownership and moral ownership. He has often said that Trusteeship means the joint Trusteeship of capitalists and labourers over the wealth of society. Legal ownership in the transformed condition will be vested in the trustee, not in the state.

It was in order to avoid confiscation that the Doctrine of Trusteeship came into play, retaining for society the ability of the original owner in his own right."[20] The choice of naming the successor "should be given to the original owner who became the first trustee, but the choice must be finalized by the state. Such arrangement puts a check on the state as well as the individual."[21] It is, therefore, not necessary that trust property will pass from father to son, in every case, or can be sold out to any one.

Now question arises—How will trusteeship be brought about? Gandhji suggests, "I will concentrate on my means. My means are non-cooperation. No person can amass wealth without the cooperation, willing or forced, of the people concerned."[22] And if, in spite of these sanctions a Trustee is adamant, the state will dethrone him and the property will go under the trust of another person or it will be nationalized.

If the doctrine of Trusteeship is accepted, the evils of both private enterprise and state enterprise would be eliminated. The inequalities and exploitation created by private enterprise as well as the violence and loss of freedom caused by state-enterprise would at once come to an end. The institution of Trusteeship would, moreover, eliminate all possibilities of class conflict and lead to the establishment of cooperative and harmonions relations between labour and capital.

Public Sector

Gandhiji was against nationalization, because it represents violence.[23] However he will agree to nationalize a few industries or firms provided the following pre-requisites are fulfilled :

1. "Nationalization presupposes that real power rests with the people, i.e. with the masses ...When the Government of the land is in the hands of such tried patriots who will be trusted to hold the interests of the millions as their first care, then alone can we claim to have a National Government and Nationalization will then ensure that the interests of the masses will be taken care of."[24] Obviously this Central Government will be a federation of Panchayats and will be effectively controlled by them.

2. Only those industries or firms will be nationalized which are producing consumption goods for masses and not which are serving a selected few.

3. Only those firms of the private sector or trusteeship sector will be nationalized which, in spite of warnings, have failed to improve.

When Gandhiji recommends nationalization, it does not apply to the industry as a whole. Individual cases are to be tested on their merits and only such trustees as are found guilty of breach of trust, will be deprived of their trust property. But other trustees or individuals, who are running their factories, in keeping with the Gandhian ideology, will not be touched.

Regarding the public utility concerns and basic industries, Gandhiji says, "The heavy machinery for work of public utility, which cannot be undertaken by human labour, has its inevitable place, but all that would be owned by the state and used entirely for the benefit of the people."[25] Explaining this point he says, "......If we could have electricity in every village home, I should not mind villagers plying their implements and tools with the help of electricity. But then the village communities or state would own power houses just as they have their grazing pastures."[26] Gandhiji would agree to nationalize a few key industries also. But only those key industries will be nationalized the goods of which cannot be produced on a small scale.

Thus Gandhian Public Sector will have three types of industries and firms :

1. Firms whose owners, in spite of repeated reminders, continue to betray the trust.

2. Public utility concerns such as transport and communication, health and sanitation, education, banking and insurance, statistics and research.

3. Key industries which cannot be run on small scale such as defence industries, power generating industries, mining, metallurgy, machine tools, heavy engineering, heavy chemicals, fertilizers and pharmaceuticals.

METHOD OF DISTRIBUTION

Gandhiji felt that one of the important causes of the present day unrest and unhappiness can be traced in the faulty method of distribution of wealth. Today the distribution of wealth among the various factors of production takes place in such a way that a few get the major share of the produce and thus live in luxury, while the majority gets so little that it is never able to satisfy even its minimum requirements of life. Hence, Gandhiji wanted to change the method of distribution.

Marxists also were not satisfied with the capitalistic method of distribution and so they suggested that state must become supreme in matter of distribution. Gandhiji could never agree to the state supermacy and method of distribution evolved in the communist world. He wants equal distribution. As he says, "My ideal is equal distribution, but so far as I can see, it is not to be realized. I therefore, work for equitable distribution."[27] To achieve this ideal he propounded a theory, which can be called the theory of equality.

The Theory of Equality

Economic equality of his conception did not mean that everyone would literally have the same amount. It simply meant that every body should have enough for him or her needs. For instance, he required two shawls in winter whereas his grand nephew Kannu Gandhi, who stayed with him and was like his son, did not require any warm clothing whatsoever. Gandhi required goat's milk, oranges and other fruits. Kannu could do with ordinary food. Kannu was a young man whereas he was an old man of 76 ; the monthly expense of his food was far more than that of Kannu, but that did not mean that there was economic inequality between them. The elephant requires a thousand times more food than the ant, but that is not an indication of in equality. So the real meaning of economic equality was to each according to his needs.[28] He further explains, "If a single man demand as much as a man with wife and four children that would be a violation of economic equality."[29]

As regards the method of bringing economic equality, Gandhiji advocates non-violent method. He wants that the rich should themselves renounce their extra wealth, because material progress of the rich, beyond a limit, is highly immoral and it retards real progress. Therefore, the rich should, by their own accord, become trustees of their properties and so help in non-violent distribution of wealth. This idea is based upon Hindu philosophy of renunciation, which was successfully and willingly practised by our ancestors for centuries. If they fail to behave properly, they should be forced to do so.

For this purpose labour unions will have to play a very important role. The unions should "aim to raise the moral and intellectual height of labour and thus by sheer merit- make labour master of the means of production instead of being the slave that it is."[30] He feels that poverty or idleness is the mother of vices. So, he wants unions to train up workers to a supplementary occupation.[31] He thought that labour organized in a strong union on his lines will be able to keep a check on the greed of the rich and through non-violence, non-cooperation and Satyagraha will, on the one hand, be able to convert them into trustee and, on the other hand, help in improving the lot of labourers.

Moreover, till the ideal state of stateless society is achieved, the state will be mainly controlled by peasants, should keep through legislations, regulations, taxation and expenditures on social service in reducing the inequalities of wealth.

Above all, to achieve the ideal of economic equality, we should have love for bread-labour

"...We must not think of earning a livelihood by desk work merely."[32] "Man must earn his bread by labouring with his hand."[33] Love for Bread-labour will not only provide work to the unemployed manual labourers[34], but will also solve to a very great extent, the present problem of the educated unemployed whose number, unfortunately, is sharply rising in every country. If one tenth of humanity, which at present is not doing physical labour, starts doing it, the world will become much more happier, healthier, and peaceful.[35] Bread-labour may be made a qualification of a voter.[36]

To sum up we can say that Gandhiji's socio-political and economic ideas followed from his concern for individual freedom and were calculated to keep the power of state to the minimum that was required for a civilized and morally satisfying life. His theory of Trusteeship was, for example, meant to end the exploitation of workers and gross inequalities of income as well as to prevent a centralization of power in the hands of the state. Gandhiji wanted the legal ownership of the means of production to vest in the trustee but the trustee could not nominate his successor except with the approval of the government. Also, the trustee's commission was to be restricted to an amount that would by reasonable for his personal needs, the rest of the income being utilized for public good.

References

1. Dhawan, G.N. "The Political Philosophy of Mahatma Gandhi", p. 94.
2. Yervada Mandir, p. 34.
3. Hind Swaraj, Ch. 13 and 19.
4. Tendulkar, D.G. Mahatma, Vol. VII, p. 188.
5. *Ibid.*, Vol. IV, p. 195.
6. *Ibid.*, Vol. III, p. 135.
7. Collected Works of Mahatma Gandhi, 1963, Vol. X, p. 581.
8. Tendulkar D.G., Mahatma, Vol. IV, p. 196.
9. *Ibid.,* Vol. II, p. 161.
10. Harijan, 31-3-1946.
11. Collected Works of Mahatma Gandhi, (1963) Vol. X, p. 58.
12. *Ibid.,* p. 59.
13. Tendulkar, D.G. Mahatma, Vol. IV, pp. 195-96.
14. Young India 13-11-1924, p. 377.
15. *Ibid.,* 3-11-1924.
16. Harijan 12-2-1938.
17. Tendulkar, D.G. 'Mahatma', Vol. III, p. 169.
18. Bose, N.K., Selection from Gandhiji (1957) p. 93.
19. Harijan 25-8-40.
20. *Ibid.,* 16-2-47.
21. *Ibid.*
22. C. Rajagopalacharya and J.C. Kumarappa, 'The Nation's Voices', p. 190.

23. Gandhi M.K. 'Economic and Industrial Life and Relations'. Vol. I, p. 124.
24. Kumarappa J.C. The Gandhian Economy and the Way to Realise It, p. 76.
25. Dantarvala, M.L., 'Gandhism Reconsidered', p. 40.
26. Harijan, 22-6-35.
27. Young India, 17-3-27, p. 86.
28. Bose, N.K., Selections from Gandhi (1957), p. 79.
29. *Ibid.*
30. Hindustan Standard, 28-10-1944.
31. Gandhi, M.K., Constructive Programme, pp. 2, 28.
32. Young India, 25-8-1921.
33. Yervada Mandir, p. 50.
34. Harijan, 19-12-1936.
35. Yervada Mandir, p. 50.
36. Harijan 2-11-35.

10

Religion and Morality

A votary of ahimsa cannot subscribe to the utilitarian formula (of the greatest good of the greatest number). He will strive for the good of all and die, so that others may live. He will serve himself with the rest, by himself dying. The greatest good of all inevitably includes the good of the greatest number, and therefore, he and utilitarian will converge in many points in their career but there does come a time when they must part company and even work in opposite directions. The utilitarian, to be logical, will never sacrifice himself. The absolutist will even sacrifice himself.

—YOUNG INDIA, DECEMBER 9, 1926.

WE have made an attempt in the proceeding chapter, to discuss the socio-politico-economic philosophy of Gandhiji. His bent, we have seen, is not political but religious. 'Most religious men I have met", says Gandhiji, "are politicians in disguise; I, however, who wear the guise of a politician, am at heart a religious man."[1] In all his thought and action Gandhiji takes his stand on the principles of religion and morality. He says, "...at the back of every word that I have uttered, since I have known what public life is, and of every act that I have done, there has been a religious consciousness and a downright religious motive."[2]

Politics is concerned with the control and use of state authority which is essentially coercive. So Gandhiji looks upon politics as an unavoidable evil. "If I seem to take part in politics, it is only because politics today encircles us like the coil of a snake from which one cannot get out no matter how one tries. I wish to wrestle with the snake... I am trying to introduce religion into politics."[8] Thus it is religion that compels him not to eschew politics. The goal of life is self-realization which, Gandhiji believes, cannot be achieved unless he identifies himself with the whole of mankind and tries to advance part in politics. For the whole gamut of man's activities today constitutes one indivisible whole, and social, economic, political and purely religious work cannot be divided into water-tight compartments.[4] Political evils, for example, political subjection, unsuitable political institutions, etc. are great hindrances to the realization of the greatest good of all, which is possible only in a non-violent state. Political freedom is essential for the emergence of this state. He has, therefore, no doubt whatsoever that "those, who say that religion has nothing to do with politics do not know what religion means."[5]

THE CONCEPT OF RELIGION

Gandhiji was deeply religious. Without religion, life for him was not worth living. Gandhiji used the term "Religion" in a very wide sense. He held that religion was a term of wide connotation. It has both negative and positive aspects. From his writings, it is abundantly clear that he laid considerable stress on both aspects of religion. There are passages in the writings of Mahatma Gandhi which tend to show his negative as well as positive attitudes towards religion. In the negative aspect of his religion, Gandhiji tries to point out what is not religion, that which is not included within the sphere of religion. In its positive aspects, he tries to show what religion is in its full connotation. Therefore, we propose to discuss both the aspects of his religion separately.

In propagating the negative aspect of religion, Gandhiji followed the Upanishadic principle, i.e., the method of negation (*Neti, Neti,* "not this, not this"). He excluded all which does not constitute religion or which has no sanction of religion. He started with negation and then defined religion which constitutes the positive aspect of his religious ideas. Gandhiji said, "By religion, I do not mean formal religion, or customary religion."[6] Again he said, "Religion does not mean sectarianism."[7] "Religion is not what you will get after reading all the scriptures of the world."[8] He went on saying, "By religion, I do not mean Hindu religion."[9] "Religion does not mean merely offering one's Namaz or going to the temple."[10] "Religion is not really what is grasped by the brain."[11] He further said, "Bluster is no religion, nor is vast learning stored in capacious brains."[12] Gandhiji still goes on saying, "Religion which takes no account of practical affairs and does not help to solve them, is no religion."[13] "To see the universal and all-pervading spirit of Truth face to face, one must be able to love the meanest of creation as oneself. And a man, who aspires after that, cannot afford to keep out of any field of life. That is why my devotion to truth has drawn me into the field of politics."

It may be useful to point out here that Swami Vivekanand and Rabindranath Tagore also held the same view about religion. They have also excluded what is not required to be included within the sphere of religion. Swami Vivekanand says, "Temples and Churches, books and forms are simply the kindergarten of religion, to make the spiritual child strong enough to take higher steps...Religion is not in doctrines, in dogmas, nor in intellectual argumentation; it is being and becoming, and it is realization."[14] Tagore states, "Leave this chanting and singing and telling of beads. Whom dost thou worship in this lonely dark corner of a temple with doors all shut ! Open thine eyes and see thy God is not before thee."[15]

From these statements of Gandhiji and others, it is obvious that they have prescribed the negative definitions of religion. In regard to Gandhiji we can safely say that by religion he did not mean a study of scriptures only. One may read scriptures but that does not mean that one is truly religious. Again, according to him, religion does not mean a set of dogmas, nor does it mean merely conformity to rites and rituals. As Nehru observed, "Gandhiji's conception of religion had nothing to do with any dogma or custom or ritual."[16] Gandhiji's religion is not mechanical. His religion is not the religion of merely uttering the name of God or Allah. Religion, according to him, is not pride, pedantry or sophistry. It does not also, according to him, mean a display of argumentative faculty or parade of logic and intellectual exhibition. Again, by religion he did not mean this or that religion, a denominational faith, or a creed or a sect. Hence, it can definitely be said that his religion is neither customary nor narrow. Religion, according to him, is not the practice of untouchability.

We have discussed the negative aspect of religion according to Gandhiji. We now proceed to elaborate his positive aspect of religion. Let us now see what he meant by positive aspect of religion. We shall discuss this aspect of his religion on the basis of his own statements made from time to time. By religion, Gandhiji meant self-realization and knowledge of self. He said, "The term 'religion' I am using in its broadest sense, meaning thereby self-realization or knowledge of self."[17] Religion means, "being bound to God, that is to say, God rules your every breath."[18] Again he said that religion meant, "a belief in the ordered moral government of the Universe."[19] "Religion means knowledge of one's self and knowledge of God."[20] By religion Gandhiji meant that "which underlies all religions, which brings us face to face with our Maker."[21] Thus we see Gandhiji has presented to us innumerable definitions of religion. He does not stop here. He still goes on to say that religion is, "that which changes one's very nature, which binds one indissolubly to the truth within and which ever purifies."[22] It is obvious that Gandhiji did not mean by religion what people ordinarily meant by it. As already stated, Gandhiji used the term in the widest connotation. It is something which embraces the whole being, the entire personality of man. As he says, "Religion is a heart grasp."[23] He further says, "Religion deals with the science of the soul."[24] According to him, religion pervades the entire texture of human life. Nobody can escape being religious. The religious consciousness is so rooted that it guides man's every moment. He remarks, "The whole gamut of man's activities today constitutes an indivisible whole. You cannot divide social, economic, political and purely religious work into water-tight compartments. I do not know any religion apart from human activity."[25] The ultimate definition of religion, he concluded, may be said to be, "Obedience to the Law of God. God and His Law are synonymous terms."[26]

On the basis of the various statements made by Gandhiji with regard to the positive aspect of his religion, we can conclude that Gandhiji's religion, as opposed to physics or the science of matter, is the Science of Soul and God. It is the union of the two. 'Religion', in the opinion of Gandhiji, is a friend of liberation and a foe to fanaticism. He argued that religion means recognizing the self *(Atman)*, recognition of the cosmic self *(Parmatma)*, recognition of Reality, seeing God face to face, attaining of *Moksha* through service to man. It is the union between man and man, and communion with the Divine. Thus, Gandhiji's God and religion are things of the heart. They reside in the heart of every individual. God and man are not two independent entities. Gandhiji himself says, "Religion binds man to God and man to man."[27] But no man has really found God. Only the prophets and *Avatars* (by means of their *tapsya)* have the glimpses of Him.

Thus, Gandhiji's religion is the law, the *dharma,* which sustains the universe. The universe is a beautiful combination of things. This combination is unique. How did this beautiful universe emerge? Who is the creator and the sustainer of this world? To this Gandhiji maintains that there is the wall, the *dharma* which sustains the universe. This sustainer is God Himself. He is the law, the *dharma,* the principle of virtue. There is complete identity between God and His law. "He and His law are one."[28] Religion is not a matter of a bare emotion. It is not a thing to be accepted by mere reasoning or thinking. It is a matter of feeling, feeling in the sense of sublime sentiment. This is how Gandhiji interpreted his different meanings of religion.

The Diverse Religions

Gandhiji, by his personal study of the great religious scriptures, found that every one of them contained good precepts capable of helping man attain a truly religious life. On the other hand, he also found that the many interpretations commentaries, and practices which have grown within each religious tradition contained things which were morally degrading and unsupportable by reason. So all religions were good as well as bad—good at the source and in ideals, bad in subsequent accretions and practices. Every person is, therefore, thrown back on his reason to select the good elements and reject the bad ones, Gandhiji, therefore, places "sober reason" above the scriptures when they tend to confuse and mislead the mind.

Religion, therefore, becomes a personal quest and a way of life. Every one should be free to choose. "Religion", says Gandhiji, "is a very personal matter." He adds, "We should be living the life according to our lights to share the best with one another, thus adding to the sum total of human effort to reach God."[29] Gandhiji, thus, sees the possibility of fellowship of all religions. He says, "Religions are different roads converging to the same point. What does it matter that we take different roads, so long as we reach the same goal? In reality there are as many religions as there are individuals." He gives his considered opinion on the fellowship of different religions when he says, "After long study and experience, I have come to the conclusions that (1) all religions are true (2) all religions have some error in them (3) all religions are almost as dear to me as my own Hinduism, is as much as all human beings should be as dear to one as one's own close relatives. My own veneration for other faiths is the same as that for my own faith ; therefore, no thought of conversion is possible. The aim of the fellowship should be to help a Hindu to become a better Hindu, a Mussalman to become a better Mussalman, and a Christian a better Christian... Our prayer for others must be NOT "God, give him the light thou hast given me," BUT "Give him all the light and truth he needs for his development." Pray merely that your friends become better man, whatever their form of religion.[30] To the Christian missionaries who were anxious to convert Indians to Christianity his request was, "Make us better Hindus, i.e. better men and women."[31] A mere change means little without a change of heart. He adds, "It is better to allow our lives to speak for us than our words. God did not bear the cross only 1900 years ago, but He bears it today, and He dies and is resurrected from day to day. It would be poor comfort to the world if it had to depend upon a historical God who died 2000 years ago. Do not then preach the God of history but show him as He lives today through you."[32]

What the world needs today are good men who can pass the higher canons of every religion. The readiness with which Gandhiji has been accepted by the best minds of all great faiths of the world as an example of their cherished ideals, shows that he passed such canons. He stands, therefore, above all faiths—yet so dear to many.

The Rock-Bottom Unity

The secret of the appreciation of a really good man by persons of all religions is that behind all faiths there is a common ethical basis—a universal religion. "It means," as Gandhiji says, "a belief in ordered moral government of the universe...This religion transcends Hinduism, Islam, Christianity, etc. It does not supercede them. It harmonizes them and gives them reality."[33] The "Study of other religions besides one's own will give one a grasp of the rock-bottom Unity of all religions and afford a glimpse also of the universal and absolute truth which lies beyond the 'dust of creeds and faiths'."[34]

Prayer in Religion

"Prayer is the very soul and essence of religion."[35] Gandhiji prayed every morning and evening without fail, like and with, the rising and setting of the sun, wherever he was and whatever he did in his life, busier than which no life could be. But, what is prayer ? "Prayer", says Gandhiji, "is not asking. It is a longing of the soul. It is daily admission of one's weakness."[36] "Our prayer" he adds, "is heart search."[37] It is "a call to self purification,"[38] and "a call to humility."[39] It is also an attempt to prepare ourselves "to share the sufferings of our fellows whoever they may be."[40]

Gandhiji, at all critical stages in his life, whenever he had to make a momentous decision, would retire to himself, and even observe silence and fast, and check his accounts and motives with the God in him—Truth, Reason, and Love—and earnestly pray, 'Lead kindly light.' He came out refreshed, determined, and invigorated. He forged ahead, with redoubled energy and love, into outward action, enthusing his followers, winning the heart of his opponents, and sweeping away, like a miracle, the age-long obstacles, hatred and shakles that degraded his countrymen and those that ruled over them. Repeated and increasing success confirmed his faith.

Gandhiji tried to place his body and mind at the service of God, efface his ego and vanity by surrendering himself to God and doing His will and His work. Because he believed that, "Perfection or freedom from error comes only from grace. Without an unreserved surrender to His grace, complete mastery of thoughts is impossible."[41] He also believed that, "To feel that we are something is to set up a barrier between God and ourselves; to cease feeling that we are something is to become one with God. That is why he did not allow his little self and its narrow desires to stand in the way of the larger interest of humanity—which was God incarnate to him. So he often exclaimed impatiently, "I must reduce myself to zero."[42] He tried to dedicate the results of his honest efforts—success as well as failure—to God, as the harvest of the Divine Will acting in him. He thus tried to escape the maddening vanity of success and the depressing effect of failure. But the harvest often pleased him and filled him with gratitude to God in him and outside. This is Gandhiji's way of realizing God, his religion or philosophy of life. For this philosophy he was greatly influenced by Gita which was his constant guide, on which he also wrote a commentary supporting in his own light Gita's doctrine of salvation through selfless action. In the introduction of this commentary he observes, "The Gita says, 'Do your alloted work but renounce its fruit—be detached and work—have not desire for reward and work ;" and "Salvation of Gita is perfect peace."

THE CONCEPT OF MORALITY

According to Gandhiji, in short, religion means "belief in the ordered moral government of the universe."[43] It is identical with morality. "True religion of True morality are inseparably bound up with each other."[44] Yet, "Religion is to morality what water is to the seed that is sown in the soil"[45]. This similie would suggest that though morality is not possible without religion, its growth, is greatly helped by religion. But, on the other hand, morality helps religion by purifying the heart of passions and prejudices that stand in the way of realizing God in one's own self and in others. "The purer I try to become the nearer I feel to be to God." So religion and morality help each other.

The realization of God to Gandhiji, is the ultimate goal of human life. But God, for Gandhiji, is not an abstract entity. He is the Truth or Reality that lives in man's own self and in the selves of others. The realization of God can, therefore, be attained best through the realization of God in one's own self and in humanity.

Every individual is a definite centre of the life of God manifested through particular physical and mental conditions. Every one is born with certain basic tendencies, good and bad, selfish and unselfish. He must try to know himself and reform himself, and gradually widen his limited circle of the existence towards the Infinite Self, God. This can be done only by considering and including the interests of others. As Gandhiji says, "Our desires and motives may be divided into two classes—selfish and unselfish. All selfish desires are immoral, while the desire to improve ourselves for the sake of doing good to others is truly moral. The highest moral law is that we should unremittingly work for the good of mankind."[46] The path to the realization of True Self or God, therefore, lies through the love of others and performance of duties towards others as such love demands.

Morality thus becomes "the essence of religion" and love the soul of morality.

Love

Love (ahimsa) is the nearest approach to God, the Truth manifested in our knowledge of Reality. Love helps the finite individual to widen his narrow self. It breaks the barrier between himself and others and makes the life of the individual include more and more of others. Love in man is the Divine Law or God inherent in him. Without this Divine Impulse man would have remained confined to his narrow ambit of selfish existence, if he could exist at all. No amount of reasoning or threat can accomplish what love can do quite spontaneously. All duties towards one's fellow-beings follow from love. The performance of duty is also made pleasant by love. Love penetrates into every sphere of life and tunes all impulses to one pleasant, orchestral harmony, Gandhiji tried to realize this truth.

Knowledge

But love itself has to be gradually perfected by knowledge and moral effort. Love, in its unenlightened form, is manifest as a blind animal appetite centred mostly in the body. Knowledge liberates love from its narrow limits. When man is ignorant of his real nature, he is moved by the cravings of the flesh with which he completely identifies himself. But when he realizes his underlying Reality, and through it his inseparable relations with the rest of existence, his love extends beyond his body and its immediate interests. Thus we find that love and knowledge of Truth help each other. Love without Truth would be blind and narrow, Truth without love would be a mere unrealized Ideal.

Gandhiji places, therefore, great emphasis on the necessity of knowledge for morality. Mere mechanical action, performed either under the influence of blind impulse or customs is not really moral. Morality implies conscious, deliberate volition. He says, "No action which is not voluntary can be called moral."[47] He adds, "So long as we act like machines, there can be no question of morality. If we want to call an action moral, it should have been done consciously and as a matter of duty. Any action that is dictated by fear or by coercion of any kind ceases to be moral."[48]

Not only this, a good action requires also the knowledge of the conditions of other fellow-beings concerned, the environmental conditions and particularly the motives behind the action. Self-analysis, therefore, acquires a great importance in the ethics of Gandhiji. Self-analysis is necessary to check our selfish motives. Without self-analysis there cannot be self-purification.

But like some modern psychologists Gandhiji is aware that self-analysis might be sometimes deceptive and that others can at times see our motives and desires more clearly by observing our behaviour. His advice is, "We must also try to see as others see us." Thus, knowledge is essential for good, as well as successful moral life.

Free Will

Freedom of will is a necessary postulate of morality, according to Gandhiji, as to most ethical thinkers. But he believes that man is not entirely free. Every man is born with certain limitations. He should know them and develop himself to the best of his capacities. All limitations cannot be totally overcome. Moreover, the laws of nature to which man is subject, prescribe some limits. But man can know these laws and learn to obey them and derive benefits from them. Man's own action, too, creates habits and tendencies; and he is driven by them too. The tendencies with which man is born are regarded by Gandhiji, like ancient Indian philosophers, as also the effects of his own action in previous lives. But inspite of all these limiting influences, and even within their arena, man has sufficient scope for exerting his will and moulding his environment, body and mind.

Soul Force

But he can draw additional strength from another source too if he has the will and faith. One of the chief sources of the weakness and helplessness of man is his egotism—his mental identification of himself with his mind and body. This isolates him from the rest of Reality. To superficial thought the ego appears as the very source of energy, and the assertion of the ego appears to be the only way of getting power and success. This is, however, a partial truth. Self-assertion is necessary and even beneficial for a person who suffers from utter inertia (tamas) and who cannot even command the physical and mental energy normally available to him. But one, who has not only perfectly mastered his body and mind but has also realized that he is an inseparable part of All-pervasive, Omnipotent Reality, can command an extra-ordinary power, particularly for the service of humanity. Such a person has much greater confidence in himself and others as part of the one whole. He has an ardent love for others by which he can serve, move and lead his fellow beings towards perfection with an ever-increasing speed. This is what Gandhiji calls soul-force which he often contrasts with brute force.

While brute-force is based on egotism which creates conflict and misery, soul-force is based on love, trust and humility which create harmony and happiness. Gandhiji lays great emphasis on humility. Genuine humility is, however, very different from consciously affected modesty. It is a natural attitude which characterises a man who has realized the insignificance and helplessness of the little self apart from God and humanity. It is to be found most in him who has surrendered his little self completely to the will of God and has made himself a mere instrument to it.

Work by Self-Surrender

"To feel" says Gandhij, "that we are something is to set up a barrier between God and ourselves; to cease feeling that we are something is to become one with God."[49] To be an instrument in the hands of God liberates man from the ever increasing bondage of selfish desires. It helps him also avoid the ordinary depression from failure and the madness from success, and helps him thereby to pursue steadily the path of duty with calm judgement.

This is the state of equality (samabhava) which is taught in Gita and which Gandhiji adopted, as his ideal. So his motto was, "work without attachment as a mere instrument to the will of God." This is true renunciation for Gandhiji. One should not run away from the world and one's duties. One should renounce the selfish desires for enjoying the fruits of action. The more one thinks of the pleasures to be attained, the less can one concentrate energy on the action. Do the will of God and let Him take care of the results. "Seek ye first the Kingdom of God and righteousness; and all of these things shall be added unto you." If the duties are rightly done, good results are sure to follow; for God's law rules the world.

But what does the will of God really mean ? God is a name we give to the best motive forces of love, sympathy, and harmony that work in man, make for unity, and prevent chaos and ruin. Conscience or the sense of duty indicates the direction of these forces. It is, therefore, called the voice of God. To work for God is to allow conscience. To the extent that man can do so, he does only what is good for all and not merely for his little ego. The true good of the individual lies in the good of all which, of course, includes him too.

God is the name, again, of the abiding Reality that expresses itself through the changing phenomena of birth, decay and death. To work for God is to work for this abiding principle. It gives strength to man to think that he is a link in the eternal principle of existence that survives death and destruction.

Dynamic Humility and Peace

A life of service, dedicated to the best and the most abiding principles of existence tends to efface the little self and it generates spontaneous and dynamic humility. For, the little self tends to be replaced by the Universal Self, the helpless life by the Cosmic Life that moves all existence. Selfish desires then hide in shame. Selfless activity brings abiding joy, and ceaseless service creates unceasing peace.

So, Gandhiji says, "A life of service must be one of Humility."[50]

SOME MORAL MAXIMS

Let us now discuss some moral maxims which Gandhiji accepted and found useful in life.

The Greatest Good of All

Gandhiji does not agree with the utilitarian motto, "the greatest good of the greatest number." The utilitarian derives his principle from the pleasure-seeking motive present in every individual. "The utilitarian to be logical will never sacrifice himself."[51] But one who bases his moral principle, not on man's selfish search for pleasure, but on the love and reason that are also present in him, sees his larger interest in the interest of all. His ideal should, therefore, be the greatest good of all. "A votary of ahimsa", says Gandhiji, "cannot subscribe to the utilitarian formula (of the greatest good of the greatest number). He will strive for the greatest good of all and die, so that the others may live. He will serve himself with the rest, by himself dying. The greatest good of all inevitably includes the good of the greatest number, and therefore, he and the utilitarian will converge in many points in their career but there does come a time when they must part company, and even work in opposite directions. The utilitarian to be logical will never sacrifice himself. The absolutist will even sacrifice himself."[52]

Gandhiji's insistence on this principle also implies that in democratic rule by majority there is always the danger of neglecting the interest of the minority if we aim at only "the greatest number" and not "all." The simplest principle that we can remember for realizing this ideal is, "As with the self, so with the Universe."

The Goal Ever Recedes From Us

Though Gandhiji was in favour of setting the ideal high, he was always aware that the goal can never be completely reached. Unlike a follower of Shankara's Advaita Vedanta, but like the Theistic Vedantians and most Western Idealists, he repeatedly affirmed the un-attainability of perfection in human life. He says, "None can attain perfection while he is in the body for the simple reason that the ideal state is impossible so long as one has not completely overcome his ego, and ego cannot be wholly got rid of so long as one is tied down by the shackles of the flesh."[53] Thus, he adds, "Man will ever remain imperfect, and it will always be his part to try to be perfect."[54] "This goal," says Gandhiji, "ever recedes from us. The greater the progress the greater the recognition of our unworthiness. Satisfaction lies in the effort, not in the attainment. Full effort is fully victory."[55]

The necessity for an unattainable ideal is to evoke greater and greater effort and to keep up the ceaseless spirit of further and further progress. As Tolstoy says, if we have to cross a swift stream we must have to aim our steering at a point much higher up the stream than where we wish to go. Changing the analogy Gandhiji often says that perfect Geometrical figures, like straight lines, can never be drawn, yet because of these ideals we draw more and more perfect figures.

One Step Enough for Me

In our ceaseless effort to reach the ideal we should not forget the present realities surrounding us and through which we have to reach the goal. The future is unknown. We can take care of only the present which is in our hands. If we utilize the present well, then alone we can ensure future progress. We must take the present step well.

We can then sing with Newman, "One step enough for me." And we may be sure from our past experience that the next step will always be in view. In other words, the impenetrable darkness is nothing so impenetrable as we imagine. But it seems impenetrable when, in our impatience, we want to look beyond that one step.[56] Gandhian maxim "One step for me" reflects his practical realism which exists side by side with his great idealism. He was fond of saying, "I am a practical idealist."

As the Means So the End

The present action of man determines his future—as the Indian Law of Karma asserts. If the present action is immoral it will degrade the doer, spoil his habits, and he cannot therefore, achieve a good and noble life. Our good habits are the most important capital of our lives. "The mere spectacular success which is sometimes attained by the adoption of foul means should not be mistaken for real success. No success is worthy of human effort if it does not ennoble man. If the man is lost, success becomes a pity and a shame. As the Bible says, "For what shall it profit a man if he shall gain the whole world and lose his own soul ?" This maxim was particularly adopted by Gandhiji in avoiding all methods of political emancipation based on hatred and violence. He felt sure that such methods though temporarily successful would degrade the nation and involve it in never ending series of future bloodshed and ruin.

The True Source of Rights is Duty

We cannot morally acquire the right to expect any consideration from others, society, or state, unless we also do our duty towards them. "If we all discharge our duties, rights will not be far to seek. If leaving duties unperformed we run after rights, they will escape us like a will-O'-the-wisp."[57]

Hate the Sin but not the Sinner

Gandhiji believes that "Man and his deed are two distinct things." It is quite proper to resist and attack a system, but to resist and attack its author is tantamount to resisting and attacking oneself. For we are tarred with the same brush, and are children of one and the same creator, and as such the divine powers within us are infinite. To slight a single human being is to slight those divine powers, and thus to harm not only that being but with him the whole world."[58] Gandhiji followed this maxim, and commended it to his associates when he had to fight against the misdeeds of individuals or public organizations or systems. Believing in the inner goodness of man, Gandhiji, like Christ, thought it wise to hate sin but not the sinner. He would, therefore, regard the misdeeds apart from miscreants whose good sense he would try to evoke by friendly appeal. A corollary to this maxim, which Gandhiji used when fighting against the British Government in India, was, "Hate not the British, but the British system." This attitude prevented much bitterness.

Heal Thyself

This is a very important maxim Gandhiji adopted and found most useful in private and public life. He strongly believes that a man cannot really reform others unless he reforms himself. Example is much more effective than precept. Moreover, if a man follows the path of love in dealing with others and correcting their misbehaviour he must inspire respect, trust, and love; and this can be done only when he honestly tries to remove his own defects. Gandhiji also realized that a man's or a nation's own faults and sins incite in others the baser passions like hatred, plunder and oppression.

In dealing with all such things Gandhiji's first step was self analysis and the second self-purification. This is the method which he applied also in his political struggles. He analysed and diagnosed the causes of India's suffering and found them to consist chiefly in communal differences, social injustice to backward classes, want of self-sufficiency, want of proper education, and above all fear of the rulers. He applied himself heart and soul to the removal of these national defects by organizing constructive work in all these directions in all parts of the country. His political action thus proceeded side by side with the constructive efforts for national self-purification. He says, "Without a large, very large, army of such self-sacrificing and determined workers, real progress of the masses, I hold to be an impossibility. And without that there is no such thing as Swaraj. Progress towards Swaraj will be in exact proportion to the increase in the number of workers who will dare to sacrifice their all for the cause of the poor.."[59]

To sum up, we can say that Gandhiji's conception of religion is not separate and apart from his social and moral concepts. There is one common thread running in almost all his ideas and thought. His religion is the religion of man. Morality, according to Gandhiji, is the 'essence of religion and love the soul of morality'.

References

1. Speeches, Appendix, II, p. 40.
2. Young India, III, p. 360.
3. Speeches, p. 807; Remain Rolland, Mahatma Gandhi, p. 988.
4. Harijan, 24-12-30, p. 393.
5. Autobiography, II, p. 591.
6. M.K. Gandhi, *My Religion,* p. 3.
7. *Ibid.,* p. 3.
8. R.K. Prabhu, and U.R. Rao, *The Mind of Mahatma Gandhi, op. cit.,* p. 178.
9. N.B. Sen, ed., *Wit and Wisdom of Mahatma Gandhi,* p. 193.
10. *Ibid.,* p. 192.
11. *Ibid.,* p. 191.
12. *Ibid.,* p. 193.
13. M.K. Gandhi, *My Religion, op. cit.,* p. 4.
14. S.M. Tiwari, "Four Questions on Gandhiji's Philosophy", p. 208.
15. R.N. Tagore, *Gitanjali, op. cit.,* p. 89.
16. N.B. Sen, ed., *Wit and Wisdom of Mahatma Gandhi, op. cit.,* p. 14.
17. M.K. Gandhi, *An Autobiography,* p. 22.
18. *Harijan*, March 2, 1934, p. 23.
19. *Harijan*, February 10, 1940, p. 445.
20. N.B. Sen, ed., *Wit and Wisdom of Mahatma Gandhi,* p. 192.
21. M.K. Gandhi, *My Religion, op. cit.,* p. 3.
22. *Ibid.,* p. 3.

23. R.K. Prabhu, and U.R. Rao, *The Mind of Mahatma Gandhi, op. cit.,* p. 178.
24. N.B. Sen, ed., *Wit and Wisdom of Mahatma Gandhi, op. cit.,* p. 194.
25. *Harijan,* December 24, 1938, p. 393.
26. N.B. Sen, ed., *Wit and Wisdom of Mahatma Gandhi, op. cit.,* p. 194.
27. *Ibid.,* p. 191.
28. *Harijan,* March 24, 1946, p. 56.
29. Ḥarijan, 28-12-36.
30. Sabarmati, 1928, pp. 17-19.
31. Young India, 11-8-27, pp. 250-51.
32. *Ibid.,* p. 251.
33. Harijan, 26-7-42, p. 248.
34. Young India, 6-12-28, p. 406.
35. Young India, 23-1-30, p. 25.
36. *Ibid.*
37. Harijan, 8-6-35, p. 132.
38. *Ibid.*
39. *Ibid.*
40. *Ibid.*
41. Autobiography, p. 388.
42. *Ibid.,* p. 616.
43. Harijan, 10-2-40, p. 445.
44. Ethical Religion, p. 49.
45. *Ibid.,* p. 36.
46. Ethical Religion, p. 36.
47. *Ibid.,* p. 43.
48. *Ibid.*

49. From Yeravda Mandir, p. 68.
50. *Ibid.*
51. Young India, 9-12-26, p. 432.
52. *Ibid.*, 20-9-29.
53. *Ibid.*, 20-9-29, p. 319.
54. The Modern Review, 1935, p. 412.
55. Young India, 8-1-25, p. 141.
56. Harijan, 20-4-34, p. 78.
57. Young India, 8-1-25, p. 15.
58. Autobiography, p. 337.
59. Young India, 24-6-26, p. 226.

11

The Philosophy of Education

By education I mean an all round drawing out of the best in child and man—body, mind and spirit. Literacy is not the end of education not even the beginning. It is one of the means whereby Man and Woman can be educated. Literacy in itself is no education.

HARIJAN, JULY 31, 1937

WE have made an attempt in the preceding chapter to discuss the nature and structure of Gandhian socio-politico economic order. Socio-politico-economic order and educational system are closely related. Every society evolves its own system of education aiming at preparing the individuals for a particular end. The modern industrial revolution in the West, with its new values and outlook, changed the system of education to suit the requirements of a capitalistic society. On the other side, Communist Russia, in persuance of its ideal of classless and stateless society, evolved its own state-controlled, rigid, stereotyped and highly polytechnized system of education.

Gandhiji too, while visualizing an ideal socio-politico-economic order as a stepping stone to the realization of God or Truth, evolved an educational system suitable to his philosophy. There is a unity running through his concrete scheme and plan making them a complete system of philosophy.

A very erroneous notion, unfortunately quite common, is that Gandhiji had neither read the works of ancient or modern educationists or philosophers of education, nor had he made any experiments in the field, he having remained extremely preoccupied with his political and social activities. By charging Gandhiji of lacking in first-hand information in the field of education, these critics want to paint him as a visionary with no touch of reality. It may, however, be pointed out that the truth is rather otherwise. Like the greatest educational philosopher of 20th century, John Dewey, Gandhiji had experimented with his ideas at Phonenix settlement and Tolstoy Farm in Africa and Sabarmati Ashram in India. He also founded the Gujrat Vidyapith in 1920. His association with students, teachers and educationists cannot be simply questioned. He was also a copious reader and there are proofs to show that he had read a lot, both, of eastern and western philosophy of education. His ideas on Basic Education, on which topic he has mainly written, and a University Education, therefore, deserve serious attention. They are practical, life-oriented and not mere academic researches of an arm-chair theorist.

EDUCATIONAL PHILOSOPHY OF MAHATMA GANDHI AND BASIC EDUCATION

There is a growing tendency among some educationists to identify Gandhiji's educational philosophy with what is popularly known as Basic Education or Wardha Scheme of Education. The Wardha Scheme of Education is no doubt, an integral part of Gandhiji's Educational Philosophy, but it is a scheme, or a programme of education not synonymous with Gandhiji's Philosophy of Education, which aims at bringing about a revolution in the hearts and minds of men all over the world. His thoughts on education well-cohere into a complete educational philosophy which is a coping-stone of his general philosophy. The Wardha Scheme, on the other hand, is primarily concerned with the education of children between 7 and 14 years of age, and that too for India of 1935.

GANDHIJI'S CONCEPT OF EDUCATION

'What is education' according to Gandhiji ? We have the answer in his own words : "By Education," says Gandhiji, "I mean an all-round drawing out of the best in child and man—body, mind and spirit. Literacy is not the end of education nor even the beginning. It is one of the means whereby man and woman can be educated. Literacy in itself is no education."[1] The literary training in a school lays more emphasis on the tools and subjects rather than on the personality of the educand which according to Gandhiji, is the main concern of education. What does Gandhiji mean by "drawing out of the best"? This best is nothing else but the inner voice of Truth. Education which draws out the best or Truth consists in development of the mind and body with a corresponding awakening of the soul. It is the function of education, therefore, to bring about a harmonious development of all the aspects of human personality, viz., body, heart, mind and spirit. "True education", says Gandhiji, "is that which draws out and stimulates the spiritual, intellectual and physical faculties of the children."[2] This concept of education is in conformity with the modern concept of education. It is universally admitted in the modern times that personality constitutes body, heart and mind, and it is the function of education, therefore, to bring about a harmonious development of all these aspects of human personality. This explanation is perhaps based on inadequate understanding of human nature, because it neglects the most important aspect of human personality, namely the spirit. Any programme of education that puts exclusive emphasis on one of these four aspects of the human personality militates against the basic principles of education. Most of the ills of our educational system, from the dawn of civilization, can be traced to unique emphasis laid on the one or more of these aspects and indifference to the others.

A very great evil of the present day all over the world is the neglect of the spiritual aspect of human personality. Gandhiji revolts against this evil of the modern education and emphasises all aspects of human personality. Thus, his concept of education is intended to remove the inadequacies of modern education and his definition of education seems to be more suitable than any other.

AIMS OF EDUCATION

Gandhiji was essentially a believer in God. But the concept of his God was much different from what is commonly understood in those days. To him God was not a superman controlling our destinies. For him God was Truth[3] and Non-violence[4], just as a scientist is in search of Truth, so Gandhi was in search of Truth. It could be served not by retiring to Himalayas but by serving his creation. He says, "...the only way to find God is to see Him in His Creation and be one with it. This can only be done by serving all. I am a part and parcel of the whole, and I cannot find Him apart from the rest of humanity."[6] He further says, "Man becomes great exactly in the degree in which he works for the welfare of his fellow men."[7]

Self realization *i.e.* Moksha can be had only through the source of humanity.[8] The ultimate aim of one's life should be self-realization. *i.e.,* utmost development of heart, hand and head (3H)[9] when this goal can be achieved only through the medium of serving humanity, and living nearer home and in the midst of society, Gandhiji could not find out any real conflict between the just interests of individual and the society, and between society and other societies. To Gandhiji all become one, helping and supporting each other. He says, "I believe in the absolute oneness of God, therefore also of humanity. What though we have many bodies, we have but one soul. The rays of the sun are many through refraction. But they have the same source."[10]

This, in short, was the philosophy of life of Gandhiji. This philosophy of life is reflected in his educational philosophy. Gandhiji, to begin with, wanted that education should be such as may lead to self-realization.

Gandhiji's aims of education are implied in the meaning of education, and are correlative to his ideal of life. The more we study Gandhiji's addresses and writings, the more strongly do we feel that he has given two sets of aims—viz, the immediate and the ultimate.

Among the immediate aims, we may mention the bread and butter aim, the cultural aim, the harmonious development aim, the moral or character development aim and the aim of liberating the educand. The ultimate aim of Gandhiji is related to the ultimate goal of life—the aim of self-realization, the realization of God or Truth. By advocating these two sets of aims, Gandhiji shows his catholicity, his greatness, his breadth of vision, his ability to embrace all aspects of human life.

The Bread and Butter Aim

The exponents of this aim maintain that the child should be able to earn his living after finishing his education. What is the use of education, they say, if it does not help provide the basic economic needs of our life. Food, clothes and shelter are our minimum needs and unless we are able to satisfy them, all talks about higher ideals of life fall on deaf ears. Gandhiji advocated this among other aims of education. It was in this context that he arrived at his theory of 'self-supporting education'. He remarks, "This education ought to be for them a kind of insurance against unemployment."[11]

Elaborating the same idea, he further says, "The child at the age of 14, that is, after finishing a seven year course, should be discharged as an earning unit. Even now the poor peoples' children automatically lend a helping hand to their parents—the feeling at the back of their minds being what shall my parents eat and what shall they give me to eat, if I do not also work with them ? That is an education itself. Even so the state takes charge of the child at seven and returns it to the family as an earning unit. You impart education and simultaneously cut at the root of unemployment."[12] It may be remembered, however, that Gandhiji never wants the child to be a little wage-earner, a boy-man. Really speaking, he wants him to learn while he earns and to earn while he learns. His labour is to be a part of his learning and is to make him fit for the kind of society in which he would be expected to live. This aim of education may seem to be base and materialistic to some people, but it can never be denied that our primary needs must be satisfied, if we are to make any progress—material, moral, or intellectual. It goes to the credit of Gandhiji that he arrives at his theory of self-sufficiency in education independent of any authoritative book on Education.

The Cultural Aim

As against the 'bread-and-butter aim of education', there is the cultural aim, according to which knowledge is worth having apart from any material use that it has for its possessor. Knowledge of this kind is the goal of liberal education The advocates of the cultural aim of education tend to think that, because a person had been engaged in intellectual work, his mind is trained to behave better ever afterwards in all new situations. It should, however, be borne in mind that knowledge is not the same thing as culture. "A man's culture is not to be judged", says Dr. S. Radhakrishnan, "by the amount of tabulated information which he has at his command, but by the quality of mind he brings to bear on the facts of life."[13]

Being practical to the core, Gandhiji would not enter into an academic discussion of culture. His conception of culture is typically Gandhian and he would not care what others think of it. In his talk to the girls of Kasturba Balikashram, New Delhi on 22nd April, 1946, he said, "I attach far more importance to the cultural aspect of education than to the literary. Culture is the foundation, the primary thing which the girls ought to get from here. It should show itself in the smallest detail of your conduct and personal behaviour, how you sit, how you walk, how you dress etc., so that anybody might be able to see at a glance that you are the products of this institution. Inner culture must be reflected in your speech, the way in which you treat visitors and guests, and behave towards one another and your teachers and elders."[14]

The Complete Development or Perfection of Nature Aim

The complete development or perfection of nature is another aim that Gandhiji advocates. According to this view, our various innate and acquired powers should be so trained as to bring about a harmonious development of all those powers. This aim accords well with Gandhiji's concept of education—"an all-round drawing out of the best in the child and man—body, mind and spirit." The development of the mind and body must go hands in hand with a corresponding awakening of the soul in order to save it (education) from being reduced to a mere lopsided affair. It is only a complete development that can give us a whole man.

In the light of this aim, we can easily see how the present education is a lopsided affair. It consists of mainly the training of the mind. The training of the soul as well as the heart is necessary, because it can lead to a refinement of emotions and impulses; it can awaken our deepest feelings of love, sympathy and fellowship—the qualities that constitute Ahimsa.

The Moral Aim

The moral aim is also emphasized by Gandhiji in the sense of character formation or character development. Gandhiji attaches so much importance to character training that he was prepared to sacrifice literary training if the choice were to be made between the two. To the question, "What is your goal of education when India obtains freedom ?" he promptly replied, "Character building. I would try to develop courage, strength, virtue, the ability to forget oneself in working towards great aims. This is more important than literacy. Academic learning is only a means to this greater end."[15]

This character is to be built up in terms of non-violence and universal love. Gandhiji believes that such moral virtues, properly cultivated, will enable the individual to realise truth.

Liberating the Educand Aim

Besides character building Gandhiji makes 'sa vidya ya vimuktaye' (education is that which liberates) one of the most important aims of education. It has been the motto of the Gujarat Vidyapith founded by Gandhiji in 1920. To a student who seriously asked what he was to do after finishing his studies, Gandhiji replied, "The ancient aphorism, 'Education is that which liberates', is as true today as it was before. Education here does not mean mere spiritual knowledge nor does liberation signify liberation after death. Knowledge includes all training that is useful for service of mankind and liberation means freedom from all manner of servitude even in the present life."[16] Thus, according to this aim, education should liberate the individual learner. It should lead to political, economic, intellectual and spiritual freedom.

Self-Realization Aim

The highest aim of education, according to Gandhiji, is realization of God or Truth *i.e.* self-realization. All other aims are subordinate to this supreme aim of life and education. We have considered different aims of education as put forth by Gandhiji. With all these aims as the bases of educational activities, Gandhiji regards self-realization as the Summum Bonum of life and education. This is the ultimate goal after which human beings ought to strive. In his autobiography, he clearly says, "Long before I understood the education of the youngesters of the Tolstoy Farm, I had realized that training of the spirit was a thing by itself. To develop the spirit is to build character, to enable one to work towards a knowledge of God and self-realization. And I held that all training without the culture of the spirit was of no use, and might be even harmful."[17] Gandhiji believes, "that those who defer preparation for this invaluable experience until the fourth stage of life i.e. Sannyasa, attain no self-realization, but old age amounting to a second and pitiable childhood, living as a burden on this earth."[18] He regards the life of a brahmachri and that of a sannyasi as spiritually similar."[19] In his letter to his son, Mani Lal, he writes, "You have realized my ideal of education, if you learn real virtues and saturate your life with them. Armed with these virtues, you will earn your living in any part of the world and will be on your way to the knowledge of God and self realization."[20]

Are Gandhiji's Aims Individual or Social ?

We have dwelt in brief on the immediate and ultimate aims of education as formulated by Gandhiji. It would, therefore, be in the fitness of things for us to consider whether his educational aim is social or individual.

Gandhiji does not hesitate to state that "the individual is one supreme consideration."[21] and "I look upon an increase of power of the state with great fear, because although while apparently doing good by minimizing exploitation, it does greatest harm to mankind by destroying individuality which lies at the root of all progress."[22]

Gandhiji has no doubt in his mind that individuality should be preserved and developed if we are to achieve any progress, either material or spiritual. At the same time, Gandhiji believes in the good of the state whose service and interests should be the aim of its individual citizens. Service, he thinks, is an essential part of education.

Gandhiji, thus, strikes a balance between the ideals of social service and individual development. He says, "I value individual freedom, but you must not forget that man is essentially a social being. He has risen to his present status by learning to adjust his individualism to the requirements of social progress. Unrestricted individualism is the law of the beast of the jungle. We have learnt to strike a balance between individual freedom and social restraint. Willing submission to social control and restraint for the sake of the well being of the whole society enriches both the individual and the society of which the former is a member."[23]

Individual development and social progress are, thus, interdependent. The individual can reach his highest development in and through a spiritual society. Acharya Kripalani, commenting on Gandhiji's synthetic viewpoint, says that the inter-relation can only be ignored at the peril of the individual and the society. Any over-emphasis on the one will be at the expense of the other. Such overemphasis destroys the balance which a true and lasting civilization needs. Sometimes the individual with his anarchic tendencies produces confusion in society. At other times society so crushes the individual that his initiative and personality are lost and he becomes a mere automation. "Humanity has been oscillating between the thesis of the individual and the anti-thesis of the society."[24] But Gandhiji succeeds in achieving the proper synthesis between individual and society in his philosophy of life and education.

THE METHOD AND PROCEDURE

How can such objective be realized ? Only a suitable method can help in realizing these objectives. The system of education as it prevails, is too literary and academic to fulfil these aims. It cannot train the whole man. Gandhiji believes that in order to train the whole man education should be craft-centred. A system of education in which a craft is the centre can lead to the highest development of the mind and the soul. The craft chosen should be manual and productive. It is "to be taught not merely mechanically as is done today, but scientifically, i.e. the child should know why and the wherefore of every process."[25] It is to be a starting point of other subjects as well—a meeting point of both physical and social environment represented by such subjects as General Science, Social Sciences and Creative and

Expressional Arts. When teaching the craft and through craft other subjects, stress should be laid on the principles of co-operative activity, planning, accuracy, initiative and individual responsibility in learning. Gandhiji attaches a spiritual significance to the craft-centred method. The notion of education through handicraft arose from the contemplation of Truth and Love permeating life's activities. True education should be easily accessible to all and should be of use to every villager in his daily life.

Craft-centred education lays emphasis on such important principles of teaching as provision of useful experiences and activity as well as correlation of subjects. All this help to develop an all-round personality in which knowledge, action and feeling are evenly balanced.

The craft-centred education will fulfil other objectives as well, such as 'the bread and butter aim'. "There are influences in the craft-centred education which are favourable to virtuous dispositions even to a richness and fulness of culture. Its effect on character in general is very wholesome, irrespective of the fact whether the craft is going to be one's vocation for life or just an antidote to that lethargy, listlessness and weakness of all which is not consistent with and which is very often generated by too much intellectual work, pure and simple." The craft is again in consonance with Gandhiji's ideal of non-violence. It will save people from exploitation, selfishness and usurpation—all expressions of violence." The craft-centred education will bring a new age from which class and communal hatred is eliminated and exploitation is eschewed.

The craft in the school should be the craft of the locality as far as possible. Only then, some positive relationship between education and life could be formed. It is thus, a method which not only stresses the importance of students' activity, experimentation, discovery and discussion rather than passive reception and absorption of information, but one which establishes an intimate relationship of the school with life and reality.

DISCIPLINE AND THE ROLE OF TEACHER

In Gandhian educational philosophy the teacher's role is very significant. "It is for the teachers to make attractive and intelligible, what to pupils may, at first appear repulsive or uninteresting."[26] It is for the teacher with all his knowledge and experience of life to point the way.

"It is the duty of the teacher" says Gandhiji, "to teach his pupils discrimination. If we go on taking in indiscriminately, we would be no better than machines. The best way to do this, in Gandhiji's opinion, "is for the teacher rigorously to practise these virtues in their own person. Their very association with the boys whether on the playground or in the class-room will then give the pupils a fine training in these fundamental virtues."[27] "It would be idle for me if I were a liar, to teach the boys to tell the truth. A cowardly teacher would never succeed in making his boys valiant, and a stranger to self-restraint could never teach his pupils the value of self-restraint."[28] Teachers who themselves do not believe in non-violence or truth or non-co-operation, cannot impart to their students the spirit of any of these things."[29] For, "even a lofty utterance, that has not the backing of sincerity and experience, will be inert and lifeless, and will utterly fail to penerate and quicken the hearts of man, which the speech that springs from self-realization and genuine experience is always fruitful."[30] So the teacher had always to be mindful of his p's and q's whether he was in the midst of his boys or not."[31] In the matter of religious instructions, no good work is ever done except by the teacher living the religion himself. "I have found", says Gandhiji, "that boys imbibe more from the teachers' own lives than they do from the books they read to them, or the lectures they deliver to them with their lips. I have discovered to my great joy that boys and girls have unconsciously a faculty of penetration whereby they read the thoughts of their teachers. Woe to the teacher who teaches one thing with his lips, and carries another in his breast."[32] Gandhiji, therefore, asks teachers "to cultivate their hearts and establish with the students a heart-contact."[33] He wants them to "fashion their (the students') hearts rather than their brains,"[34] and so, calls for intimate contact, all the time, both inside and outside the school, between the educator and the educand. He says, "I have felt that teachers work lies more outside than inside the lecture room. In this work-a-day life, where teachers and professors work for the wages they get, they have no time to give to the students outside the class-room and that is the greatest stumbling block in the development of the life and character of the students today."[35]

Whereas Gandhiji emphasizes the role of the teacher, he also stresses the need for discipline among the students. He says, "It is not for a pupil, therefore, once he has joined a school, to choose what and how he will learn."[36] He further says, "He may respectfully put his doubts before his teachers. He need not believe what does not appeal to him. But if he has respect for his teachers, he will do without believing what he is asked to do, not out of fear, not out of churlishness, but with the knowledge that what is dark to him today, will some day be made clear to him."[37] So, Gandhiji requests the students to have the same faith in teachers as they have in him."[38] "A student is like a soldier...who may not argue about matters of discipline, when he has put himself and chooses to remain under it...Here there is no under-rating or despising the intelligence of the student. It is an aid to his intelligence for him to come voluntarily under discipline."[39]

But it does not, in any way, imply that the students should give blind obedience to whatever is taught or done by the educator. Gandhiji makes this point quite clear when he says, "I can conceive of occasions when implicit obedience, without waiting for reasoning out causes, is a necessity. ...But occasions for such obedience are, and must be, rare in any well ordered society. The worst thing that can happen to boys in school is to have to render obedience to everything that the teacher says. On the contrary, if teachers are to stimulate the reasoning faculty of boys and girls under their care, they would continuously tax their reason and make them think for themselves...teachers of national schools will take note of the warning I have uttered and prevent their pupils from lazily basing their actions upon statements, without testing, of men reputed to be great."[40]

In fact, he wants students to resist teachers' order if they are not moral.[41] Thus, for instance, if a principal running counter to public opinion recognise a day of universal rejoicing as a holiday, which both parents and their school or college going children may desire, students will be justified in declaring a strike for that day...In my opinion, students of a college are in duty bound to resist such breach of honour by their principal...It is impossible to render to a teacher that unreserved respect to which he is entitled by reason of his honourable calling, when he is found to be guilty of breach of honour...They (the students) have a right to be left free to hold, and actively to advocate, what political opinion they choose."[42] "Students must be granted the greatest freedom of opinion and speech."[43]

Gandhiji is convinced that teachers can only point out to their pupils what they consider is the best way. Having done so, they have no right to curb their pupils' thought and feelings. Discipline has nothing to do with artificial restraint upon the students' all-round growth. Indeed, Gandhiji would give the students so much freedom of opinion that if they find teachers lacking in vitality, he says, they may, far from submitting to the teacher, burn them in their fire of righteousness,[44] and if they have a real grievance against the teachers, they may have the right to strike and even picket their school or college, though only to the extent of politely warning the unwary from attending their classes."[45] But Gandhiji does not justify political strikes and demonstration by students,[46] what he favours and enjoins, is that they should rebel against whatever is morally repugnant. For example, he considers it, "the duty of every pure-minded student to rebel against obscenity."[47] Justifying the decision of his daughter-in-law to omit to learn obscene and erotic passages which filled pages and pages in the text-books prescribed for her University examination, Gandhiji says, "It is a mild strike on her part, but this is an occasion which not only justifies a strike on the part of the students and pupils, it is in my opinion, their duty to rise in revolt against such literature being forced on them...Such a strike would not be boisterous. It would simply consist in the students notifying boycott of examinations, which require a study of objectionable literature."[48]

It is important, thus to remember that while Gandhiji advocates indoctrination in education, he immediately adumbrates the necessary checks and balances to prevent its abuse. The discipline to which he would subject the stud-sent is purely voluntary discipline, arising out of love and respect for the teacher and his views. 'Restraint, self-imposed, is no compulsion. A man who chooses the path of freedom from restraint, i.e. of self-indulgence, will be a bound slave of passions, whilst the man who binds himself to rules and restraint releases himself. All things in the universe, including the sun and the moon and the stars, obey certain laws.

Without the restraining influences of these laws, the world would not go for a single moment. You, whose mission in life is service of your fellow-men will go to pieces if you do not impose on yourselves some sort of discipline...It is discipline and restraint that separate us from the brute. If we will be men walking with our heads erect, and not walking on all fours, let us understand and put ourselves under voluntary discipline and restraint.[49] Of course, voluntary submission to authority is one-thing and forced obedience quite another. The first is reminiscent of the moral influence of the saint and the expert, the second of the brute authority of the policeman. While the first is liberating, the second is suffocating, choking, killing the soul of man.

Higher Education

No doubt, Gandhiji is not in favour of so-called higher education which consists of mere intellectual training unrelated to the real needs of the society and the individual, he is not against higher education, if it is improvd. He says, "I would revolutionize college education and relate it to national necessities."[50] He adds, "Thus, I claim, I am not enemy of higher education...under my scheme there will be more and better research institutes...There will be truly original work instead of mere immitation."[51]

As regards universities, Gandhiji says that, "state universities should be purely examining bodies, self-supporting, through the fees charged for examination."[52]

They should guide the whole field of education and should prepare and approve courses of studies in various departments of education. But he wants university charters to be given liberally to any body of persons of proved worth and integrity.[53] It is his opinion that "it is not for a democratic state to find money for founding universities. If the people want them, they will supply the funds. Universities so founded will adorn the country which they represent."[54] "All education in a country has to be demonstrably in promotion of the progress of the country in which it is given."[55] Education should be based on realities. "To be based on realities, is to be based on national, i.e. State requirements."[56] Gandhiji considers it "criminal to pay for a training which benefits neither the nation nor the individual and held that the "university becomes self-supporting when it is utilized by the state."[57]

"The state must pay for it", he says, "whenever it has definite use of it", but this does not mean that there will not be many institutions which are conducted by voluntary contributions. Higher Education, being selective, whether in industries, or fine arts, can and must normally be left to private enterprise, but it "does not absolve the state from running such seminaries as may be required for supplying state needs."[58]

It is his firm conviction that the vast amount of so-called education in arts, given in our colleges, is sheer waste and has resulted in unemployment among educated classes. "The aim of university education", according to Gandhiji, "should be to turn out true servants of the people, who would live and die for the country's freedom."[59]

CONCLUSION

In his philosophy of education Gandhiji rises above dualistic thinking and tries to resolve all anti-thesis between various opposing aims.

Gandhiji's system of education develops an all-round vigorous personality, physically and mentally alert, keenly aware of its environment and fired with the desire to improve it. If such persons could be multiplied by the million and Gandhiji feels they can be, the face of India rather the whole world can be changed. Gandhiji planned this system of education "as a spearhead of a silent social revolution fraught with most far-reaching consequences". And all this would be accomplished without the horror of a bloody class-war, because the schools will be the co-operative communities where students will learn lessons of love, truth, justice, co-operative endeavour, equality and brotherhood of man and social service. With these ideals in view, students will grow into citizens who will form a society known as the 'Sarvodya Smaj' in which the aim is to attain a new humanism based on non-acquisitiveness, non-violence and truth.

References

1. Harijan, 31-7-37.
2. *Ibid.*, 11-9-37.
3. 'My Experiments with Truth' pp. 4, 308; Young India, April 3, 1924 and March 5, 1925.
4. Young India, April 3, 1924; Harijan, July 29, 1940; Yervada Mandir, p. 13.
5. Harijan, August 22, 1936.
6. Harijan, August 29, 1936.
7. Gandhi M.K., 'Ethical Religion', p. 56.
8. Harijan, August 29, 1936.
9. Young India, September 1, 1921.
10. Young India, September 25, 1924.
11. Harijan, July 31, 1937.
12. Radhakrishnan, S. Freedom and Culture, p. 23.
13. Mahatma Gandhi, To the Students, p. 291.
14. Variton Washburna, Rewards of Mankind (1932), pp. 104-105.
15. Harijan, Oct. 3, 1946.
16. Harijan, 10-3-46.
17. Autobiography, p. 413.
18. *Ibid.*
19. Young India, 29-1-25.
20. Patel, R.M., Gandhi in Sadhṇa (Gujarati), p. 114.
21. Young India, 13-11-24.
22. Modern Review, 1935, p. 413.
23. Harijan, 27-5-89.
24. The Latest Fad., p. 77.
25. Harijan, 31-7-37.
26. Young India, 23-9-26.
27. *Ibid.*, 12-12-28.

28. Autobiography, II, p. 202.
29. Young India, 15-7-26.
30. Harijan, 21-11-36.
31. Autobiography, II, p. 202.
32. Mahadev Desai, With Gandhiji in Cylon, p. 109.
33. Young India, 4-4-29.
34. *Ibid.*
35. *Ibid.*
36. *Ibid.*, 23-9-26.
37. *Ibid.*, (Today prestige suggestion is considered as important factor in learning by many psychologists).
38. Speeches, p. 512.
39. Young India, 14-10-26.
40. *Ibid.*, 24-6-26.
41. "Man needs society, but under conditions of imperfection, he must defend himself against society"—Jeffreys, p. 55, In the School Community too, the same thing applies, indeed, in either case, the guarantee of freedom lies in this right to rebel against injustice.
42. Young India, 24-1-29.
43. Harijan, 2-10-37.
44. Speeches, p. 512.
45. Harijan, 4-5-39.
46. "Whilst I have pleaded for the removal of restrictions on speech and movements of students, I am not able to support political strikes or demonstrations....they may openly sympathise with any political party they like. But in my opinion, they may not have freedom of action whilst they are studying. A student cannot be an active politician and pursue his studies at the same time." Of course, Gandhiji qualifies this statement of his, immediately by one observation, "It is difficult to draw hard and fast lines at the time of big national up-heavals. Then they do not strike or, if the word 'strike' can be used in such

circumstances, it is a wholesale strike; it is a suspension of studies. Thus what may appear to be an exception is not one in reality."—Harijan, 2-10-37.

47. Harijan, 15-10-38.
48. *Ibid.*
49. Young India, 23-1-30.
50. Harijan, 31-7-37, p. 197.
51. *Ibid.*, 9-7-38, p. 176.
52. Harijan, 2-10-37.
53. *Ibid.*
54. *Ibid.*, 2-11-47.
55. *Ibid.*, 7-9-47.
56. *Ibid.*, 30-7-38.
57. *Ibid.*
58. *Ibid.*, 2-10-37.
59. *Ibid.*, 25-8-46.

12

The Nature of the Ideal Man

The ideal man is non-attached man. Non-attached to bodily sensations and lusts. Non-attached to his craving for power and possessions. Non-attached to his anger and hatred; non attached to his exclusive loves. Non-attached to wealth, fame, social position.

—HUXLEY, ENDS & MEANS, P. 3

WE have discussed the nature and the structure of Gandhian socio-politico-economic order. What Gandhiji wants is to build a society in which the individuals will play their part for the good of the community without losing their individuality, that is to say, in which individual freedom and social-walfare are identical. Unlike Communists, Gandhiji believes that the redemption of social order depends on creating proper persons and not an artificial society. He is against any social order, however good it may be, which is brought about by the use of force. He says, "It will be a sad thing if India also tries to build up the new society based on co-operation by means of violence. Good brought about through force destroys individuality. Only when the change is affected through the pursuasive power of non-violent cooperation i.e. love, can foundation of individuality be preserved and real abiding progress be assured for the world."[1] Acharya Kriplani puts this idea differently. "To avoid unregulated anarchic individualism of the capitalistic system and also the crushing concentration of the communists, Gandhiji proposes to build the economic and social structure on decentralized agriculture and industry."[2]

The brick of this new structure is the Satyagrahi individual, and he has to be reared by education in non-violent values. Habits of obedience, self-respect, self-reliance, self-sacrifice, sense of order, equanimity and other virtues are to be developed in him by a Satyagrahi. No doubt, these virtues are to be achieved by the soldier whose path is violence. But whereas in military training and career, the soldier has to obey an external authority; in the case of a Satyagrahi, the obedience is to his own internal conscience and ideal. Diwakar rightly remarks. "The Satyagrahi requires more of self-discipline than the mechanical discipline of the soldier, though he cannot do without a good deal of that too. It is not really easy to get into the habit of loving all, refusing to be angry, and suffering without ill-will. A severe course of meditation and prayer and a recasting of the values of life alone can give a man a grounding in such a new outlook of life."[3] Physically a non-violent soldier should be healthy enough to stand pain and suffering and morally he should be bold, loving and truthful. His pledge is, "I shall not fear any one on earth. I shall fear Truth or God alone. I shall bear ill-will towards none. I shall submit to no injustice wherever it might be. I shall conquer untruth with truth. While conquering untruth with truth, hate with love, injustice with justice, I shall put up with all suffering quite cheerfully and with good will towards all."[4]

VOWS FOR A SATYAGRAHI

Gandhiji lays down certain vows for the observance of a Satyagrahi. He has taken the idea of vows from the Jainas. A Jaina must observe the five minor vows (Anuvratas), the three Gunavratas and the four sikshavratas. Anuvratas are that he must not destroy any kind of life, must not tell a lie, must not use others' property without permission, must be chaste, must limit the necessities of life and avoid the use of such food as involves unnecessary killing of living creatures. "The three Gunavratas are special vows relating to the limitation and determination of his daily work, food and enjoyment. The remaining four vows relate to his worship in the morning, noon and evening, to his keeping fast on certain days and to his duty of daily giving charity in the form of knowledge, medicine, comfort and food."[5]

But the intense rigourism of Jaina Vrata (vows) is not acceptable to Gandhiji. He accepted some of the Jain's vows in a modified form to suit the modern circumstances. In the terminology of Gandhiji, a Satyagrahi must have a living faith in the vows which he prescribed for his Ashram people.

They are :

अहिंसा[2] सत्य[1] अस्तेय[5] ब्रह्मचर्य[3] असगह[6] ।
स्वधर्मसमानत्व[10] स्वदेशी[11] न अस्पृश्यता[8] ।
शरीरश्रम[9] अस्वाद[4] अभय[7] व्रत आश्रम ।

(Truth, non-violence or love, Brahmacharya or celibacy or chastity, control of the palate, non-stealing, non-possession, fearlessness, removal of untouchability, bread labour, tolerance that is equality of religions, Swadeshi are the vows in the Ashram).

These vows fall into two categories, principal and subsidiary. The principal vows are truth, ahimsa, celibacy, control of the palate, non-stealing and non-possession. Truth must be done, said and thought. It is not enough that one does not ordinarily resort to untruth. Ahimsa is not mere non-killing. Harbouring on evil thought is also Himsa or Violence. A votary of Ahimsa will oppose the tyranny but never hurt the tyrant. Celibacy is needed because without it Truth and Ahimsa cannot be fully achieved. If a Satyagrahi is married, he must look upon his wife as his life-long friend and partner. This relation of pure friendship must not be spoiled by sexual congress. The palate must be controlled and a Satyagrahi must realize that eating is necessary only for sustaining the body. Non-stealing does not simply mean that a Satyagrahi must not thieve others' property. It is theft if he uses articles which he does not need. The vow of non-possession is voluntary poverty. It is not enough not to possess much, but it is necessary not to keep anything which is not absolutely necessarv for one's daily needs.

The subsidiary vows are Swadeshi and fearlessness. What is Swadeshi ? In Gandhiji's words, "Swadeshi is that spirit within us which restricts us to the use and service of our immediate surroundings to the exclusion of the more remote. Thus in the matter of religion, I must restrict myself to my ancestral religion, that is, the use of my immediate surroundings in religion. If I find my religion to be defective I should serve it by purging it of its defects. In the domain of politics I should make use of the indigenous institutions and serve them by curing them of their proved defects. In the field of economics, I should use only those things that are produced by my immediate neighbours, and serve those industries by making them efficient and complete where they might be found wanting."[6] Last, but not the least, is fearlessness. He, who is truly fearless, will defend himself against all untruth by the soul force.

Most of these vows are the same as have been enjoined by Hindu. Shastras, but some of them Gandhiji has defined in his own way. These vows are undoubtedly based on universally recognised principles which, in the ethical terminology, are known as positive morality and hence can be taken as vows.[7] In this connection it must be admitted that in the present social set-up some of them may not be observed completely by the common man and hence it may be argued that such vows should not be taken. But Gandhiji observes that, "The taking of vows does not mean that we are able to observe it completely from the very beginning, it does mean constant and honest effort in thought, word and deed with a view to fulfil it."[8]

GANDHIJI'S IDEAL MAN AND HUXLEY'S NON-ATTACHED MAN

We may call Gandhian Ideal Man, non-attached as Prof. Huxley calls him. According to him, "The ideal man is the non-attached man. Non-attached to his bodily sensations and lusts. Non-attached to his craving for power and possessions. Non-attached to the objects of these various desires. Non-attached to his anger and hatred; non-attached to his exclusive loves. Non-attached to wealth, fame, social position."[9]

But, it does not mean that non-attached is a negative virtue, rather it is a positive one. Explaining non-attachment as a positive virtue Huxley writes, "Non-attachment is negative only in name. The practice of non-attachment entails the practice of all the virtues. It entails the practice of charity (love), for example, for there are no more fatal impediments than anger (even righteous indignation) and cold blooded malice to the identification of self with the immanent and transcendent more than self. It entails the practice of courage, for fear is a painful and obsessive identification of the self with its body. (Fear is negative sensuality, just as sloth is negative malice). It entails the cultivation of intelligence, for insensitive stupidity and disinterestedness; for avarice and the love of possessions constrain their victim to equate with mere things."[10]

GANDHIJI'S IDEAL MAN AND GITA'S STHITH-PRAJNA

In his evening prayer, Gandhiji used to recite some of the verses of Gita,[11] which describe the distinctive qualities of Sthithprajna (स्थित् प्रज्ञ) or a Man of Stable Intelligence. In brief we may say that Sthithprajna is one who is free from selfish desires, passions, fear and rage; whose mind is untroubled in the midst of sorrows and is free from eager desire amid pleasures, who does rejoice or loathe as he obtains good or evil, who draws away the senses from the objects of senses on every side, who acts free from longing without any sense of mineness or egotism, who live the life of disinterested service.

Gandhian Ideal Man may be called a Sthithprajna, a Man of Stable Intelligence who attains the state of Brahma Nirvana (oneness with God) as stated try the Gita. Explaining the meaning of Brahma-Nirvana Gandhiji says, "Nirvana is not utter extinction. So far as I have been able to understand the central fact of Buddha's life, Nirvana is utter extinction of all that is base in us, all that is vicious in us, all that is corrupt and corruptible in us. Nirvana is not like the black dead peace of the grave, but the living place, the living happiness of a soul conscious of itself and conscious of having found its own abode in the heart of the Eternal". This "abode in the heart of Eternal,"[12] is Brahma Nirvana.

GANDHIJI'S IDEAL MAN AND VAISHNAVA

The Ideal Man of Gandhiji may also be called the Vaishnava as characterised in his famous devotional song. It is described in the following way :

He is the true Vaisnava who knows and feels anothers' woe as his son's. Ever ready to serve, he never boasts.

He bows to every one, and despises no one, keeping his thought, word and deed pure. Blessed is the mother of such a man.

He looks upon all with an equal eye. He has got rid of his lust. He reveres every woman as his mother. His tongue would fail him if he attempts to utter untruth. He covets not another's wealth.

The bonds of earthly attachment hold him not. His mind is deeply rooted in detachment (renunciation). Every moment his intent is on reciting the name of Ram (God). All the holy places are ever present in his body.

He has conquered greed, hypocricy, passion and anger. A sight of such a Vaishnava, says Narsaya, saves a family through seventy one generations.[13]

To sum up, Gandhian Ideal Man has no personal and private ambition or desire of his own, rather he always identifies himself with the eternal—the whole universe and consciously strive for the welfare of the whole universe. He is always ready to make any sacrifice even that of his own life for his mission. He is non-attached and a man of stable intelligence. There is a complete harmony in his thought, word and deed.

IT IS AN IDEAL

It is not too much to expect from the masses to live the life of this Ideal Man ?

Surely it is a difficult one. But an ideal is an ideal. Man as such can only try to reach the ideal and he can never fully realise it. Gandhiji says, "Between the ideal and practice there must be an unbridgeable gulf. The ideal will cease to be one if it becomes possible to realize it."[14]

But even an ideal—a logical abstraction, and academic conception—has its practical utility. Is the point or straight line of a mathematician a reality? Certainly not. But is not the huge concrete and real edifice of engineers based on this unreal and ideal abstraction ? Therefore, what is needed is, Gandhiji says, "Let us be sure of our ideal. We shall never fail to realize it. But we should never cease to strive for it."[15]

Gandhiji wants us "not to take fright or give up the effort in despair or degrade and cheapen the ideal and thus practise untruth and lower ourselves."[16] A few most courageous and bold persons should come forward and should put their hearts and souls to materialize this dream. Gandhiji says, "what a few do, other will copy and the movement will grow like the coconut of mathematical problem".[17] Here Gandhiji agrees with Gita, when it says :

यद्यदाचरति श्रेष्ठः तद तदेवेतरो जनः ।
स यत प्रमाणम् कुरुते लोकस्तदनुर्वतते ।।

(Whatsoever a great man does, the same is done by others as well. Whatever standard he sets, the world follows).[18]

Thus is the whole edifice of Man or Individual built up by Gandhiji. Essentially it is a requirement for perfection, self-discipline, nobility in thought, word and deed, and divinity.

References

1. Harijan, 9-3-47.
2. The Latest Fad, p. 84.
3. Diwahar R. Satyagraha, p. 77.
4. *Ibid.,* p. 74.
5. Jaint J., Outlines of Jainism, p. 69.
6. Andrews, C.F., Mahatma Gandhi's Ideas, p. 120.
7. From Yeruda Mandir, pp. 9, 73, 78.
8. *Ibid.,* p. 27.
9. Huxley, Ends and Means, p. 3.
10. *Ibid.,* p. 4.
11. The Gita, Chapter II, Vs., 55-72.
12. Young India, 24-11-27.
13. Taken from Seven Months with Mahatma Gandhi by Shri Krishna Dass, p. 294 (Narsaya is the Composer of this song.)
14. Harijan, 14-10-39, p. 303.
15. Speeches, p. 301.
16. From Yeravda Mandir, p. 27.
17. Hind Swaraj, p. 86.
18. The Gita, Chapter III V., 21.

13

Epilogue

The greatest blander that we have committed is paying homage to Gandhiji as a formality, year after year, putting his statues, or visiting his Smadhi every year, offering him garands, extolling him to sky on his birthday and martyrdom day, but denying him and his teachings in our action. We are not sincere to Gandhiji. We have betrayed him. What is required the most is to study him deeply and follow his teachings in our life.

—AUTHOR

MAHATMA GANDHI belongs not to India alone but to the whole world. He belongs not to our generation alone, not to the twenty first century alone, but to posterity as well. In life as in death Gandhiji has been revered by millions of his compatriots in India and millions abroad. Most of us of the present generation look upon him as a great political leader. As such, Gandhiji would, no doubt be classified with the great makers and moulders of nations—Cromwell, Napoleon, Mazzini, Washington and Lincoln. However, Gandhiji was a great social reformer, one of the greatest political activists the world has ever seen, and a social and political thinker who was profoundly disturbed by the inadequacies of contemporary social organization and values. Millions of people have found in this many-splendoured life a 'spiritual power' that has given not only its unity and coherence, but also the majesty that has made Gandhiji a Mahatma.

Gandhijl was a multi-faceted personality. The outward simplicity of his life and his single-minded devotion to nonviolence clocked Innumerable deep currents of ideas, disciplines, loyalties and aspirations. He was at once saint and revolutionary, statesman and social reformer, economist and man of religion, educationist and satyagrah, devotee alike of faith and reason, Hindu and inter-religious, nationalist and internationalist, man of action and a dreamer. He was a great reconciler of opposites, and he was that without strain or artificiality.

No one has yet attempted a complete analysis of his complex and magnificent personality. His life was long and ceaseless saga of endeavour in which he added bit by bit and piece by piece, to his stature culminating in advancing fullness of his personality. There was nothing mystic or miraculous about his development and growth, from a common man into the unsurpassed Mahatma of our history whose teachings are relevant today and were remain so for ever.

Whereas we Indian have forgotten Gandhiji, rather betrayed him, the people in other parts of the world have made a deep study of Gandhijis teachings and have developed a great respect for him.

EMINENT FOREIGN SCHOLARS ON GANDHIAN PHILOSOPHY

The world over eminent scholars have done deep study and research of Gandhian philosophy and have found that Gandhian principles are as relevant today as they were before his assangination. They believe that most of the problems of the modern world can be solved only by following Gandhian principles.

Summary of the views of some scholars is given below :

Dr. Rodrigo Carazo president of the University of Peace, United Organization, santa rica CA, in his article 'Gandhi—A Man who Changed 1 the Course of History'[1] observes that "Gandhi gave a clear definition of India's identity through his spirituality and simplicity. But at the same time he was also a universal figure; though, the symbols he used to communicate with his people were local, the principles he inspired have permanent application for every nation of the planet." He continues, "Truly, Gandhi is the man that changed the course of history by leading his country to an indisputable victory, with the indestructible weapon of nonviolence. Likewise, Gandhi has changed the course of history by showing that the poor nations can utilize non-violence as well as showing the rich nations and their leaders that it is never too late to implement justice."

Prof. Jan Tinbergen, Noble Laureate in Economies, Erasmus University, Netherland, in his article 'A new life style and Gandhian Thought'[2] points out that, The problem of poverty in Third World countries, decreasing importance of western countries coupled with problems created by abundance, has led to degeneration due to more egotism and abundant leisure. Aware of the unacceptable poverty in some parts of the world, of new scarcities and of the past situation created by stubborn ideologies whether capitalist or communist, this movement for a new life-style tends towards a more modest level of prosperity, less inequality and more tolerance. New life style needs an ethical, intellectual and cultural base".

Mr. Haflin Samdin Coordinator, sarvodaya centre, Batticala Sri Lanka in his article 'Gandhiji and Contemporary Ideologies Regarding Freedom, Peace and Equality'[3] has analyzed his contribution to various problems that face the attainment of this ideal. He remarks that Gandhi has brought a clearer, truer, richer, and completer meaning to each one of the great pnnciple so frequently handled about in political discourses and in the comity of nations; namely Peace, Freedom and Equality.

Mr. J.P. Pathirana, Managing Editor, DANA Jayanthipura, Sri Lanka, in his article 'Gandhiji and the Concept of Power'[4] describes Gandhiji as a 'champion of human dignity' who clearly analyzed the evils inherent in the materialistic modern culture and observes in his article: No other current ideology, neither democratic Capitalism, nor democratic Socialism, nor dictatorial Communism places before mankind the bright and noble idea of moral and spiritual development.

Mr. Terence W. Miller won 'Mother Teresa Gold Medal' in the International Essay Competition on 'The Modern Search For Peace: the Gandhian Way'.[5] Tracing the history of conflict in Ireland in this essay, he observes that oppression of a minority is one of the factors. Violence has vitiated the minds of children. He advocated the use of Gandhian methods and use of non violence, which should become a way of life. Ahimsa means a spirit of tolerance, truth and love. Gandhiji's strategy was that the immediate cause of Satyagraha should be selected within the larger cause. The next step should be to love the people – and that people should feel part of the organization, and this can happen only when they contribute towards its continuance.

Mr. R. Scott Kennedy The Thanas Merton Unity center, 892 Camino del Sur Isla Vista, CA. 93017 in his article 'Love is Real And Active'[6] dwells upon the vital issues of nonviolence as a force of social change and as means of seeking truth. Gandhi and the New Testament suggest that to be effective and active, truth has to be lived in deeds. Even truths expressed most eleoquently and profoundly cannot match simpler but lived truth. The testing of truth can be performed only by strict adherence to Ahimsa or love-action based upon refusal to do harm and readiness to undergo self-suffering. This kind of Satyagraha has universal appeal and application.

Mr. William stuarl Nelson, U.S.A expressed in his article 'Gandhain concept of Non-Violence'[7] that Nonviolence is not just the renunciation of violence. It is not a single value of a single quality of life; it is a spirit, a way of life, a religion and the law of one's very being. It begins with a life which includes not only one's acts and behavior but one's speech and thought as well and embodies the qualities of compassion, selflessness, forbearance and fearlessness. It dictates a way of struggle against the civil forces in society and it decries violence and its accompaniment, malice, in all their shades and ramifications. These are the ends to which Gandhi dedicated his life in thought and action. Little wonder then that Albert Einstein could say that a thousand years from today men will scarcely believe that such a one as this ever lived.

In his article 'Gandhi for Mere Mortals'[8] Mr. Murphy Secretary – Treasurer, International Gandhain Movement, Hachett, Australia, remarks that defying Gandhi, that we consciously or unconsciously often attempt, would do no service to the promotion of Gandhian ideals. Becoming Gandhi may not be possible, but becoming Gandhian is. One may not be able to do and achieve everything that Gandhi did, but one may become Gandhian. Even one step in the desired direction is better than no step at all. Sings of true Gandhian 'seeker' are 'belief in God, devotion to service of God's creation, devotion to truthfulness, practice of nonviolence, nonviolent resistance to injustice, devotion to simplicity, service and sacrifice and non-exploitation of lower species.'

Prof. George Paxton, Editor, The Gandhi Way Quarterly News letter, Gandhi Foundation, United Kingdom. In his article 'Gandhi and War'[9] gives an account of how Gandhi's ideas about nonviolence evolved into an abiding article of faith over time and how his initial ambivalence with regard to war culminated into making him a confirmed pacifist. Violence cannot be destroyed by counter violence. Mankind has to get out of violence only through nonviolence and love. Counter hatred only increases the surface as well as the depth of hatred. Gandhi, however, considered cowardice worse than war and should there be a choice between the two, preference must go to the latter.

Prof. Gunnar Myrdal, Noble Laureate in Economies from Sweden, in his articles, 'Poverty, Inequality and Gandhi'[10] while discussing the problems of poverty, refers to Gandhiji's emphasis on radical change in the social and economic order and decentralization, revolution and changes in the direction of education. Developments in post-independent India have belied Gandhiji's expectations. Prof. Myrdal observes that it is unthinkable that today he would remain silent and idle. He would again take to roads and village lanes and begin anew his crusade. Gandhiji's approach of all-embracing planning (integrated planning) is needed which suggests a lower level of consumption of luxury goods in the upper strata—"austerity in consumption and living patterns of the rich".

Prof Amalenda Guha, Chairman, Mahatman M.K. Gandhi Foundation for Non-Violent peace, Oslo, Norway, in his essay on 'From Gautama Buddha and Gandhi to Ikeda-Mission and Visions of Peace and Truth'[11] analyses that "All these three great preachers for peace—Gautama Buddha, Gandhi and Ikeda opt for horizontal dialogues and approaches for removing wrongdoings, misunderstandings and crisis formation, as well as for reconciliation and self-realization. Non-Violence develops a culture of peace which (i) develops human instinct of propensity to forgive, (ii) removes the instincts of taking revenge, (iii) develops the rationality of tolerance and (iv) overcomes as well as prevents the evil spirit of direct violence." Earlier the author remarks that "nonviolence is neither a submissive and passive acceptance of violence pressed by the aggressor on nonviolent people, nor a coward and subjugated act of the helpless in the society." Mr. Daisaku Ikeda, the Japanese thinker has been quoted: "Gandhi's struggle in the name of nonviolence was a battle to make the people strong and wise...Gandhi was a rare leader who chose to live in the midst of the masses, sharing their sorrow and happiness and working to dispel the fear of authority bred by long years of colonial life."

Prof. Unto Tahtinen of Finland in his article 'Gandhi on Natural Law'[12] remarks that three experiments – racial discrimination in South Africa, colonial status of India and legal injustice involved in Hindu customs shaped his approach and "Gandhi came to realize that certain positive laws, even the whole system of law, as well as traditional social and religious institutions can be in conflict with an ethical law. The ethical law, however, is higher in authority and in the case of conflict, takes precedence.

Mr. Horace Alexander of U.S.A., a close associate of Mahatma Gandhi, in his article 'Non-violence and The Rule of Law',[13] remarks that Gandhi was not an anarchist in the sense that he has had no respect for rule of law. The fact is that he was himself a student of law and a legal practitioner of great repute and as such held the rule of law in high esteem. He was opposed only to such laws as were unjust and against the common interest of the society at large. His violations of law were specially significant just because he was a believer in the rule of law. Overtly in the name of maintaining law and order many governments are reigning rule of terror and tyranny. The conception of a nonviolent war-free world can materialize only through an adherence on the part of the nation states to the rule of law. Nations must learn to compromise a part to their individual selfish interests and chauvinistic sentiments to join and run global institutions like the U.N. The author, in the end, makes a passionate appeal for enforcing the rules of the game both within the nation and internationally too.

Prof. K.L. Seshagiri Rao, Professor of Religions studies, University of Virginia, U.S.A. in his article 'Gandhi's Religious Quest in South Africa'[14], observes that the basic tenets of Gandhian religion are truth, nonviolence, love, simplicity, dignity of labour, selfless service, equality and fearlessness. His religion admits of no rituals, dogmas and bigotry. Gandhiji's stint in South Africa was like a workshop of his religious formulations. Not only did he study major religions of the world there, he also came in contact with the writings of John Ruskin and Tolstoy which together exercised very profound influence on evolution and strengthening of Gandhi's ideals. Two Ashrams–Phoenix and Tolstoy Farm in particular, and the African society in general served as laboratories for experiments and confirmation of his religious hypothesis.

Mr. Stephen Murphy, Secretary – Treasurer, International Gandhian Movement, Hackett, Australia, in his article 'The Last Hours of Mahatma Gandhi[15], gives a detailed account of Gandhi's activities on 30th January, 1948, the day he attained martyrdom. Early that morning Gandhi had said to Manu, "If someone fires bullet at me and I die without a groan and with God's name on my lips, then you should tell the world that here was a real Mahatma..." Did Gandhi have premonition about his mortal end and his journey to immortality? For answer read this absorbing tale by Stephen Murphy.

Prof. Amalendu Guha, Chairman, Mahatma M.K. Gandhi Foundation for Non-Violent peace, Oslo, Norway in his article 'Non-Violent Philosophy and Culture of Peace: Gandhi's Contribution',[16] observes, "Human Peace is a culture which is the outcome of the feelings of humanity and humanism." He discusses the role of nonviolence, training in nonviolence and peace, and in his concluding remarks observes that Gandhi's concept and philosophy of peace is considered to be secularist and humanist. He quotes Gandhiji: "I must love my enemy, I must apply the same rules to the wrong-doer who is my enemy or stranger to me, as I would do to my wrong doing father or son."

Arun Gandhi, M.K. Gandhi Institute for Non-violence, Brother University, 650 East Parkway, South Memphis, T.N. 38104 in his article 'Non-Violence in the 21st Century:

Challenges and Choices',[17] states that "Non-violence, therefore, can be described as an honest and diligent pursuit of truth." In the article he further explains the four essential principles of Gandhiji's philosophy to be "Truth, Ahimsa, Trusteeship and Constructive Action."

Mr. Michelle Myres, Founding President of the Global Peace Society, U.K. in his' article 'Why Gandhi's Principles of Non-violence are Relevant Today'[18] makes a fervent appeal to encourage peace studies and academics. The fact that the people belonging to various races and religions can live together in harmony, and conflicts can be resolved without war and violence, should be demonstrated in practice as Gandhiji actually did. Violence breeds more violence, similarly peace would breed more peace. Hence shun violence and practice peace, counsels the author.

Prof. Jan Tinbergen, Noble Laureate in Economics, Netherland, in his article 'The New International Order and Gandhian Thought'[19] observes, "To put in bluntly, Gandhi's ideas are by no means outmoded, as some believe, and, on the contrary, might well be applied more often in to-day's world". In another article, 'Equality as an Aim of Policy', the author deals "with the instruments of socio-economic policy that can be applied, in economies at different stages of development, in order to reduce inequality." Describing Gandhiji's relevance Prof. Tinbergen remarks in his last article in this collection, titled 'Gandhi's Relevance' that "Gandhian thought was not of a passive nature; it did constitute a revolution in thinking".

Mr. Paras Ramoutar PRO, Mahatma Gandhi Foundation, Trinidad, in his article 'Need to Revisit Gandhi's Message'[20] remarks that to a world tormented by violence, unpeace, threat of nuclear holocaust, exploitation, inequality and terrorism etc., Gandhi and his ideals are the only hope. Abiding faith in God, truth, love, nonviolence, Satyagraha and their practice in actual dealings in life can rid the world of its present predicament and foster a culture of peace and universal brotherhood.

RELEVANCE OF GANDHIAN TEACHINGS AND PRINCIPLES TODAY

A Question is often asked: "Is Gandhian thought relevant to the present times?" In my view, this question itself is wholly irrelevant. I am convinced that Gandhiji's ideas on various subjects are based on certain essential principles which were relevant during his lifetime, are equally, if not more, relevant today and will continue to be relevant for centuries to come. This is because the Mahatma was a realistic idealist and possessed a very logical and scientific mind. He called even his Autobiography 'The Story of My Experiments with Truth.'

When we discuss about the relevance of the teachings and principles of Gandhian thought today, we should not forget the fact that the scheme of things, Gandhiji wanted to envisage was not given serious consideration in India at the time of drafting of the Constitution. The kind of political system and industrialization Gandhi had in mind, became a suspect since no serious efforts were made to restructure the economy and politics as he wished. The efforts of the new rulers were to build up the castles on the existing foundations left behind by the British. It is a fact that structural changes which Gandhiji had suggested, were never taken seriously. The well-planned and balanced industrialization that he advocated involved restrictions of several kinds, particularly on aspects such as unlimited growth and undue profit. Gandhiji expressed, 'The Earth provides enough to satisfy every man's need, but not for anybody's greed".

It is in this context that we should care for Gandhi when India is in the grip of the culture of consumerism creating a big gulf between the rich and the poor. On the other hand Gandhiji had emphasized, "I shall work for an India in which the poorest shall feel that it is their country. In whose making they have an effective voice, an India in which there shall be no high class and low class of people... an India in which all communities shall live in perfect harmony...there shall be no room in such an India for the curse of untouchability...women shall enjoy the same right as men. This is the India of my dream."

Gandhiji struggled for the freedom of the masses and in the pursuit of search for truth and justice he had to fight against imperialism, capitalism, indiscrimination, injustice and exploitation. The beauty of this great man was that he never claimed that he had discovered or invented new ideas or a new philosophy. However, his contribution lies in developing the age-old knowledge and ideas and infusing in them new meanings. He applied Satyagraha to change our society. He was fully convinced that real social change implied change in our values, ethos and ideologies and it was sheer nonsense to think that one could change anybody's mind or ideas by external or physical force. On the contrary, physical force is counter-productive resulting in anger, hatred, jealousy, revenge and bloodshed. Violence destroys many, divides the survivors who are infected with rage, intolerance, confusion, restlessness, constant fear and hatred. As a result, there is no peace, no rest, no individual freedom and as a result no development has taken place. On the other hand, the issue of development has been put on shelf and the people are engaged in devising the methods of destruction.

Similarly, Gandhiji's emphasis on the purity of means is quite relevant today as majority of today's politicians and statesmen have been trying to adopt the Machiavellian approach to achieve their end and don't bother about using unfair means from bad to worse. However, Gandhiji never approved of Machiavellian statement that the end justifies the means and he rather always opposed such kind of approach and argued, "Just as one cannot obtain rose by planting noxious weed, one cannot attain good end by adopting bad means. On the other hand, we reap exactly as we sow."

It implies that our participation in politics must not be motivated by pursuit of power, but by service to humanity as politics can only be a means for promoting the good of others. It is in the light of this fact that he made an effort to spiritualize politics for the service of the humanity. It is again on this account that he did not find any contradiction between religion and politics, so he could openly say that he was introducing religion into politics. He was fully convinced that politics minus moral values would be just a dirt and he perhaps was quite right when stated that politics bereft of religion was a death trap or dirt.

In this respect, Gandhiji warns the ambitious politicians that the choice of means is very important and decisive for the success of democracy. If in the heart of elections, moral values are put on the shelf and all kinds of means are adopted to defeat the opponent in the electoral contest, democracy itself becomes the first casualty. Therefore, judicious combination of ends and means has a significant role to play in the present context where majority of the people believe in fraud and cheating. The 'Hawala Racket' and many other scams are an eye opener to one and all. Gandhi never thought of such a state of affairs in a democracy. The politicians of today have belied the faith of the poor masses. Don't you think that Gandhiji is very much relevant today? He had already given a warning to the Congress Party in this regard long time back. It has been discussed in detail in the prologue of this book.

Terror and violence are spreading like cancer threatening the very existence of the nations. The State, despite all the measures it has been taking seems to be under heavy pressure. The sheer size of the nation and the deep penetration, the forces of violence and terror have made, also sent shock waves all around. Innocent citizens are blown up and the heartless perpetrators of violence are rejoicing. While all this is happening, the citizens who are caught up in the cross firing remain fear-struck and helpless.

What we hear from different parts of the world, is the deliberate manipulation of religious, communal, ethnic and political feelings to rouse tension from which a very few, who lurk behind the curtain, make gains. These forces pose severe threats to systems, in a hitherto unknown dimension.

Today, man kills men directly or indirectly by employing and testing of nuclear and biochemical weapons and air missiles at ground, air and in water. The vast military consumption of fossil fuels adds to the wastes produced by nuclear power contamination.

The resource depletion and toxic wastes produced by industries that are deemed necessary to produce weapons and services for modern warfare, further contribute to environmental degradation and devastation. So great is the environmental destructiveness of global militarization and associated disrespect for ecological vitality that environmentalist Barry Commoner has warned the humanity that we are in a suicidal "war with the planet" and that the planet inevitably will win. He warns that "survival depends equally on ending the war with nature and on ending war among ourselves...To make peace with the planet we must make peace with the people who live in it."

It was by the end of 20th century and beginning of the 21st century, when the concept of nuclear weapons emerged as one of the biggest challenges. Instead of spending money, power and energy on the nuclear weapons every day, if we spend half of the same for the welfare of human kind, then one thing can definitely be said that basic problems of the mankind can be solved without much difficulty and within a very short period. However, the basic question arises again that how to stop the mad race of nuclear weapons? Even the scientists, who were and are presently working on nuclear projects, are quite familiar with the destructive nature of nuclear weapons but still they are producing them.

It is quite significant and relevant to mention here that the manner in which violence is spreading in the emerging global context is the biggest concern not for any individual but for the whole humanity.

Under such circumstances Gandhiji's concept of non-violence is very much relevant today. Non-violence is a universal phenomenon having its relevance and significance for all times. It has been very effective and instrumental in solving all kinds of conflicts in society. However, its result depends upon its understanding and proper application. The present scenario of violence and exploitation all over the world has become a very serious issue.

Furthermore, Gandhiji's emphasis on humility, religious tolerance, patience, self-discipline, bread labour, prohibition, constructive programme and communal harmony, fight against untouchability, crime and violence against women and many other social evils, is quite relevant. He wanted to build a society in which every man would have equal status, opportunity and freedom where economic progress and social justice could go together.

Today, we are living in an age of disbelief, mistrust, suspicion, tension and constant fear. To raise the question like the relevance of Gandhiji's principles and teachings is like asking the question, "What is the relevance of the Sun to the Solar System?" His principles are for endless time or for the eternity. He gave us the priceless gifts of self-respect and the matchless weapon of Satyagraha—a message of peace for the whole world.

A PROPHET OF THE TWENTY FIRST CENTURY

Indeed, the more sensible approach to the population, poverty and other problems would be to consider them in a wider context or in a total 'civilizational" context, as Gandhiji does. In his earliest work Hind Swaraj, Gandhi described modern industrial civilization as "satanic," for, as he saw it and as we also see it now, it is based on exploitation, domination, inequality, violence and elitism. We have a situation where, in the Third World, millions of people toil under the boiling sun from morning till dusk for miserable rewards and premature death without ever discovering the reasons why."[21] At the same time, there is surplus in the developed countries, which, if diverted to the developing world, could help wipe out the phenomenon of hunger.

According to Chief Awolowo, former Chancellor of the University of Life, "the per capita real income remains as low as ever. Poverty, ignorance and disease are in evidence everywhere, more particularly in the vast rural area."[22]

In India, about one half of the population was below the poverty line, according to the report of a high-level seminar held in 1981 "five million persons were being added to the poverty population each year." According to a noted statistician, "economic strategies followed during the last thirty years have only sharpened the polarization of Indian society into a dual society as a small elite group and a large mass of poor group."[23]

It is clear that the developmental strategies in the majority of the Third World countries borrowed from the "affluent" countries, and based on high technology and capital-intensive industries, resource-depletion and unmindful of distributive justice and the need for the amelioration of the condition of the masses and high consumption and domination by a centralized and organised elite, are utterly incapable of delivering the goods. There is, therefore, an urgent need for a new alternative model of development, production, consumption and distribution based on decentralisation, conservation, labour-intensive production (with simple tools), equitable distribution, democratisation, and mass participation in government at all levels, cooperation, mass education in the three "Rs", basic ethics and useful arts and crafts and not in the art and science of weaponry in which, according to the Tinbergen Report, "half the world's scientific and technological manpower" is currently engaged. Such is the order of the society that Gandhiji conceived. Let India—free India which Mahatma Gandhiji, more than anyone else, brought into being—prepare for it as it moves into the twenty first century, and, instead of borrowing models and technologies from others, present it to the rest of the world for the sake of human survival and sanity, and peace and harmony now and in the future.

There is such a grandiose fanfare to usher in the twenty-first century with super computers, giant industrial plants, and wholesale automation and mechanization in all departments of life. First, to talk of the start of twenty-first century, as if it would be a landmark in the world history, is a myth. The year 2009 would be just like any other year. Momentous events do some time shake the globe, but they do not neatly fit in with the physiognomy of numbers or statistical contours.

But, Gandhian Non-Violence would have to be accepted as the world's creed. Even Mr. Gorbachev, the leader of one of the world's two most militarised nations, advocated nonviolence and peaceful co-existence as two of his ten principles in the joint communique. As Nehru once said, the alternative to co-existence is co-destruction. Either the world accepts nonviolence as the method of settling international disputes or there would be no world left. The armaments in the nations' arsenals can destroy this poor humanity many times over. Even the atom bomb of Hiroshima has been rendered obsolete like a single barrel gun. We have taken such giant strides towards the goal of wholesale annihilation. In the next nuclear war, there would be no victors or vanquished, but all would perish in a general holocaust, the whole air of our little planet would be poisoned—and our earth, like moon, would blindly spin in space, without life or activity.

The celebrated British philosopher C.E.M. Joad was the first to note the new Gandhian hope for humanity. He said that in the barbaric days, inter-personal disputes were decided on the principle of "might is right." Whether this land or house is my property or that of my enemy was decided by single combat. It showed not the superior justice but the superior force of the winning party. Today we apply that barbaric practice in the adjudication of inter-country conflicts. C.E.M. Joad said that Gandhiji sought to extend the principle of peaceful and just settlement of inter-personal disputes to conflicts among nations.

Others had preached nonviolence and peace like Buddha, Mahavir, and even Christ. It was left to Gandhi to give a practical demonstration of the efficacy of the principle of nonviolence by winning independence from the British imperialism for what then was one fifth of the human race. Never had such a Himalayan experiment been tried before and never had such a colossal success been achieved to vindicate the power of nonviolence. Future historians will evaluate the significance of the great Indian nonviolent revolution as they have done of Lenin's revolution. It is a harbinger of a new trend to change the direction of the world.

Imperialism and colonialism never die. They only change their name or shape. Once it was one King grabbing the territory of the neighbouring ruler, enslaving people's body and soul. The British Empire was a more civilised and subtle way; for a while, it gave the slaves a pride in their status and association with the ruling power. Today imperialism takes the shape of "spheres of influence". There is a race between super powers to make more and more conquests of new land and new people. They are free in all local matters; only they must toe the line in the global strategy of the super powers. Gandhian ideology, by preaching the message of love and mutual service and welfare blunts the edge of this ambition to conquer the world or larger parts of it, since it is sterile of any good result, but breeds war, violence, hatred, and a sense of pride in the victor and humiliation in the vanquished. The world's defence budget is now increasing day by day. These astronomical sums, if spent on people's welfare instead of mass slaughter of humans, could bring heaven on earth for every family. Gandhian ideology would lead to a change of heart and change the direction of the wind. Of course, we Indians do not rightly value our own great men and things, unless these get a foreign certificate.

Another element of Gandhian thought is its opposition to the big machine—the Charkha being the symbol. Computers and big plants, we are assured are inevitable. Yes, but inevitability is no proof of anything's desirability or its capacity to lead to human happiness. We are moving into the computer age, we are told. Computers would do all the jobs and man would find his occupation gone. Man gets happiness and self-fulfillment through a job well done. When he is just reduced to be a cog in the machine, he finds all his self-importance, dignity and indispensability robbed. The result is soul-killing boredom through repetitive work that gives him no joy of "making something beautiful", and that leads to heart troubles, nervous disorders and cancer through ennui. There may be some justification in the West for such labour-saving machines, where men are in short supply and money abundant to buy very expensive machines to do the work. But in India and the Third World, opposite is the case; no money (only borrowings or foreign loans) to buy super computers and no end of manpower, hungering for a job and bread. In any case, man—once the lord of creation—is now just a slave of the big machine whose whole job is to attend on machines, nurse them to normalcy when they are sick and to keep them at normal temperature and happy mood, lest they become angry and spread death, the destruction all round, as at Bhopal or Chernobyl. Gandhian economy is not primitivism, but a very practical device to give work, joy of creation, self-respect and feel of importance and usefulness to each human being.

Under industrialisation, modern financial management, economic structures, and monetary strategies have become so hopelessly complicated that the modern man can hardly understand their working, far less control them. The *summum bonum* is maximum production and maximum wealth (beyond certain limits money becomes counter-productive and leads to worries, heartache and disease), but human happiness. And that can be secured only by the Gandhian way. But the modern industrial man has become so frightfully busy that he has no time to stand and stare and think of the fundamentals. He just allows himself to be carried by the strong current that is carrying others like him. Machine culture has dehumanised him and robbed him of all happiness—see American billionaires knocking at the Ashrams of our Sadhus (genuine and fake) in search of peace of mind and joy of living.

Most of the people have become neurotic and use sleeping pills to have sleep, even then fail to have sleep. This is the result of cut-throat competition among Nations, business enterprises and even ordinary individuals, creating tensions among them. The solution does not lie in knocking at the Ashrams of our Sadhus but in following the teachings and principles of Gandhiji.

Gandhi Still Lives

It is significant that the International Seminar on Gandhian Thought has significant relevance for the modern world and that many things which have happened since he passed away have not diminished but heightened its relevance. "The Message", issued by the Seminar at the end of the deliberations, reads:

"The crisis that Gandhi faced is obviously not over but has been deepening, and the solutions that he proposed have not become outdated...Gandhi is still a living challenge to the economic thinking, planning and action not only in his own country but in all the countries of the world."

Before answering the question, Is Gandhian thought relevant to the present time, it is necessary to study the situation of the world. Only then we can answer this question.

Now let us analyse the world situation as it exists to day.

MODERN AGE AN AGE OF PARADOES

The modern age is an age of paradoxes. Two world wars have been fought 'to end wars', but the shadow of the third is haunting us. The sky all over the world is coloured with hypocricy, suspicion, hatred, misunderstanding and cut-throat competition for material gains. This is the age of cold war. Cold war may, at any moment, change into hot war and a single atom may atomize the whole universe.

The First World War was fought by the Allied Countries in the name of Democracy and was won. But after this war the world witnessed the emergence of totalitarian forms of government with their various symbols—red, black and brown—but each designed to establish a despotism over the bodies and minds of men and each founded on the principle that man is created for the state. They replaced the democratic slogan of liberty, equality and fraternity by their own slogan of duty, discipline, sacrifice, man for the state, and regimentation.

The Second World War was fought to end these totalitarian regimes which were a challenge to individual freedom and dignity of man. No doubt, the war brought destruction of the black and brown forms of totalitarianism (Fascism and Nazism), but paradoxically it strengthened the red regime (U.S.S.R.) which emerged to challenge the democracies that had fought to preserve the ideals of freedom, with its own slogan of 'class-struggle, violent revolutions, proletariat dictatorship, withering away of the state and ultimately classless and stateless society free from exploitation and oppression.'

Communism is trying to establish a classless and stateless society to save the individual from exploitation and oppression. According to the communists a classless and stateless society is the *raison deter* of peace, progress and prosperity and proletarian dictatorship is a stepping stone towards this goal. Once the transfer of the means of production into the hands of the community has been achieved, the state—that is to say, the instrument of coercion—will no longer be necessary. It will wither away. Theoretically, the dictatorship of the proletariat, no doubt, was to create conditions for 'withering away' of the state. But, paradoxically the state has become all powerful and all pervasive. It has its iron hand not only on the political and economic life but also on the moral, cultural and intellectual life, nay its words are final in the domain of art and literature, philosophy and science. Under such a dictatorship of the communist party (rather the leadership of the communist party) the individual is degraded, oppressed, tortured and controlled by fear. It seems that the state will never 'wither away' and the goal of classless and stateless society will remain only a dream. This sorry state of affairs is not confined to the U.S.S.R. alone, it also finds its full expression in the Russian satellites and Red China—the greatest challenge to the world. The hall-mark of this system is that the Individual seems to be deprived of liberty and freedom for which the human soul cries so loudly.

America is aware of the fact that communism is enemy number one of individual freedom and dignity of man, but she does not realize the increasing likeness of methods and developments, towards which the struggle with the communist bloc is driving her. The Individual freedom guaranteed by the constitution and protected by the Supreme Court still permeates American life and ideology. But the powers of the Committee for the Un-American Activities of the Federal Investigation Bureau, under the so-called Loyalty Order of 1947, and the pressure of publicity campaigns by newspapers and other organs of public opinion, subject statesmen, public servants, scientific workers and teachers to growing restrictions and intimidations under the label of communist sympathies or associations. The 'Voice of America' rivals with that of Moscow and Peking in abuse. Today, the ideological gap between American and Communist states is still very wide, but so far as methods in practice are concerned, both are coming close to each other. Behind all the tension and fury of the modern age, there has always been a measure of common values between the two camps. There is the same faith in boundless possibilities of technological perfection, a pride in the sheer bigness of scientific and industrial development, a naïve optimism about man's ability to produce heaven on earth, by mastering nature and circumstances. Thus, not only totalitarian communism, but big-scale capitalism is also leading to a very similar system of control, and the very existence of the individual is likely to be jeopardized,

Trade unionism was started as a measure of collective self-defence of the under-previledged working class against the exploitation of capitalism, but even in the most developed industrial countries it has now reached the stage in which the individual worker is left with less and less freedom. In practice, if not in theory, he must join the union or he will lose his livelihood. Under trade-unionism the innocent workers are exploited by the so-called labour leaders who are more dangerous than the capitalists, who are bigger parasites on society and who are a challenge to the society with their slogans of strike and violence.

Universal education is being provided to liberate the masses, so that they may think or act independently, following their own judgement and conscience, but paradoxically they are losing their independent thinking, because they are more exposed than ever to the press, the radio, the television, the wireless, the film and the organized political mass meeting.

This is the age of Democracy—"Government of the people, for the people and by the people", but paradoxically even in the modern democratic states the average citizen usually speaks of "they", not "we", when referring to Government action of taxation, defence or other matters. It is significant that in the last few decades leading political and social thinkers of different countries have studied the growth of the new "elite", a new oligarchy of rulers dominating the masses. The sociological studies of Frenchman Georges Sorel, the Italian Vilfredo Pareto, the Spainish Ortega Y Gasset, German Oswald Spengler find their counterpart in Aldous Huxley's picture of a completely mechanized and standardized 'Brave New World', together with the superficial trends towards democracy and the greater participation of the people in the political affairs, the technical means by which the small groups of people can guide and rule the masses have grown immensely, in quantity and quality. Thus, the modern democracy is democracy only in name.

THE MODERN AGE OF STATISM

We talk of democracy, socialism, communism and democratic socialism, but in fact, it is the age of statism, in the sense that the state (Whether capitalist or socialist or communist) is gaining more and more say in our lives. "It was said in the beginning of this century that the modern state was Jenghiz Khan, with telegraph lines. Today it is more than that. It is Jenghiz Khan with distant controls exercised by a hundred methods. It speaks with a million voices on the radio. It overhears our conversation on the telephone. It pries into our secret thoughts by censoring our letters. It controls the water we drink, the food we eat, the light we use, our modes of transportation and infact, practically everything in our lives". One may be proud of human rights enshrined in the constitution of almost all the countries of the world. But, what chance has the individual against such an institution, that is, highly centralized modern state—impersonal, all pervasive, unmoved by sentiments, armed both by the power of law and by every possible instrument of authority and coercion?

The Individual at Stake

In this modern age of paradoxes the Individual is degraded, oppressed and controlled by fear, and he has become the victim of hatred, jealousy, violence and suspicion. He tends to suffer from neurosis. The old ideals and philosophies of life which have brought him so far are unable to push him any further. He is trying to find out something and experiments with whatever crosses his mind. All that is nothing but a search in the darkness and instead of solving problems, he is only making them more and more complicated. The individual is losing all hope and is feeling insecure. Slowly and slowly all the inner and finer qualities of man are leaving him, making him increasingly gross and self-centred. As a consequence, in all spheres of activities—moral, social, intellectual, economic, political, educational and cultural—he finds nothing, but confusion. In such a state of confusion the very existence of the human is at stake. He does not know what to do.

The Problems of the Modern Age

Some of the problems which the individual is facing today are :

(*a*) How can the individual regain the sense of wholeness, so that he ceases to be neurotic ?

(*b*) How can he regain awareness of his essential oneness with his fellow beings ?

(*c*) How can a non-violent sanction for a society be developed that may take the place of the external sanctions by which society is at present regulated?

Gandhiji was not a born Mahatma. He grew into one. He was a common man who pulled himself up to the most uncommon heights. He was no god, but became a god-man. Gandhiji knew this about himself and that was why he called his biography, 'The story of the Experiments with Truth.' Experimentation was one of the deepest passions of his life. He experimented with food, health and cure, clothes and dress, politics and economics, education and reform, organization and revolution, ethics and spirituality, with almost everything that his life knew as part of life. When we look into the splendid mosaic of his thoughts and deeds, there is one thing which stands out as unique and all other thoughts and deeds revolve around that.

Mahatma Gandhi was essentially a man of faith. His conception of new social order, i.e., Sarvodya, is rooted in religion and sustained by the faith in the moral law, the divinity of man. The fulcrum of Gandhi's teaching is religion. He could live without anything and everything except his faith in God, the highest object of religious consciousness. Gandhiji himself confesses: 'I may live without air and water but not without Him. You may pluck out my eyes, but that cannot kill me. You may chop off my nose, but that will not kill me. But blast my belief in God, and I am dead." Thus religion is the support, the basis, the background, the nucleus, the centre, the fulcrum, the prop and the pivot of Gandhiji's teaching. Religion, in the opinion of Gandhiji, is a friend of liberalism and a foe to fanaticism. It is conquest of passion and quest for compassion. Religion means man's equation with his Maker. It is to see God face to face, to attain Moksha through service to Man. It is union between man and man, and communion with the Divine. Religion binds man to God and man to man. It is a cohesive force and not a disintegrating power.

For Gandhiji religion is truth, the only truth, nothing but truth. Gandhiji himself says: "I often describe my religion as the Religion of Truth." There is no religion other than truth." Truth alone is religion and everything else is irreligion. Truth is Gandhiji's religion and Ahimsa is the only way of its realization. Truth is the end and Ahimsa is the mean. The central principle of Gandhian Philosophy is his doctrine of the End and the Means.

The crisis in the modern civilization is the direct result of loss of faith. We have today a generation of men who are smart, superficial, trim, alert ready to question and doubt, unwilling to believe in anything, and have no moral earnestness or love for truth. Our knowledge is diffuse, directionless, and we are all distraught in mind and tired in body and listless in outer manners. We have a civilization built upon untruth and lovelessness. We have given ourselves to the cult of violence. We just shift and drift and cleverly erect defences to hide out real nature. The best lack all convictions and the worst are all of passionate interests. When the best lack all convictions and the worst are full of passionate interests, when the exponents of different isms, propagandists of contradictory socio-politico-economic values and enthusiasts of diametrically opposed parties do not hesitate to slaughter their opponents, humanity can be saved only by practicing Truth and Non-Violence in life in such a way as was advocated by Gandhiji.

Despite equality, brotherhood and world-peace been so ubiquitous, and yet never has humanity or human values stood nearer to the brink of total destruction than they do today. The world is now passing through the after-effects of the two great world wars which have revealed the brute in man and shaken all confidence in his inner goodness. The world is getting caught up again in a long and grim cold war of which even the most pacisist nations are engaged in coolly devising the most powerful instruments for the destruction of fellow beings. Today, even democratic governments are being unconsciously led to adopt autocratic methods for saving democracy. The same is being done to get rid of terrorism, Thus, the modern world faces a paradox.

The explanation for the paradox lies in the contradiction between the ends and the means that characterize the present age. When we use brute force to settle a problem, it sets into motion an opposite force of a like character. This in turn necessitates the use of greater force, and so the chain of retaliation and counter-retaliation lengthens and strengthens.

Is there a way of breaking this vicious circle? Is there a force different and better suited for resolving tensions than brute force? Gandhiji showed us one. 'Satyagraha' i.e. the power of Truth was the name he gave to it. He also called it 'soul force' because it pits against the material force of the opponent the power of the spirit.

Recovery of Spiritual Values

The paradoxes of the modern world are because the material aspect of the world is almost completely divorced from its spiritual aspect. The material which knows no moral law, has become a law unto itself.

Gandhiji's great regret is that today, so much human energy, time, and money is being spent in discovering the truths of outer material nature, but very little is being done to reveal and utilize the deeper truths of human nature. Even the most advanced people blindly assume the truth of the brute in man, plan human relations on this crude basis, and then apply all scientific talents to the perfection of destructive implements that can take care of brute, by threat and violence. In this process of killing the brute in the enemy by violence, man turns both himself and his enemy into greater brutes.

As we have already seen in the course of this study, Gandhiji's social and political experiments are all based on the recognition of the moral foundation of human nature and human society. Human progress can be assured only if the life of the individual, society, country, and the world as a whole be more and more based on the fundamental moral principles of Truthfulness, Non-violence, Non-stealing, Self-control and Non-possession. The regeneration of moral life requires, as Gandhiji tried to show, the progressive planning of social, economic and political life on these moral principles. Thus, if the physical world is to be established and saved from self-destruction, it must become part of a unified world order. It must, that is to say, be brought under the control of moral and spiritual law. It is to the recovery of spiritual values that we must look for the solution of our major, national and world-problems.

Problems of the Modern Age and their Solution

In the end the investigator attempts to answer the questions (problems of the modern age) posed at the beginning of the study in the light of Gandhian philosophy.

Problem One

How can the individual regain the sense of his wholeness, so that he ceases to be neurotic?

Answer

By the practice of the gospel of selfless action.

Problem Two

How can the individual regain awareness of his essential oneness with his fellows?

Answer

By sustained practice of the law of Love and by building a social order based on the practice of this principle.

Problem Three

How can a non-violent sanction for society be developed that will take the place of external sanctions by which society is at present regulated?

Answer

By progressive identification with all that lives.

Crises of Individual essentially spiritual

Since the crisis of the 'Individual' today is essentially spiritual, the tenets of Gandhian Individual alone can come to his rescue. Man can survive only if he has faith in himself. It is by this faith and determination that Gandhiji, born an ordinary man, made himself so great and became the moral leader of millions, and achieved by the method of truth and love which looked like miracles in the modern age.

Gandhiji would have us set our course by the twin stars of Truth and Non-Violence; which means we must act in accordance with principles. Appeasement, even for the sake of peace, must be ruled out, because appeasement implies sacrifice of principles. Gandhiji would also have us work ceaselessly for the realization of 'common-human' values, as the sociologists say, for the triumph of the common-human way of life.

His well begun but unfinished work calls out to every ordinary man and woman of the world—particularly to the young people of this new world—to take up the moral leadership of the world. Let the message of Gandhiji always linger in our minds.

The greatest blunder that we have committed is paying homage to Gandhiji, as a formality year after year, putting his statues, or visiting his Smadhi every year, offering him garlands, extolling him to sky on his birth day and martyrdom day, but denying him and his teachings in our action. We are not sincere to Gandhiji. We have betrayed him. What is required the most is to study him deeply and follow his teachings and principles in our life.

References

1. Published in Gandhi Prasang, Vol. 1, No. 2 : January 1999.
2. Published in Journal of Gandhian Studies, Vol. 9, October 1982.
3. Paper contributed at the 'International Seminar on contemporary Idealogies regarding Freedom, Peace and Equality' held in October 1986 under the auspices of Gandhi Bhawan, University of Allahabad, Allahabad.
4. Published in Journal of Gandhian Studies, Vol. II; October 1983/January 1984.
5. Published in Journal of Gandhian Studies, Vol. 5; April 1978.
6. Published in Journal of Gandhian Studies, Vol. 3; January 1976.
7. Published in Journal of Gandhian Studies, Vol. I; October 1973.
8. Published in Gandhi Prasang, Vol. 1, No. 1; October 1998.
9. Published in Gandhi Prasang. Vol. 2, No. 1; October 1999.
10. Published in Journal of Gandhian Studies, Vol. 2; July 1975.
11. Published in Gandhi Prasang, Vol. 6, No. 2; January 2004.
12. Paper contributed at the International Seminars on Contemporary Idealogies regarding 'Freedom, Peace and Equality' held in October 1986 under the auspices of Gandhi Bhawan, University of Allahabad, Allahabad.

13 Published in Journal of Gandhian Studies, Vol. 1; January 1974.

14. Published in Journal of Gandhian Studies, Vol. 1; April 1974.

15. Published in Gandhi Prasang, Vol. I; No. 2, January 1999.

16. Published in Gandhi Prasang, Vol. I, October 2000.

17. Published in Gandhi Prasang, Vol. 2; January 2000.

18. Published in Gandhi Prasang, Vol. 6; No. 1, October 2003.

19. Published in Journal of Gandhian Studies, Vol. 5; October 1977.

20. Published in Gandhi Prasang, Vol. 5; No. 1, October 2002.

21. Jan Tinbergen, Reshaping the International order.

22. J. Omo-Fodaka, "Development : the Third Way", Alternative (Delhi) Vol. 1, No. 1, 1975, p. 27.

23. P.K. Bose, "Development of the Rural Poor", Gandhi Marg, December 1980, p. 412.

APPENDICES

APPENDIX ONE

A Brief Life Sketch of Gandhiji

A brief study of the life sketch of Gandhiji is a prerequisite to understand his principles and actions.

Mohandas Karamchand Gandhi, whom the world called *Mahatma* or 'Great soul', was born on October 2, 1869 at Porbandar, a small town on the western coast of India. His father, Karamchand Gandhi, Dewan of Porbandar, was a truthful, courageous, and intelligent person with a stern character. His mother, Putlibai, was a religious and gentle soul who left a deep impression on the mind of her son who wroshipped her.

As a child Mohandas went to an elementary school in Porbandar where he was a 'mediocre student', extremely shy, timid and averse to games. At school he met Sheikh Mahtab whose athletic build and physique fascinated Mohandas who himself was of a comparatively slight build and was scared of ghosts, thieves and snakes. Mahtab convinced Mohandas that 'the mighty Englishman' was able to rule over the 'puny

Indian' because the Englishman derived his 'Herculean' strength from animal flesh. So, Mohandas who came from an orthodox vegetarian family tasted cooked meat clandestinely. This was his first experiment in patriotism, but it proved too heavy a burden on his conscience.

At the age of thirteen, while still at school, Mohandas was married to Kasturba who was also thirteen. His father died in 1885 when he was just sixteen. Two years later, he matriculated and entered a college in the nearby state of Bhavnagar, since there were no colleges in Rajkot. He found studies tedious, the English medium difficult and the atmosphere uncongenial. A friend of the family suggested that if he hoped to take his father's place in the state service he had better become a barrister in England. Mohandas jumped at the idea and began raising money to study in England. His mother, however, was unwilling to part with her darling boy and expose him to all sorts of temptations. In order to reassure her, Mohandas took a vow not to touch wine, women and meat and sailed for England on September 4, 1888. The glamour of English life overwhelmed him during the early period of his stay. He got new clothes made, bought a silk hat, spent ten pounds on an evening dress made in Bond Street and flaunted a double watch-chain of gold. He took lessons in elocution and French and spent three guineas to learn ballroom dancing. He was introduced to the theosophical thought of Madame Blavataky and Annie Besant. It was through them that he came to know of the Bhagavad Gita in Edwin Arnold's English rendering which opened for him 'a new view of life.'

Later, in Johannesburg he found the company of Theosophists congenial. Their interest in Hindu sciptures and, in particular, Bhagavad Gita stimulated him to turn to his own religion for a deeper source of strength.

After three years and having been called to the bar and enrolment in the High Court on June 11, 1891, the young barrister sailed back home. His sojourn in England had been both profitable and stimulating. In India, he came to know that his mother had passed away in his absence. Since there was little scope for making a fortune from legal practice at Rajkot, he came to Bombay, (now Mumbai) to practise law. He was engaged to defend a petty suit in a small Court. As he rose to cross-examine the plaintiff's witness, he became nervous. He sat down in confusion and returned the fees to the client's agent. He never went to court again and sought a part-time job as an English teacher instead. When the Principal found that Mohandas did not have a university degree in teaching, 'he regretfully refused' him.

After a luckless trial of six months in Bombay, Mohandas wound up his small establishment and returned to Rajkot where with the help of his brother and other contacts he was able to earn a modest income by dratfing petitions and memorials. At this juncture, a Muslim firm of Kathiawar, which had large business interests in South Africa, offered to send him there for one year to assist their counsel in a big law-suit. He readily accepted the offer and sailed for Durban in April 1893.

Once in Durban, Mohandas found that though the British and Dutch together were a small minority in Natal, they treated both native Africans and Indians as less than human. Indians, who had been originally brought in 1860 at the request of the European settlers to help build their plantation economy, had been lured as indentured labourers on a five-year contract with the right to stay on as free residents on their own. Merchants and traders also followed the native Negro mainly because they found them more industrious and competitive to the whites.

Mohandas had his first humiliating experience in South Africa when a white passenger boarding the train objected to the presence of a 'coloured man' in the compartment. he was ordered by a railway official to shift to the'van compartment'. On his refusal to do so, a constable pushed him out. It was winter and bitterly cold. Mohanda's overcoat was taken away with the luggage and he lacked the courage to ask for it. So, he sat in the dark waiting-room, shivering the whole night, thinking, 'Should I stand up for my rights or should I go back to India?' Again, while travelling from Charlestown to Johannesburg, he was asked by the white conductor, to sit on a dirty sack-cloth on the footboard. When he refused, the conductor rained blows on him while he clung desperately to the brass rails.

Having seen for himsefl the plight of his countrymen in that country, Gandhiji on reaching Pretoria, addressed a meeting of the Indian community. It was the first public demonstration of his art as a speaker at which, later he became adept. He advised the audience to organise themselves into an association and to meet regularly to discuss their problems, to formulate and represent the grievances of their community. Gandhiji guided the Indian community to resist the bill to disfranchise them. A petition was drafted and sent to the Prime minister, the Speaker, the British Secretary of the State for Colonies, and other important members of the government. The London Times upheld the Indian claim as valid, and for the first time people in India were made aware of the hardships and ignominy of their countrymen in South Africa.

Gandhiji got himself enrolled as an advocate of the Supreme Court of Natal. An organisation, known as the Natal Indian Congress, was formed and it became an effective instrument to rouse the conscience not only of Indians but also of the liberal elements in England. After a brief stay in India, Gandhiji returned to South Africa. Once when an English barber declined to cut his hair he did not take offence but started cutting it himself. Thus, self-help became the basic tenet of his social philosophy. This was the first step in his evolution as the Mahatma.

In 1903, Gandhiji started a weekly, known as Indian Opinion, in four languages—English, Gujarati, Hindi and Tamil. In 1904, the Indian community in Johannesburg was afflicted by a sudden outbreak of plague. As soon as he came to know of it, he rushed to the aid of the victims with Dr. Godfrey. In this process, he also came in contact with Albert West and Henry Polak. It was Polak who introduced him to Ruskin's Unto the Last which had profound influence on him.

In May 1919, accompanied by a delegation, Gandhiji visited London where the prospective Union of the South African colonies was being considered by the British Parliament. he interacted with the politicians and the Press and pleaded for justice to the Indians. There he also met the revolutionary-minded Indians like Madan Lal Dhingra. True patriotism, according to him, "means the welfare of the whole people, and if I could secure it at the hands of the English I should bow down by head to them." Back in South Africa, Gandhiji started his civil resistance movement.

When Gandhiji returned to India, he was a transformed person. From being a timid and shy boy afraid of voicing his own feelings, he now emerged as a man with an iron will. By this time, Gokhale, Tilak and other famous leaders had roused the people of India to voice their feelings of discontent against the British. Gandhiji discerned this simmering discontent of the Indian masses against the Raj. He started participating in the Congress Party's sessions and in 1917, he launched an agitation in Champaran, a small town in Bihar, known for its indigo plantations.There, the tenants were bound by law to plant three out of every twenty parts of the land with indigo for the landlord. This system was known as the 'Tinkathia System', as three 'kathias' out of twenty (which make one acre) had to be planted with indigo.

When the British Indian Government passed the Rowlatt Act (1919), its recommendations startled Gandhiji, and he formed a 'Satyagraha Sabha' with the help of Sardar Vallabh Bhai Patel, Sarojini Naidu and others. A general hartal and satyagraha were observed in April 1919. A peaceful meeting helf at Jalianwala Bagh, Amritsar, to protest against the Rowlatt Act, was fired upon mercilessly, without any warning, on the orders of General Dyer. Hundereds of innocent persons were killed and many more injured. Even the children and women were not spared. Horrified by the incident, Rabindranath Tagore, whom Gandhi called 'Gurudev' and who gave the epithet of 'Mahatma' to Gandhiji, 'flung to the face of the Government his title of knightood'. In 1920, Mahatma Gandhi participated in the Khilafat Movement.

Shocked by the events that took place after the passage of the Rowlatt Act and the Jallianwala Bagh massacre, Mahatma Gandhi as he had begun to be addressed then, launched the Non-cooperation Movement. It envisaged renouncing government titles, boycotting government service, legislatures, schools, colleges and non-payment of taxes. The movement evoked a spontaneous response among the people in the country but it also resulted in violence at some places, particularly at Chauri Chaura in Uttar Pradesh where people set fire to a police station causing the death of twenty-two policemen. To avoid further bloodshed he withdrew the movement. For Gandhiji, a believer in satya (truth) and ahimsa (non-violence) violence of any kind was the most abhorrent expression of human anger.

When the British Government realised that the Reforms of 1919 has not satisfied the Indian people, a Commission was appointed under the chairmanship of John Simon. Since it was an 'all white' Commission, it was boycotted on its arrival in India. Bapu, as Mahatma Gandhi was affectionately called, spearheaded the movement. The Congress Party adopted the 'Purna Swaraj Resolution' (a resolution to achieve complete independence) in 1930 at its Lahore Session. On 6th April, 1930, Gandhiji started the Civil Disobedience Movement with his historic march to Dandhi to break the Salt Law imposed by the British-Indian Government. The movement, aiming at organising strikes, boycott of British goods and a general attitude of civil disobedience towards authority spread to all parts of the country.

On March 5, 1931, the Gandhi-Irwin Pact was signed and Gandhi agreed to end the Civil Disobedience Movement without any conditions. On August 29, 1931, Gandhiji sailed for London to attend the Second Round Table Conference which opened in London on September 7, 1931. He had earlier visited England four times and had walked the streets in the conventional dress of a pre-war English gentleman, in a well-cut morning coat and silk hat. Clad only in dhoti and a chadar the Mahatma or the 'half-naked seditious fakir' now became a legend, and fantastic stories—some kind and some unkind—spread about him. Winston Churchil's niece, Clare Sheridan, a sculptor, who sculptured Lenin's head in 1920, made studies of Bapu' Gandhiji's head while sat spinning or meeting people at the Knightsbridge house where he spent the hours in-between the Conference at St James' Palace. She said: "Gandhi, whom I place in the first rank of contemporary greatness, is also comparable with Lenin but in a different way, that is to say, spritiual rather than physical or intellectual ... To my mind, Gandhi's greatness is spiritual, and for this reason, he is greater, more formidable than any of the famous men of today. He has a spiritual awareness which humanity must develop if the world is ever to be raised out of the hell of its own making". Bapu braved the harsh London winter clad only in his dhoti and a chadar. Some journalists asked him: "Well, Mr Gandhi, Don't you think you are somewhat underclad?" "Well", Gandhiji quipped, "the King has enough clothes on his person sufficient for both of us". On his return to India, Gandhiji once again started the Civil Disobedience Movement and was duly arrested.

Poets, saints and social reformers had, for centuries condemned untouchability in Hindu society but what Mahatma Gandhi did will always be remembered. When, in August 1932, the Communal Award was announced providing separate electrorates for the 'untouchables', Bapu Announced his intention to go on a fast unto death shocking millions of people into realising that they were guilty of promoting untouchability. After five days of suspense, leaders of upper-case Hindus and of the so-called 'untouchables', whom Gandhiji had christened Harijans or children of God, signed a pact under which the proposal for separate electrorates was given up for an increased share of reserved seats. The British Government accepted this formula as well and Gandhiji broke his fast.

Gandhiji settled down in a mud hut in a village near Wardha and devoted his thought and energy to the upliftment of Harijans and the development and propagation of the country's rural economy and education. With the outbreak of war in 1939, he was dragged back into the political maelstrom. He was not the man to sit back and shirk responsibility when danger threatened his people and a crists seemed imminent. There were many within and outside the Congress who felt that this was the hour to strike, since Britain's difficulty was India's opportunity. But to Gandhiji such an attitude seemed immoral and inconsistent with the Congress creed."We do not seek our independence out of Britain's ruin", he said.

In march 1940, the All India Muslim League, under the presidentship of M.A. Jinnah passed a resolution saying that Muslims were not a minority but a separate nation and the concept of Pakistan came into being Gandhiji was distressed. His wife, Kasturba, who had supported him through his pursuits, passed away. He was sad and heart-broken, yet his indomitable spirit did not sag. He continued his struggle, courting arrest and holding meetings at Sabarmati Ashram, near Ahmedabad. The Congress Party, at its meeting in Wardha in July 1942, passed a resolution asking the British Government to withdraw from India and threatned to launch a struggle. In August 1942, Gandhiji launched the 'Quit-India Movement' in an effort to bring the British to the negotiating table. He was arrested along with other leaders precipitating a mass revolt. In 1945, the then British viceroy, Lord Wavell, was called to London for consultations. The British Government tacitly accepted the two-nation theory, which culminated in the creation of India and Pakistan.

But unfortunately, even before the two-naticn theory was accepted, riots broke out between Hindus and Muslims. These riots, engineered by fanatics belonging to both religions, deeply disturbed Gandhiji. When he found that these riots were becoming uncontrollable he undertook a fast unto death. As his condition deteriorated, wiser counsel prevailed among the people. The riots stopped and Gandhiji broke his fast. The country was partitioned into India and Pakistan and India won her freedom on August 15, 1947. But Bapu was assassinated on Jaunary 30, 1948.

APPENDIX TWO

An Out Line of Gandhiji's Life

NORTHWEST INDIA, (GUJARAT), 1869-88:

DATE	AGE	
1869		October 2nd: born in Porbandar, a town of *ca.* 70,000 on the northwest coast of India; the youngest child of the prime minister of a small and fairly prosperous Indian state.
1876	7	For the sake of his father's career the family moves 120 miles east to Rajkot.
(sometime)		Impressed by a the drama, *Harishchandra*, extolling truthfulness.
early 1880s		Is routinely present as his father conducts the bureaucratic and diplomatic work of governing.
1881		Enters secondary school (English-language).

1882	12	May 12th: Married to Kasturba; continues to attend school.
1883		With encouragement from a friend, furtively becomes carnivorous, but then resolves to be faithful to his parents' vegetarianism while they live.
		The family's income is much reduced as his father resigns his post and becomes bed-ridden with illness.
1885	15 or 16	Experiments with smoking, pilfers some money and a piece of gold jewelry, repents, and is tearfully forgiven by his father.
		Upon his father's death (at 63), feels remorse for having left the bedside a few minutes beforehand in order to lie down with his wife.
1886		A few weeks later, their first child is born and dies.
1888	18	Attends a nearby branch of the University of Bombay, but cannot follow the lectures as they are in advanced English.
		(First surviving child,l Harilal, born.)
		Sails for England (unaccompanied) to study law and thus become qualified by modern standards for a government post such as his father and grandfather had held. (His caste excommunicates him for going abroad.)

ENGLAND (MAINLY LONDON), 1888-91:

1888	19	Enrolled as a law student, beings to adapt to British culture *e.g.* by taking music and dance lessons and to waste money, while

		keeping a vow—made to assuage his mother's anxiety—not to touch wine, woman or meat.
1888-90		Finds a vegetarian restaurant; joins the London Vegetarian Society, curbs his spending.
		Describes England as 'the land of philosophers and poets, the very center of civilization.'
		Reads the Gita (in English), *The Light of Asia*, some books on Theosophy, and much of the Bible. Attends Bradlaugh's funeral.
1891		Licensed to practice British law, sails for Bombay.

INDIA (MAINLY BOMBAY AND RAJKOT), 1891-93

1891		Learns that his mother has died the year before. Is introduced to Rajchandra.
		(The caste elders at Rajkot, but not those in Bombay, end his excommunication.)
1892	22	In Bombay, fails as a courtroom lawyer; applies unsuccessfully to work as a part-time school-teacher; quarrels with his wife and sends her back to her parents for a while.
		Second son, Manilal, born.
		Moves to Rajkot and finds work drafting legal documents, but in calling upon the local British political agent, offends him and is forcibly ejected—thus dashing his hopes of a bureaucratic career.

1893		Receives and immediately accepts an offer of employment assisting an Indian-owned business firm in South Africa in some litigation with another Indian-owned firm.

SOUTH AFRICA (MOSTLY), 1893-1914

1893	23	Sails to South Africa, is subjected to the color-bar in various ways such as being thrown off a train because he would not leave the first-class seat for which he had a ticket, and resolves to say and fight it.
1893-94		Studies the Bible, the Koran, Tolstoy's *The Kingdom of God is Within You* and some 80 other books on religion and mysticism, attends Bible classes.
1894		Founds an Indian cultural-political association. Becomes the first Indian allowed to argue legal cases before the local high court.
		Persuades the litigants in his big case to submit their case to an arbitrator, who decides in favor of Gandhi's client, thereby initiating his prosperous career as a lawyer in South Africa.
		Founds the Natal Indian Congress to struggle for civil rights.
1895		Impressed by the simple life of Trappist monks and nuns.
		Writes and publishes *The Indian Franchise: An Appeal to Every Briton in South Africa.*
1896		Sails to India to agitate in behalf of his South African cause; returns to South Africa with his wife and sons.

1897	Upon his return to South Africa is lynched and nearly killed at shore by non-Indians influenced by a false newspaper account of a pamphlet he wrote in India. Declines to prosecute the attackers, but writes about the incident to the appropriate Cabinet secretary in London.
	Third son, Ramdas, born.
1897 or 98	Quarrels with his wife on account of her opposition to their cleaning the chamber-pot of an 'untouchable' born Christian guest.
1899-1901	In the Boer War, raise and leads an ambulance corps (on the British side) of more than 1000 Indian volunteers; is awarded war medal.
1900	Fourth and last son, Devadas, born.
1901	Returns to India to practice law there and to win support for the cause of Indians in South Africa, *e.g.* by proposing successfully a resolution at a meeting of the Indian National Congress.
1902	Meets Gokhale his political mentor.
	Receives a telegram from Indians in South Africa and returns there.
1903	Founds a political weekly in South Africa, *Indian Opinion,* in four languages.
	Begins to learn the Gita by heart.
1904	Reads Ruskin's *'Unto This Last'* and deeply impressed, founds Phoenix Settlement—100 acres in a rural area—with facilities to produce *Indian Opinion* and with a home for the staff and their families.

1905		Delivers four lectures on Hindu religion; is obliged to deny that these were critical of Islam.
1906		Leads the Indian Ambulance Stretcher-Bearing Corps assisting the British during the Zulu Rebellion.
	36	Vows chastity with his wife's consent and introduces rule of chastity at Phoenix Settlement.
		September: organizes in Johannesburg a protest meeting where everyone vows to God to fight to death, if necessary, with 'passive resistance" against a proposed South African law unjust to Indians.
		This undertaking will prove to be very complex, with many phases, broken promises, beatings, jail terms etc., but with a negotiated compromise settlement in 1914.
1907		Dissatisfied with the phrase 'passive resistance,' conducts a contest for a better term: *satyagraha* 'holding on to Truth'.
		Organizes the first satyagraha campaign.
1908		Jailed; released upon negotiating a verbal compromise with Smuts. Attacked and wounded for this compromise by an Indian extremist.
		Smuts does not keep the agreement.
		Organizes another satyagraha campaign.
		No longer accepts employment as a lawyer.
		Nailed for two months with hard labor.

1909	Jailed for three months (alone in a narrow cell); visits England for negotiations, which are unsuccessful.
	Reads Edward Carpenter's 'Civilization, Its Cause and Cure'. On shipboard returning to South Africa, writes Hind Swaraj 'Indian Home Rule', condemning modern Western civilization.
1909-10	Corresponds with Tolstoy.
1910	Established near Johannesburg 'Tolstoy Farm', a self-supporting commune for the families of jailed resisters.
1913	Closes Tolstoy Farm. Fasts taking only one meal daily for four months against someone's lapse from the rule of chastity at Phoenix Settlement.
(1913)	Satyagraha; jailed; released for negotiations.
1914	Fasts for two weeks against another lapse from chastity at Phoenix Settlement.
	Negotiates a written compromise with Smuts; leaves South Africa for England, thence India, First World War begins.

INDIA (MOSTLY), 1915-48:

1915	Establishes Satyagraha Ashram in Gujarat; admits 'untouchables.'
	Travels throughout India at Gokhale's suggestion, finds extreme poverty.
1916	Declines to participate in Home Rule League, hoping that loyalty during the Great War will induce Britain to grant home rule.

1917		Helps bring an end to the recruiting of Indians to become indentured laborers in South Africa.
	47	Campaigns successfully for a modicum of economic justice for peasants on indigo plantations in a remote district of north India. Arrested and tried, explains in court his role, whereupon the government withdraws its case for the sake of moral decency.
		Indians generally take to addressing him as Mahatma 'Great Soul'.
1918		Advises striking cotton-mill workers at Ahmedabad the leading industrial city of Gujarat; arbitrates voluntary semlement.
1918		Campaigns for peasants in a poor district of Gujarat.
		Urges Indians to fight for England in the First World War.
		Falls gravely ill; learns spinning during his convalescence.
1919		Britain grants very little to India in the way of home rule, instead curtailing civil rights even more than during the war.
		Organizes a brief national satyagraha. Fasts against the ensuing violent anti-British protests, saying he made a 'Himalayan miscalculation'.
		Becomes editor of *Young India* and of a similar Indian-language weekly, *Navajivan*.
		British perpetrate massacre at Amritsar and other brutalities.

1920 Elected president of All-India Home Rule Leauge. Plans and initiates mass Hindu-Moslem satyagraha campaign for Indian independence predicting success within one year and for restoration in Turkey of the caliphate.

Founds a university at Ahmedabad.

1921 Launches campaign for everyone to make homespun cotton daily; presides at a bonfire of British-made clothing; resolves to wear henceforth only a loincloth; has his head shaven.

Fasts against anti-British violence in Bombay.

Mass civil disobiedence, thousands in jail.

Invested by Congress with 'sole executive authority.'

1922 Suspends the satyagraha campaign altogether as he cannot maintain non-violence among some of his millions of ostensible supporters.

Arrested for writing seditious articles in *Young India*; eloquently pleads guilty; sentenced to six years in jail.

52 Writers in Europe and India—Romain Rolland, Sarojini Naidu—begin to describe his moral stature as comparable with that of Jesus.)

1923 Starts writing *Satyagraha in South Africa*.

1924 Hospitalized; released from jail.

Fasts for three weeks against religious violence.

Chosen president of the Indian National Congress (**195**)

1925		Undertakes a year of political silence yet still urging that everyone spin cotton daily.
		Fasts against a lapse from chastity at the ashram.
		Starts writing autobiography.
1928		Moves Indian-National-Congress resolution calling for a satyagraha campaign if independence is not granted within a year.
		Fasts against a moral lapse at the ashram.
1929		December 31st: moves Congress resolution declaring complete independence as national goal.
1930	60	March: begins anti-salt-tax march to the sea.
		April: illegally picks up some salt at seashore.
		May: jailed without trial.
		Some 90,000 other satyagrahis are jailed in this year. British methods of torture are described in *Y*, 12/vi.
1931		Released from jail, reaches hopeful agreement with the viceroy; participates in an unsuccessful 'Round Table Conference' in London (where he claims that he and not Ambedkar represents the untouchables.
		En route home, visits continental Europe, meets Romain Rolland.
1932		Because of Gandhi's consciousness-raising in India, only ¼ of British cotton exports are now to India, instead of ½ as before the war.

January: jailed until 1933.

September: fasts to obtain the 'Poona Pact' whereby (1) a British proposal supported by Ambedkar to establish separate electorates for 'untouchables' is revised and 2. conservative religious leaders say that untouchability will no longer be practiced.

1932 February: founds a new periodical, 'Harijan', to succeed 'Young India'.

May: released from jail, fasts for three weeks for self-purification.

July: disbands Satyagraha Ashram.

1933 August: jailed but soon released after fasting against a ruling not to grant him the facilities he had previously had in jail for his Harijan work.

64 November: begins an eight-month 'Harijan-uplift' tour.

1934 August: fasts for a week to atone for arousing hatred toward religious conservatives.

October: resigns from Congress, (196) launches All-India Village Industries Association.

1935 In the wake of the 'Poona Pact' and with a new administration in London, the British accept a degree of Indian self-rule with provincial elections to be held in 1937.

Rejects an appeal from Margaret Sanger to sanction birth control.

1936 Makes his home later named 'Sevagram Ashram' in a poor village near Wardha, a town where the Madras-Delhi and Bombay-Calcutta rail lines cross in central India.

1937 Indian National Congress Candidates win most of the provincial elections.

1938 Upset when his wife attends a temple closed to Harijans.

1939 Britain declared India to be at war with Germany. The provincial government ministers from the Congress resign *en masse*.

1941 May and again June: fasts against religious strife.

November: devises a campaign of 'individual satyagraha' by selecting representatives walking unaccompanied to villages and shouting, 'It is wrong to help the British war effort with men and money. The only worthy effort is to oppose war with non-violent resistance.'

1942 Japan conquers Burma. Britain proposes that India—after the war if Britain wins—may devise a constitution, provided that every province and princely state may have 'full status' of independence from India.)

72 At Gandhi's urging, the Indian National Congress adopts a 'Quit India' resolution. The leaders are immediately detained and prohibited from communicating with their followers.

1943 Fasts to protest British allegations that Congress is responsible for the current widespread anti-British violence in India.

1944	February: his wife dies in detention.
	May: very ill, released from detention.
	June: D-day, August: Paris liberated.
	July: Churchill sends the viceroy 'a peevish telegram to ask why Gandhi had not died yet.' (197)
1945	Germany and Japan defeated. Churchill voted out of office. The new British administration seeks 'an early realization of self-government in India.'
	The leader of the Moslem League, Jinnah, proposes an independent nation with a state religion and with ¼ of the territory then comprising India.
1946	Urges 'every Brahmin girl' to marry a harijan; vows to attend only weddings between a Harijan and Non-Harijan.
	August, September, October, November: a storm of religious violence, launched by Jinnah, makes inevitable the establishment of Pakistan.
	Fasts for four days to atone for a having caused a misunderstanding in negotiations with the Moslem League.
	Undertakes private, super-chastity experiments with young women. 'If I can master this, I can still beat Jinnah.' (198)
	November: begins four-month walking tour of violence-torn districts of Bengal to mitigate religious violence there. Praises "Ishwar-Allah" in his daily prayer meetings.
1947	August: on Independence Day, fasts to lament the separation of Pakistan.

		September: fasts against religious violence in Calcutta.
1948	78	January 13-18: fasts, in the name of Truth but not of God, to obtain pledges from Hindu leaders to stop the violence against Moslems in Delhi.
		January 30: assassinated by a member of a Hindu group opposed to his “pro-Islamic” activities.

APPENDIX THREE

Gandhi's Satyagraha Movements : An Analysis

1. SOUTH AFRICAN SATYAGRAHA MOVEMENT

Duration: July 1, 1907 to June 30, 1914.

Issue: The segregation policy of the South African Colonies and the various measures resulting therefrom.

Directed Against: 1. Officials of the Transvall Asiatic Department, and subsequently also those of the Imperial Government; and subsequently also those of the Imperial Government: and 2. The White Population (European).

Method Employed: 1. Wait and watch; 2. Negotiations; 3. Protest Meetings; 4. Formation of political associations; 5. Satyagraha-pledge; 6. Prayer for self-purification; 7. Ultimatium; 8. Ceremonial March; 9. Pamphlets and Newpapers; 10. Hartals; 11. Strikes; 12. Civil Disobedience; 13. Courting Imprisonment; 14. Boycott; 15. Picketing; 16. Satyagrahi-sahayog; and 17. Symbolic Acts of Satyagraha.

Results: 1. The Indian Relief Act of 1st July, 1914, finally and successfully closed the struggle. General Louis Botha, the Prime Minister of the Union of South Africa admitted that it was solely due to the Satyagraha efforts of the Indian community that the Government had to revise or repeal the Discriminatory laws and prevent their further enactment; 2. General Smuts (the Union Minister for Interior), Patrick Duncan (author of the Asiatic Registration Act), Percy Fitzpatrick (the worst opponent of the Indian cause), the Government officials; the legislator, the Magistrates, Jail-authorities, police, and a very large number of white Europeans realized that the Indians' cause was just, and they not only co-operated with them in several ways, but also conceded their demands substantially; 3. His methods not only roused public opinion in favour of the Indian cause, but also brought considerable political awakening among the masses and knit them together; and 4. The movement strengthened Ganhdi's belief in the efficacy of Satyagraha as a surer way of solving social and political conflicts.

2. FIRST PENITENTIAL FAST

Duration: November 10, 1913 to November 16, 1913 .

Issue: Moral lapse of two of his Ashram-inmates at Phoenix.

Directed Against: The erring Ashram-inmates.

Methods Employed: 1. Prayer for self-purification; and 2. fasting for seven days.

Result: The Ashram-inmates realized 'What a terrible thing it was to be sinful'.

3. SECOND PENITEMIAL FAST

Duration: April 1914.

Issue: Mora lapse of an inmate at the Phoenix Ashram.

Directed Against: The erring Ashram-inmate.

Methods Employed: 1. Prayer for self-purification; and 2. Fasting for fourteen days.

Result: The Ashram-inmates realized 'What a terrible thing it was to be sinful'.

4. VIRAMGAM QUESTION

Duration: January 16, 1915 to November 4, 1917.

Issue: harassment of passengers proceeding from Kathlawad and other villages bordering Gujarat, by levying customs duties on them.

Directed Against: Officials of the Government of India.

Methods Employed: 1. Assessment of facts by public enquiry; 2. Negotiations; and 3. Protest Meetings.

Result: In view of the imminent possibility of Satyagraha, Lord Chelmsord announced the abolition of Viramgam Customs on 4-11-1917.

5. INDENTURE IMMIGRATION QUESTION

Duration: March 20, 1916 to March 12, 1917.

Issue: India's demand for the abolition of the Indenture immigration question.

Directed Against: Officials of the Government of India.

Methods Employed: 1. negotiations; 2. Protest Meetings; and 3. Ultimatum.

Result: In view of the imminent possibility of Satyagraha, the Governor-General-in-Council's decision prohibiting labour emigration from India under Defence of India Act was gazetted on 12the March, 1917.

6. CHARMAPARAN SATYAGRAHA

Duration: April 16, 1917 to October 6, 1917.

Issue: Harassment of and unfair impositions on the Champaran ryots by the British Indigo Planters.

Directed Against: 1. British Indigo Planters: 2. Officials of the Bihar Government.

Methods Employed: 1. Assessment of facts by public enquiry; 2. Negotiations; 3. protest Meetings: 4. Prayer for self-purification; 5. Ultimatum; 6. Personal Disobedience of the District Magistrates orders restraint; 7. Technical trespass on the wrongly forefeited fields, squatting thereupon, and looting the onion crops therefrom; and 8. Satyagrahi-sahayog.

Results: 1. Champaran Agrarian Enquiry Committee with Gandhi as one of its members was appointed by the Government. The recommendations of this Committee were subsequently carried out through the enabling Act of 26th April, 1918; and 2. The Movement brought social and political awakening amongst the peasantry and knit them together.

7. AHMEDABAD SATYAGRAHA

Duration: February 26, 1918 to March 18, 1918.

Issue: Ahmedabad mill-workers' demand for increase in their wages to make up for the special wartime plague bonus, which was arbitrarily withdrawn by the mill-owners.

Directed Against: The mill-owners of Ahmedabad.

Methods Employed: 1. Negotiations; 2. Protest Meetings; 3. Arbitration; 4. Satyagraha-pleoge; 5. Prayer for self-purification; 6. Ultimatum; 7. Pamphlets; 8. Strike; 9. Fasting for three days; and 10. Satyagrahi-sahayog.

Results: 1. On Arbitrator's Award, workers' demand for 35% increase in wages was accepted by the mill-owners; 2. The

Satyagraha brought social and political awakening among the workers and knit them together; and 3. The indefinite fast undertaken by Gandhi against the mill-workers in order to encourage them in their strike indirectly exercised moral pressure on the mill-owners as Gandhi had with them very close and cordial relations.

8. KHEDA SATYAGRAHA

Duration: March 22, 1918 to June, 6, 1918.

Issue: kheda peasants' demand for suspension of land revenue recovery on account of failure of crops and the Government's refusal thereto.

Directed Against: Officials of the Government of Bombay.

Method Employed: 1. Assessment of facts by public enquiry; 2. Negotiations; 3. Protest Meetings; 4. Formation of political associations; 5. Satyagraha-pledge; 6. Prayer for self-purification; 7. Ultimatum; 8. Pamphlets; 9. No-tax campaign; 10. Courting imprisonment; and 11. Satyagrahi-sahayog.

Results : 1. The recovery of land revenue was suspended from those peasants who were unable to pay it; and 2. There was wide-spread awakening among the peasantry in Gujarat. In fact, they shed their lethargy and learnt the lesson of self-reliance and self-confidence. They realized that they had certain rights which they could enforce by mass-action.

9. ROWLATT ACT SATYAGRAHA

Duration : March 1, 1919 to April 18, 1919.

Duration: march 1, 1919 to April, 1919.

Issues: 1. Indians' demand for the withdrawal of the Anarchical Crimes Act of 1919 and prevention of the passage of the II Bill of the similar character; and 2. Intensification of political awareness for Independence.

Directed Against: Officials of the Government of India.

Methods Employed: 1. Negotiations; 2. Protest-Meetings; 3. Formation of political associations; 4. Satyagraha Training Centres: 5. Satyagraha-pledge; 6. Prayer for self-purification; 7. Ultimatum; 8. National Days and Weeks; 9. Pamphlets; 10. Hartals; 11. Civil Disobedience; 12. Protest Resignations; and 13. Satyagrahi-sahayog.

Results : 1. The Anarchical Crimes Act was never implemented and the second Bill was never brought before the Central Legislature; 2. Through Satyagraha Sabha, Gandhi raised a corps of volunteers and commenced the work of educating the public with regard to the meaning and practice of Satyagraha; 3. The campaign brought unprecedented political awakening among the masses; and 4. He had to suspend the civil disobedience movement hi order effectively to assist the Government in restoring law and order despite the fact that satyagraha had neither been the cause nor the occasion for the outbreak of violence.

10. FIRST ANTI-VIOLENCE FAST

Duration: April 14, 1919 to April 16, 1919.

Derailment of a train at Nadiad by some anarchists.

Directed Against : The anarchists and the Ahmedabad mill-labourers on whose behalf he had earlier offered Satyagraha.

Methods Employed: 1. Prayer for self -purification; and 2. Fasting for three days.

Result : The disturbances at Ahmedabad came to an end on April 14, and the Government withdrew the military proclamaiton.

11. FIRST NON-VIOLENT NON-CO-OPERATION MOVEMENT

Duration : August 1, 1920 to February 12, 1922

Issues : 1. Government of India's failure to protect the innocent people of Panjab and punish offenders guilty of unsold-diery and barbarous behaviours towards them; 2. Imperial and Indian Government's failure to allow the authority of the Turkish Empire to remain as it was at the commencement of the I World Wan and 3. the Attainment of Swaraj for India.

Directed Against : Officials of the Government of India.

Methods Employed : 1. Assessment of facts by public enquiry; 2. Negotiations; 3. Protest meetings; 4. Formation of political associations; 5. Satyagraha training camps; 6. Satyagraha-pledge: 7. Prayer for self-purification; 8. Ultimatum; 9. National Days and Weeks; 10. Pamphlets and Newspapers; 11. Hartals; 12. Civil Disobedience; 13. Courting imprisonment; 14. Boycott; 15. Picketing; 16. Dharna; 17. Protest meetings; 18. Constructive Programme; 19. Satyagrahi-sahaycg; and 20. Symbolic acts of Satyagraha.

Results : 1. The Movement failed in its immediate objectives and had to be suspended due to violence at Chauri-Chaura; 2. The whole of India, particularly the hitherto politically indifferent and inert peasantry, became acquainted, as never before, with the deep-seated disease of alien domination; 3. The people learnt lessons in the practical art of fearlessness and self-restraint; and 4. the spirit of religious unity was created between the Hindus and Muslims, which was Gandhi's biggest sin in the eyes of the British bureaucracy.

12. SECOND ANTI-VIOLENCE FAST

Duration : November 19, 1921 to November 22, 1921.

Issue : Ananrflists' activities in protest of the visit of the Prince of Wales to India.

Directed Against : The anarchists.

Methods Employed: 1. Prayer for self-purification; 2. Fasting for th'rec days: and 3. Newspaper propaganda.

Result: Peace was restored and consequently on November 22, Gandhi broke his fast in the midst of Hindus, Muslims and Parsis.

13. THIRD ANTI-VIOLENCE FAST

Duration : February 12, 1922 to February 17, 1922.

Issue : Outbreak of violence at Chauri-Chaura.

Directed Against: The Anarchists.

Methods Employed : 1. Prayer for self-purification; 2. Fasting for five days; and 3. Newspaper propaganda.

Results : Riots rapidly subsided.

14. VYKOM SATYAGRAHA

Duration: March 1924 to June 17, 1925.

Issues : 1. Prohibition upon the use by untouchables of roadways passing the Vykom Shiva temple; and 2. To rid Hinduism of the blot of untouchability.

Directed Against: 1. The orthodox Hindus of Travancore; and 2. The Maharaja, the Dewan, and the members of the Legislative Council of Travancore.

Methods Employed : 1. Negotiations; 2. Protest meetings; 3. Newspaper propaganda; and 4. Courting of imprisonment.

Results: 1. Roads were declared open for all on 17th June, 1925: and 2. Subsequently, on 12th November, 1937, the Maharaja of Travancore declared all the temples open for all, and the so-called untouchables were willingly welcomed by both the priest and the *savarna* Hindus.

15. FIRST HINDU-MUSLIM UNITY FAST

Duration : September 18, 1924 to October 8, 1924.

Issue : Hindu-Muslim riots in Delhi, Gulbarga, Kohat, and Lucknow.

Directed Against : The communal fanatics.

Methods Employed: 1. Negotiations; 2. Protest Meetings; 3. Prayer for self-purification; 4. Newspaper-propaganda; and 5. Fasting for twenty-one days.

Results : 1. The riots rapidly subsided; and 2. The Unity Conference at Delhi passed a resolution appointing a National Panchayat Board of 15 members for settling communal disturbances.

16. THIRD PENITENTIAL FAST

Duration : November 24, 1925 to November 30, 1925.

Issue : Moral lapse of some of his Ashram-inmates at Sabarmati.

Directed Against : The erring Ashramites. Methods Employed : 1. Prayer for self-purification, and 2. Fasting for seven days.

Result : Gandhi succeeded in bringing the youngsters to the sense of their error.

17. NEILL STATUE SATYAGRAHA

Duration : September 1, 1927 to October 13, 1927.

Issue : Peoples' demand for the removal of the statue of Neill—a British General responsible for the brutalities during the 1857 rebellion.

Directed Against : Officials of the Madras Government.

Methods Employed : 1. Negotiations; 2. Protest meetings; 3. Newspaper propaganda; and 4. Courting imprisonment

Results : 1. The Satyagraha had to be discontinued after some time due to lack of public enthusiasm; and 2. Eventually in 1937, the Congress Ministry got the statue removed.

18. BARDOLI SATYAGRAHA

Duration : February 12, 1928 to August 4, 1928.

Issue : Bardoli peasants' demand for the revision and suspension of land revenue assessment, arbitrarily enhanced by the Government by 22%.

Directed Against : Officials of the Revenue Department, the Police of the Bardoli District and the Government of Bombay.

Methods Employed: 1. Protest Meetings; 2. Negotiations; 3. Satyagraha Training Camps; 4. Satyagraha-pledge; 5. Ultimatum; 6. Pamphlets and Newspapers; 7. No-tax campaign; 8. Courting imprisonment; 9. Boycott; 10. Dharna; 11. Protest Resignations; 12. Non-possession; 13. Constructive Programme; 14. Satyagrahi-sahayog; and 15. Symbolic Acts of Satyagraha.

Results : 1. Broomfield Enquiry Committee appointed and on its recommendations the enhanced rate was reduced to 6i%; 2. Closer co-operation was established between the Hindus and Muslims; and 3. There was wide-spread awakening among the peasantry.

19. SALT SATYAGRAHA

Duration : March 12, 1930 to March 4, 1931.

Issues : 1. Demand for the repeal of Salt Acts providing for Government monopoly of salt, resulting in hardships especially to the poor; and 2. Demand for *Purna Swaraj* for India.

Directed Against: The Officials of the Government of India. Methods Employed : 1. Protest meetings; 2. Formation of political associations; 3. Satyagraha training centres; 4. Satyagraha pledge; 5. Prayer for self-purification; 6. Negotiations; 7. Ultimatum; 8. Ceremonial March; 9. Pamphlets and Newspapers; 10. Hartals; 11. National Days and Weeks; 12. Non-violent Non-co-operation; 13. Civil Disobedience; 14. No-tax campaign; 15. Courting imprisonment; 16. Boycott; 17. Picketing; 18. Dharna; 19. Peaceful Raids on Salt-pans and works; 20. Protest Resignations; (21) Non-possession; (22) Constructive Programme; (23) Satyagrahi-sahayog; and (24) Symbolic acts of Satyagraha.

Results : 1. The Satyagraha was discontinued in order to enable the government to implement the Gandhi-Irwin Pact; 2. The Pact provided that in further discussions on Indian Constitutional reforms, the Congress representatives would be associated; 3. The campaign marked a distinct moral victory which created self-confidence among the people and confidence in the weapon of Satyagraha, 4. Young Muslims and Hindus showed increased toleration towards each other." They came to realize that the prevailing Hindu-Muslim antagonism was due to the extremists (on both sides) who were "advanced hi age and few in number"; and 5. Though the immediate and the long-range objectives of the Satyagraha were not realized, the Government did permit certain classes of people to collect or make salt for domestic consumption or for sale within their villages.

20. KARNATAK SATYAGRAHA

Duration: March 1931 to May 1931.

Issue : Demand of the peasants of Sirsi, Siddapur and Hirekerur Talukas of Karnatak for the suspension of land revenue recovery on account of failure of crops, and the government's refusal thereto.

Directed Against: Officials of the local government.

Methods Employed : 1. Protest Meetings; 2. Negotiations; 3. No-tax campaigns; 4. Courting imprisonment; and 5. Peacetul picketing.

Result : Relief was granted to those who were unable to pay the assessed land revenue.

21. SECOND NON-VIOLENT NON-CO-OPERATION MOVEMENT

Duration: January 4, 1932 to April 7, 1934.

Issue : Attainment of *Puma Swaraj* for India.

Directed Against: Officials of the Imperial and Indian Governments.

Methods Employed : 1. Negotiations; 2. Protest meetings; 3. Political associations; 4. Prayer for self-purification: 5. Ultimatum; 6. Holding of banned meetings and processions; 7. Ceremonial March; 8. National Days and Weeks; 9. Non-violent Non-co-operation; 10. Courting imprisonment; 11. Boycott; 12. Picketing; 13. Sarya-grahi-sahayog: and 14. The symbolic acts of Satyagraha.

Results : 1. Due to unprecedented allrouud repression by the Government, the movement failed to achieve its objective of *Puma Swaraj* and had finally to be abandoned; and 2. Phenomenal mass awakening throughout the country.

22. FIRST ANTI-UNTOUCHABILITY FAST

Duration: September 20, 1932 to September 26, 1932.

Issue : To lodge protest against the Macdonald Award aimed at creating separate electorates for the depressed classes.

Directed Against: Officials of the Imperial and Indian Governments.

Methods Employed : 1. Negotiations; 2. Prayer for sett-purification; 3. Ultimatum; and 4. Fasting for six days.

Results : 1. On 24th September, 1932, a complete agreement was reached between Gandhi and the British officials, and on 26th September the British Prime Minister announced his acceptance of the Yervada Pact, substituting the Mac-donald Award; and 2. The fast "roused mass consciousness, directing public opinion to the field of social reform".

23. SECOND ANTI-UNTOUCHABILITY FAST

Duration : December 3, 1932.

Issue : To express sympathy with Appasaheb Patwardhan, who had asked for the scavenger's work in the Ratnagiri Jail, but was refused by the authorities.

Directed Against : Officials of the Government of India.
Methods Employed: 1. Negotiations; 2. Prayer for self-purification: 3. Ultimatum; and 4. Fasting for one day.

Result : Exercised moral influence on his adversaries.

24. THIRD ANTI-UNTOUCHABILITY FAST

Duration : May 8, 1933 to May 29, 1933.

Issue : To hasten the removal of untouchability.

Directed Against : The *savarna* Hindus.

Methods Employed : 1. Negotiations with the Government of India; 2. Prayed for self-purification: and 3. Fasting for 21 days.

Results : 1. The fast exerted a sort of purifying influence on the adversaries and on those in whose behalf it was under-taken; and 2. In view of his fast, he was unconditionally released on 8th May, 1933.

25. FOURTH ANTI-UNTOUCHABILITY FAST

Duration : August 16, 1933 to August 23, 1933.

Issue : Bombay Government's refusal to permit Gandhi to continue Harijaii work, from inside the jail.

Directed Against : Officials of the Government of India.

Methods Employed : 1. Negotiations; 2. Prayer for self-purification; 3. Ultimatum; 4. Newspaper propaganda; and 5. Fasting for seven day.

Result: In view of the seriousness of his condition he was released on 23rd August, 1933, unconditionally.

26. FOURTH ANTI-VIOLENCE FAST

Duration : August 7, 1934 to August 14, 1934.

Issue : An act of violence on the part of a young Congress-man, who had struck Swami Lal Nath (a Sanatani Hindu) on his head.

Directed Against : The young Congressman.

Methods Employed : 1. Prayer for self-purification; 2. Newspaper propaganda; 3. Fasting for seven days.

Result : Enabled him to realize more fully that untouchability could be removed only by those who had a pure character.

27. RAJKOT SATYAGRAHA

Duration : March 3, 1939 to May 17. 1939.

Issue : 1. Breach by Rajkot Ruler of an agreement entered into between him and his people, and his subsequent ordinances aimed at suppressing the Satyagraha activities; and 2. Peoples' **demand for** representative Government in princely states.

Directed Against : The native and British rulers of Rajkot.

Methods Employed : 1. Assessment of facts by public enquiry; 2. Negotiations; 3. Protest meetings: 4. Prayei for self-purification; 5. Ultimatum: 6. Newspaper propaganda; 7. Fasting for four days; and 8. Satyagrahi-sahayog.

Result : Failed in achieving its immediate objective, and Gandhi had to renounce the Gwycr Award for he realized his unconscious fault of offending the Rajkot Thakore and Durbar Shri Virawala by seeking the Viceroy's intervention.

28. INDIVIDUAL SATYAGRAHA

Duration : October 17, 1940 to December 4, 1941.

Issues : 1. Indians' demand for the freedom to preach non-co-operation with the Government in their II World-War efforts; and 2. To attain *Puma Swaraj* for India.

Directed Against : Officials of the British Government in India.

Methods Employed : 1. Negotiations; 2. Protest Meetings; 3. Political Associations; 4. Satyagraha pledge; 5. Prayer for self-purification; 6. Ultimatum; 7. Newspaper propaganda; 8. Courting imprisonment; 9. Non-violent Non-co-operation; and 10. Satyagrahi-sahayog.

Results : 1. The Satyagrahis successfully preached non-cooperation and cheerfully courted imprisonment; 2. Towards the end of 1941 public enthusiasm had waned and consequently the movement was discontinued.

29. QUIT INDIA MOVEMENT

Duration : August 9, 1942 to June 21, 1945.

Issues : Indians' demand for the immediate ending of the British Rule in India and the attainment of the *Purna Swaraj.*

Directed Against : The officials of the British Government in India.

Methods Employed : 1. Negotiations; 2. Protest meetings: 3. Political associations: 4. Satyagraha-pledgc; 5. Prayer for self-purification; 6. Holding of banned meetings, processions and demonstration; 7. Hartals; 8. Fasting for 21 days; 9. Non-violent Non-co-operation; and 10. Satya-grahi-sahayog.

Result : The Government crushed the movement with all the weight at their command.

30. SECOND HINDU-MUSLIM UNITY FAST

Duration : September 1, 1947 to September 4, 1947.

Issue : Hindu-Muslim Riots in Calcutta and Punjab.

Directed Against : The communal fanatics, particularly the militant Hindus.

Methods Employed : 1. Negotiations; 2. Protest meetings; 3. Tours, including the *pad yatra:* 4. Prayers for self-purification: 5. Newspaper propaganda: and 6. Fasting for three days.

Result : The fast stirred the people and the riots rapidly subsided.

31. THIRD HINDU-MUSLIM UNITY FAST

Duration : January 13, 1948 to January 18, 1948.

Issue : Hindu-Muslim riots in Delhi.

Directed Against : The communal fanatics, particularly the-militant Hindus.

Methods Employed : 1. Negotiations; 2. Protest meetings; 3. Prayer for self-purification; 4. Newspaper propaganda; and 5. Fasting for five days.

Results : 1. Representatives of Hindus and Muslims signed a joint declaration assuring Gandhi the restoration of peace; and 2. Riots rapidly subsided.

APPENDIX FOUR

(Gandhi's Satyagraha Movements : A Classification)

PART I : COLLECTIVE MOVEMENTS

A : On National Questions :

1. South-African Satyagraha Movement: July 1, 1907 to June 30, 1914.
2. Rowlatt Act Satyagraha : March 1, 1919 to April 18, 1919.
3. First Non-violent Non-co-operation Movement : August 1, 1920 to February 12, 1922.
4. Salt Satyagraha: March 12, 1930 to March 4. 1931.
5. Second Non-violent Non-co-operation Movement: January 4, 1932 to April 7, 1934.
6. Quit India Movement: August 9, 1942 to June 21, 1945.

B : On Local Questions

1. Champaran Satyagraha : April 16. 1917 to October 6, 1917.
2. Ahmedabad Satyagraha: February 26, 1918 to March 18. 1918.
3. Kheda Satyagraha: March 22, 1918 to Jane 6, 1918.
4. Rajkot Satyagraha: March 3. 1939 to May 17. 1939.

PART II: INDIVIDUAL MOVEMENT

A : On Naitonal Quesitons

1. First Hindu-Muslim Unity Fast: September 18, 1924 to October 8, 1924.
2. First Anti-Untouchability Fast: September 20, 1932 to September 26. 1932.
3. Second Anti-Untouchability Fast: December 3. 1932.
4. Third Anti-Untouchability Fast: May 8, 1933 to May 29, 1933.
5. Fourth Anti-Untouchability Fast: August 16, 1933 to August 23, 1933.
6. Individual Satyagraha: October 17, 1940 to December 4,. 1941.
7. Second Hindu-Muslim Unity Fast: September 1, 1947 to September 4, 1947.
8. Third Hindu-Muslim Unity Fast: January 13, 1948 to January 18, 1948.

B : On Other Questions

1. First Penitential Fast: November 10. 1913 to November 16. 1913.

2. Second Penitential Fast : April 1914.
3. First Anti-Violence Fast: April 14, 1919 to April 16, 1919.
4. Second Anti-Violence Fast : November 19, 1921 to November 22, 1921.
5. Third Anti-Violence Fast : February 2, 1922 to February 17, 1922.
6. Third Penitential Fast: November 24, 1925 to November 30, 1925.
7. Fourth Anti-Violence Fast : August 7, 1934 to August 14, 1934.

PART III : MOVEMENT SHORT OF SATYAGRAHIC MEHTODS

1. Viramgam Question : January 16, 1915 to November 4, 1917.
2. Indenture Immigration question: March 20, 1916 to March 12. 1917.

PART IV : MOVEMENTS STARTED BY OTHERS AND SUPPORTED BY GANDHI :

1. Vykbm Satyagraha: March 1924 to June 17, 1925.
2. Neill Statue Satyagraha : September 1, 1927 to October 13, 1927.
3. Baidoli Satyagraha: February 12, 1928 to April 4, 1928.
4. Kamatak Satyagraha: March 1931 to May 1931.

APPENDIX FIVE

Gandhi's Imprisonments

1. JOHANNESBURG IMPRISONMENT

Method of Courting Imprisonment : By disobeying the orders to leave the Colony within the prescribed time-limit.

Imprisonment Awarded : Two months' simple imprisonment.

Actual duration of Imprisonment: Twenty days simple imprisonment (January 10 to January 30, 1908).

Ground of Release : In view of the Gandhi-Smuts Agreement regarding the voluntary registration and its validation.

2. VOLKSRUST IMPRISONMENT

Method of Courting Imprisonment : By entering Transvaal without Registration certificates and by refusing to give his finger and thumb impressions.

Imprisonment Awarded : Seven days simple and two months rigorous imprisonment.

Actual Duration of Imprisonment : Seven days simple and two months rigorous imprisonment. (October 7 to October 14, 190S) and (October 14 to December 12, 1908).

Ground of Release : Completion of the awarded imprisonment.

3. VOLKSRUST-PRETCRIA IMPRISONMENT

Method of Courting Imprisonment: By entering Transvaal without registration certificates and by refusing to give his finger and thumb impressions.

Imprisonment Awarded : Three months simple imprisonment.

Actual Duration of Imprisonment: Three months' simple imprisonment (February 25 to May 24, 1909).

Ground of Release : Completion of the awarded imprisonment.

4. PALMFOD-VOLKSRUST IMPRISONMENT

Method of Courting Imprisonment : By inducing strike of Ballengeich Indian miners and Ladysmith Railwaymen and by taking them to stage a March from Newcastle to the Transvaal without requisite registration certificates to protest against £-3 tax.

Imprisonment Awarded : Nine months' rigorous imprisonment.

Actual Duration of Imprisonment : One month and eight days' rigorous and three *days* simple imprisonment (November 6. 9, 10, 1913 and November 11 to December 18, 1913).

Ground of Release: Recommendations of the Solomon Commission.

5. FIRST YERVADA IMPRISONMENT

Method of Courting Imprisonment: By writing four articles in his *Young India,* amounting in the Government's opinion to sedition.

Imprisonment Awarded : Six years' simple imprisonment.

Actual Duration of Imprisonment: One year, ten months and twenty-seven days' simple imprisonment (March 10 to March 17, 1922 and March 18, 1922 to February 5, 1924).

Ground of Release : In view of the seriousness of his health.

6. SECOND YERVADA IMPRISONMENT

Method of Courting Imprisonment : By violating salt laws at Dundi and at Aat and by asking others to do the same for achieving *Purna Swaraj* or complete independence for India.

Imprisonment Awarded : During Government's pleasure.

Actual Duration of Imprisonment : Eight months' and twenty-two days' simple imprisonment (May 4, 1930 to January 25. 1931).

Ground of Release : In the "hope of restoration of peaceful conditions".

7. THIRD YERVADA IMPRISONMENT

Method of Courting Imprisonment: By dispatching to the Viceroy an ultimatum to revive civil disobedience movement for the attainment of *Purna Swaraj* for India.

Imprisonment Awarded : During Government's pleasure.

Actual Duration of Imprisonment: One year, four months and five days (January 4, 1932 to May 8. 1933).

Ground of Release : "In view of the nature and object of the fast" Gandhi imposed on himself on this day.

8. FOURTH YERVADA IMPRISONMENT

Method of Courting Imprisonment: By continuing and intensifying the civil disobedience movement for the attainment of *Puma Swaraj* for India.

Imprisonment Awarded : During Government's pleasure.

Actual Duration of Imprisonment: Three days (August 1 to August 4, 1933).

Ground of Release : After being served with a restraint order requiring him to reside within the limits of Poona City.

9. FIFTH YERVGDA IMPRISONMENT

Method of Courting Imprisonment: By disobeying the restraint orders requiring him to reside within the limits of the Poona City.

Imprisonment Awarded : One year simple imprisonment.

Actual Duration of Imprisonment: Twenty days simple imprisonment (August 4 to August 23, 1933).

Ground of Release : When he was considered to have entered the danger zone, he was released unconditionally (on medical grounds).

10. AGA KHAN PALACE IMPRISONMENT

Method of Courting Imprisonment : Although this time Gandhi did not want to court imprisonment, the Government, by precipitating the inauguration of Quit India Movement, arrested and detained him under the Defence of India Rules.

Imprisonment Awarded : During Government's pleasure.

Actual Duration of Imprisonment: One year, eight months and twenty-nine days. (August 9, 1942 to May 6, 1944).

Ground of Release : His anaemic condition had worsened and blood-pressure fallen.

SUMMARY OF IMPRISONMENT

Total Imprisonment Awarded : Twelve years, two months, six days.

Total Simple Imprisonment Awarded : Eleven years, three months, six days.

Total Rigorous Imprisonment Awarded : Eleven months.

Total Actual Imprisonment: Six years, four months, twenty-four days.

Total Actual Simple Imprisonment: Six years, one month, sixteen days.

Total Actual Rigorous Imprisonment : Three months, and eight days.

Total Actual Imprisonment in South Africa : Seven months and eight days.

Total Actual Imprisonment in India : Five years, nine months and sixteen days.

APPENDIX SIX

Gandhi's Fasts

1. FIRST PENITENTIAL FAST

Issue of Fast : Against moral lapse of two of his Phoenix-Ashram inmates.

Announced Duration of Fast : Seven days.

Actual Duration of Fast : Seven days (March 10 to March 16, 1913).

Ground of Terminating Fast : Expiry of the period for which the fast was undertaken.

2. SECOND PENITENTIAL FAST

Issue of Fast : Against second moral lapse of an inmate of his Phoenix-Ashram.

Announced Duration of Fast : Fourteen days.

Actual Duration of Fast : Fourteen days (April 1914).

Ground of Terminating Fast : Expiry of the period for which the fast was undertaken.

3. AHMEDABAD FAST

Issue of Fast: In order to encourage the Ahmedabad Mill workers in their strike.

Announced Duration of Fast : Indefinite.

Actual Duration of Fast : Three days (March 15 to March 18, 1918).

Ground of Terminating Fast: Settlement between the mill-workers and the owners was arrived at, and Mr. A. B. Dhruva was appointed the arbitrator.

4. FIRST ANTI-VIOLENCE FAST

Issue of Fast : Against die attempts of some anarchists to derail a train at Nadiad.

Announced Duration of Fast : Three days.

Actual Duration of Fast: Three days (April 14 10 April 16, 1919).

Ground of Terminating Fast: Expiry of the period for which the fast was undertaken.

5. SECOND ANTI-VIOLENCE FAST

Issue of Fast: In order to check anarchists' activities on the occasion of the arrival of the Prince of Wales.

Announced Duration of Fast : Indefinite.

Actual Duration of Fast: Three days (November 19 to November 22, 1921).

Ground of Terminating Fast : Peace was restored.

6. THIRD ANTI-VSIOLENCE FAST

Issue of Fast : Against violent activities at Chauri Chaura.

Announced Duration of Fast : Five days.

Actual Duration of Fast : Five days (February 12 to February 17, 1922). Ground of Terminating Fast : Expiry of the period for which the fast was undertaken.

7. FIRST HINDU-MUSLIM UNITY FAST

Issue of Fast : Against Hindu-Muslim riots in Delhi, Gulbarga, Kohat and Lucknow.

Announced Duration of Fast : Twenty-one days.

Actual Duration of Fast : Twenty-one days (September 18 to October 8. 1924).

Ground of Terminating Fast : Expiry of the period for which the fast was undertaken.

8. THIRD PENITENTIAL FART

Issue of Fast : Against moral lapse of some 01 his Sabarmati-Ashram inmates.

Announced Duration of Fast : Seven days.

Actual Duration of Fast : Seven days (November 24 to November 30, 1925).

Ground of Terminating Fast : Expiry of the period for which the fast was undertaken.

9. THIRD ANTI-UNTONCHABILITY FAST

Issue of Fast : Against MacDonald Award creating separate electorates for the depressed classes.

Announced Duration of Fast : Unto death.

Actual Duration of Fast : Six days (September 20 to September 26, 1932).

Ground of Terminating Fast : British Prime Minister accepted the Yervada Pact in place of the MacDonald Award.

10. SECOND ANTI-UNTOUCHABILITV FAST

Issue of Fast : Sympathetic fast with Appasaheb Patwardhan, who asked for scavenger's work in jail but was refused by the jail authorities.

Announced Duration of Fast : One day.

Actual Duration of Fast : One day (December 3, 1932).

Ground of Terminating Fast : Expiry of the period for which the fast was undertaken.

11. THIRD ANTI-UNTOUCHABILITY FAST

Issue of Fast : A purificatory fast for Harijan work and welfare.

Announced Duration of Fast : Twenty-one days.

Actual Duration of Fast : Twenty-one days (May 8 to May 29, 1933).

Ground of Terminating Fast : Expiry of the period for which the fast was undertaken.

12. FOURTH ANTI-UNTOUCHABILITY FAST

Issue of Fast : Against Government's refusal to allow him to continue Harijan work from inside the Yervada Prison.

Announced Duration of Fast : Unto death.

Actual Duration of Fast: Seven days (August 16 to August 23, 1933).

Ground of Terminating Fast : On his unconditional release from jail on medical grounds.

13. FOURTH ANTI-VIOLENCE FAST

Issue of Fast : Against a young Congressman who had struck a sanatani on the head.

Announced Duration of Fast : Seven days.

Actual Duration of Fast: Seven days (August 7 to August 14, 1934).

Ground of Terminating Fast: Expiry of the period for which the fast was undertaken.

14. RAIKOT FART

Issue of Fast : Against the Rajkot Thakore's refusal to honour his agreement with the people, to release Satyagrahi prisoners, and to withdraw the repressive ordinances.

Announced Duration of Fast: Unto death.

Actual Duration of Fast : Four days (March 3 to March 7, 1939).

Ground of Terminating Fast : The Viceroy conceded to intervene and appoint Chief Justice Maurice Gwyer to resolve the deadlock between the Rajkot ruler and Sardar Patel (and also Gandhi).

15. AGA-KHN PALACE FAST

Issue of Fast : As a protest to the Viceroy's refusal to convince him of his errors or to release him from the prison so that he does not remain a helpless witness to what was going on in the country.

Announced Duration of Fast : Twenty-one days.

Actual Duration of Fast : Twenty-one days (February 10 to March 3, 1943).

Ground of Terminating Fast : Expiry of the period for which the fast was undertaken.

16. SECOND HINDU-MUSLIM UNITY FAST

Issue of Fast: To prevent Hindu-Muslim riots in Calcutta and Punjab and particularly to protect the Muslim minority against the Hindu majority.

Announced Duration of Fast: Unto death.

Actual Duration of Fast: Three days (September 1 to September 4, 1947).

Ground of Terminating Fast: Peace was restored and a pledge was signed by the representatives of Hindu and Muslims, and a car-load of hand-grenades and arms were surrendered to him as a token of repentance, on the part of those who had taken part in the reprisals and counter-reprisals.

17. THIRD HINDU MUSLIM UNITY FAST

Issue of Fast : To prevent Hindu-Muslim riots in Delhi, and particularly to protect Muslims from being forcibly turned out of Delhi by their Hindu brethren.

Announced Duration of Fast : Unto death.

Actual Duration of Fast : Five days (January 13 to January 18, 1948).

Ground of Terminating Fast : Peace was restored and pledge was signed by the representatives of various communities to prevent then further outbreak.

TOTAL ACTUAL PERIOD OF FASTING

138 days (4 months, 18 days).

BIBLIOGRAPHY

PRIMARY SOURCES

BOOKS BY GANDHIJI AND COMPILATION OF HIS WRITINGS

1. An Autobiography : The story of my Experiments with Truth	Vol. I, translated from Gujarati by Mahadev Desai Ahmedabad, Navajivan Publishing House, 1927. Vol. II, translated by Mahadev Desai and Pyarelal Nair Ahmedabad, Navajivan Publishing House, 1929.
2. Bapu's letters to Mira :	Ahmedabad, navajivan Publishing House, 1949.
3. Basis Education :	Ahmedabad, Navajivan Publishing House, 1951.
4. Christian Mission :	ed. by the publisher Ahmedabad, Navajivan Publishing House, 1957.
5. Delhi Diary :	ed. Jivanji, D. Desai Ahmedabad, Navajivan, Publishing House, 1948.

6. Ethical Religion :	translated by Ramiyer Madras, Ganesh and Co., 1922.
7. From Yeravda mandir : Ashram observances.	translated from Gujarati by Valji Desai, 3rd. ed. Ahmedabad, Navajivan, Publishing House, 1945.
8. Gandhiji's Correspondence with the Government (1942-44):	Ahmedabad, Navajivan Publishing House, 1945.
9. Harijan (Weekly) 1933-40, 1942, 194-48:	Files of Harijan upto-date published from, Ahmedabad.
10. Hind Swaraj or Indian Home Rule :	rev. ed., (Ahmedabad, Navajivan Publishing House, 1939).
11. Hindu Dharma :	ed. Bharatan Kumarappa Ahmedabad, Navajivan, Publishing House, 1950.
12. Non-Violence in Peace and war :	ed. Bharatan Kumarappa, 2. vols. Ahmedabad, Navajivan Publishing House, 1948-49.
13. Rusk's Unto This Last : A Paraphrase :	translated from Gujarati by Valji, G. Desai Ahmedabad, Navajivan Publishing House, 1951.
14. Sarvodya—Its Principles and Programme :	Ahmedabad, Navajivan Publishing House, 1954.
15. Sarvodya :	ed. Bharatan Kumarappa Ahmedabad, Navajivan Publishing House, 1951.
16. Satyagraha in South Africa :	trans. From Gujarati by Valji, G. Desai Stanford, Academic Repritns, 1951.
17. Self-Indulgence Versus Self-Restraint :	Ahmedabad, Navajivan Publishing House, 1947.

18. Speeches and Writings	ed. by the publisher, 4th. ed., Madras, G.A. Natesan, 1933.
19. The Collected Works of Mahatma Gandhi :	ed. by the government of India, Vols. I and II. New Delhi, Publication Division, Ministry of Information, 1958-69.
20. To Pacifists :	ed. Bharatan Kumarappa, Ahmedabad, Navajivan Publishing House, 1949.
21. Towards New Education :	ed. Bharatan Kumarappa, Ahmedabad, Navajivan Publishing House, 1953.
22. Towards Non-Violent Socialism	ed. Bharatan Kumarappa Ahmedabad, Navjivan Publishing House, 1951.
23. To the students :	Ahmedabad, Navajivan Publishing House, 1949.
24. To the Women :	ed. Hingorani, A.T. Karachi, 1945.
25. Young India :	Vol. I 1919-1922, ed. S. Ganesan, New York. B.W. Huebsch, 1924.
	Vol. II, 1924-1926, ed. S. Ganesan, New York. Viking Press, 1927.
	Vol. III, 1927-28, ed. by the Publisher, Madras, S. Ganeshan, 1935.

BOOKS BY OTHERS ON GANDHIJI

26. Andrews, C.F :	Mahatma Gandhi's Ideas, London, Allen Univin, 1929.
27. Abid Husain, Sayed :	The Way of Gandhi and Nehru, Bombay, Asia, Publishing House, 1959).

28. Bose, N. K. (Ed) : Selections from Gandhiji, Ahmedabad, Navajivan Publishing House, 1948.
29. Bose, N.K : Studies in Gandhism, 2nd ed., Calcutta, Narendra Chaterjee, 1947.
30. Chakravarty, Amiya: Mahatma Gandhi and the Modern World, Calcutta, The Book House, 1945.
31. Datta, Dhlrendra Mohan: The Philosophy of Mahatma Gandhi, Madison, University of Wisonsin Press, 1953.
32. Dhawan, Gopinath : The Political Philosophy of Mahatma Gandhi, 2nd. ed., Ahmedabad, Navajivan Publishing House, 1951.
33. Dhiman, O.P. Gandhian Philosophy : A Crilicae and comprehensive Study, The Indian Publication An edutt. 1971.
34. Diwakar, Ranganath, R : Satyagraha, Bombay, Hind Kitabs, 1946.
35. Fischer, Louis : A weak with Gandhi New York, Duel, Solan and Pearce, 1942.

    The Life of Mahatma Gandhi, New York, Harper, 1950.
36. Gregg. Richard B : The Power of Non-Violence, Philadelphia, J.B. Lippin cott Co., 1934.
37. Kripalani J.B : The Gandhian Way, Bombay, Vora and Co. Ltd., 1934.
38. Majumdar, Biman bihari, ed : Gandhian Concept of State, Calcutta, M.C. Sarkar and Sons, Private Ltd; for Bihar University, 1957.
39. Mashruwala, K.G : Gandhi and Marx, Ahmedabad, Navajivan Publishing House, 1951.

40. Nag, Kalidas : Tolstoy and Gandhi, Patna, Pustak Bhandar, 1950.

41. Nair, Pyarelal : Mahatma Gandhi : The Last Phase, 2 Vols., Ahmedabad, Navajivan Publishing House, 1956-1958.

SECONDARY SOURCES

42. Admas, Sir John : Educational Theories, London. Bend's Six Penny Library, 1927.

43. Aristotle : Politics, translated by Benjamin Jowett, Oxford, 1908.

44. Aslrvathan, E : Political Theory, Lucknow, U.P., The Upper India Publishing House, 1949.

45. Barker Ernest : Principles of Political and Social Theory, Oxford, Clarendon Press, 1952.

46. Broad, C.D : Determinism, Indeterminism Libertariansim, Cambridge, at the University Press, 1934.

47. Bronstein, Krikorian, Wiener : Basic Problems of Philosophy, ed. by 2nd ed., Prentice Hall, Inc., 1955.

48. Cassier, Earnest : The Myth of the State, London 1945.

49. Chagla M.C. : The Individual and the State.

50. Dewey, John : Democracy and Education, New York, Macmillan, 1916.

51. Dhiman, O.P. Principles & Techniques of Education, Kalpaz Publication, Delhi 2007.

52. Dhiman, O.P. Understanding Education : An Overview of Education, Kalpaz Publication, Delhi 2008.

53. Haas, Francis J : Man and Society, New York, Appleton-Century-Crofts, 1952.

54. Hunter Mead : Types and Problems of Philosophy, 3rd ed., New York, Henry Holt and Company, Inc. 1959.

55. Hunley, Aldons : Ends and Means, London, Chatto and Windus, 1938.

56. Jeffreys, M.V.C. Education, Christian or Pagan, London, U.L.P., 1946.

57. Kant, E : Kant's Critique of Practical Reason, trans. by T.K. Abbott, London, Longmans, Green and Co., 1898.

58. Laski, Harold, J : A Grammar of Politics, 3rd Edition, London, George Allen and Unwin, 1934.

59. Lenin, V.I. The State and Revolution, reprinted, Moscow, Foreign Longuage Publishing House, 1949.

60. Maclver, R.M : The Modern State, Oxford University Press, 1947, reprint.

61. Marx, Karl : Capital, A critique of Political Economy, Saraswati Library.

62. Modern Review : Calcutta, June 1945.

63. Mill, J.S : On Liberty and Considerations on Representative Government, Oxford, R.B. Mc. Callum, Basil Black-Well, 1946.

64. Nehru, Jawarlal : An Autobiagraphy, London, The Bodloy Head, 1936.

65. Nunn, Sir Percy : Education, its Datta and First Principles (London, Edward, Arnold 1945).

66. Plato : The Republic of Plato, translated by B. Jowett, Oxford 1888.

67. Radhakrishan S : History of Philosophy Eastern and Western 2 vols., London, George Allen and Unwin Co., 1953.

68. Ross, J.S : Ground Work of Educational Theory, London, Harrap, 1952).

69. Rusk, Robert R : The Philosophical Basis of Education, London, U.L.P., 1928.

70. Thilly Frank : A History of Philosophy, New York, Henry Holt and company, 1951.

71. Threau, Henry David : They Duty of Civil Disobedience, Bombay, Satyagraha Sabha, 1919.

72. Taylor, A.K : Elements of Metaphysics, London, Methuen and Co. Ltd., 1903.

73. UNESCO SEMINAR : Gandhian out-look and Techniques, Ministry of Education, Govt. of India New Delhi.

74. Unnithan T.K.N. : Gandhi of Free India, Vora and to C. Publishers, Bombay.

75. Wallas, Graham : The Great Society, London Macillan, 1936.

INDEX